cordon bleu
COOKBOOK

recipes for freezing and entertaining
by Rosemary Hume and Muriel Downes

Hamlyn

LONDON · NEW YORK · SYDNEY · TORONTO

in association with Phoebus

Jacket shows: potage velouté aux fèves
(page 108); chicken sauté chasseur (page 67)
with chicory and orange salad (page 50)
and maître d'hôtel potatoes (page 28); and
galette au chocolat Cordon Bleu (page 6).
The soup tureen was kindly lent by the
Worcester Royal Porcelain Co. Ltd., and the
Waterford wine glasses came from The
General Trading Co. (Mayfair) Ltd.

Published 1977 by
The Hamlyn Publishing Group Limited
London · New York · Sydney · Toronto
Astronaut House,
Feltham,
Middlesex, England

ISBN 0 600 31959 8

Made and printed in Great Britain by
Waterlow (Dunstable) Limited

ABOUT THIS BOOK

We are so often asked by today's busy cooks for recipes which can be prepared in advance, for dishes which can be cooked, then stored in the freezer and which thaw out without losing either texture or flavour, and for new ideas for quick, last-minute dishes when unexpected guests arrive. We are well aware that today's cook, in many cases, needs to keep her eye on the purse strings as well as the larder. We also appreciate that no guest can fully enjoy even a Cordon Bleu meal if the hostess is flustered, pink-faced, and looks as if she has been cooking since dawn.

In this book, therefore, we have concentrated on producing menus that are planned to the last detail, starting with eight complete three-course dinner parties—with alternative suggestions for some of the courses to give variety. Then there are dishes which can specifically be cooked ahead and frozen. Freezing and thawing instructions are given in each suitable recipe, but you do not need to own a freezer to cook them. Then we have worked out menus for all kinds of occasions from a simple family supper to a reception for fifty, including three complete sets of weekend menus, each with a plan of work for the cook to adapt.

We would like to thank all the people who have helped in the production of this book, especially Michael Leale, for taking such splendid photographs, Sarah Nops, our co-principal, for preparing all the food we photographed, and Joy Langridge, for putting it all together.

Rosemary Hume

Muriel Downes

CONTENTS

COOKING NOTES

Recipes: these have all been tried and tested at the London Cordon Bleu Cookery School. Spoon measures are level, unless otherwise stated; flour used is plain, unless otherwise stated; where cream is used, if double cream is specifically required, this is stated, otherwise double or single cream will do.

Quantities: the eight dinner party menus are planned to serve six, but quantity adjustments for eight are given where necessary. If no quantity adjustment is given, the recipe as it stands should serve either. In the other sections, refer to the relevant introduction at the head of each section as the quantities vary.

Freezing and thawing: instructions for this have been given in the relevant methods and the thawing times added as a guide. Make sure, when reheating a thawed-out dish, that the food is heated through thoroughly, and casseroles are allowed to bubble or boil before serving. Remember that seasonings and flavourings intensify during storage (recommended length of time for storing basic foods is on page 126), and thickened and semi-liquid foods tend to become thicker, so make suitable adjustments. This symbol ★ next to a recipe on menus indicates that the finished dish can be stored in the freezer.

Metrication: the recipes in this book are given in Imperial measures and tablespoons. For those who have only metric scales, the following information will be of use.

Exact conversion from Imperial to metric measures does not usually give convenient working quantities, so we suggest you follow the practice of rounding off the grams per ounce to the nearest multiple of 25. This means the quantity of the finished dish may be slightly different. The table gives recommended equivalents.

Note: when converting quantities over 20 oz (1 pint), add together the appropriate figures in the centre column, then round off to the nearest unit of 25. Rule of thumb: 1 kg (1,000 g) equals approx. 2 lb 3 oz; 1 litre (1,000 ml) equals approx. 1¾ pints.

Ounces/ fluid ounces	Approx. g and ml to nearest whole figure	Recommended conversion to nearest unit of 25
½ ¼ ¾	14	15
	21	20
1	28	25
2	57	50
3	85	75
4	113	100
5 (¼ pint)	142	150
6	170	175
7	198	200
8 (½ lb)	226	225
9	255	250
10 (½ pint)	283	275
15 (¾ pint)	425	425
16 (1 lb)	454	450
17	482	475
18	510	500
19	539	550
20 (1 pint)	567	575

ALL TAKEN FROM THE FREEZER

The main dishes for our first three-course dinner party menu can all be cooked and then frozen — saving time and trouble on the day of the party itself. We start with a deliciously creamy fish soup (see above). For this, smoked haddock is combined with cream, potatoes and tomatoes to make a smooth starter. Then you have a boned shoulder of lamb, stuffed with a mixture of orange, walnuts and raisins. Serve this with plain boiled potatoes, delicate mangetout peas, or glazed carrots. For dessert, there is a chocolate meringue cake filled with chocolate cream and cherries. And there's a timetable on page 9 to help you plan your work in the kitchen.

For good measure, Rosemary Hume and Muriel Downes have suggested alternatives for the first two courses. Instead of fish soup, try a smoked mackerel pâté served with Melba toast and its own special cucumber relish. This freezes well, as does the alternative main course of savoury chicken paupiettes filled with ham and herbs. We would suggest a white wine to drink with this lighter, more summery, menu. The recipes are on page 10.

★ *Potage Crème de Poisson*

★ *Epaule d'Agneau Farcie*
Glazed Carrots
Mangetout Peas
Potatoes

★ *Galette au Chocolat Cordon Bleu*

Red wine – Côtes de Bourg (Claret)

Potage crème de poisson

½ lb smoked haddock fillet
6 medium-size leeks (well washed)
¾ lb potatoes (peeled)
salt and pepper
2½ oz butter
1 (7½ oz) can tomatoes

To finish
1 pint milk
1 tablespoon arrowroot
2–3 tablespoons extra milk
¼ pint double cream
1 tablespoon chopped parsley

Method
Place the fish in a bowl with 1 pint of boiling water, allow to stand for 10 minutes, then drain and flake, reserving the water. Meanwhile, slice the leeks and potatoes, season and cook slowly in the butter, without allowing them to colour, for about 10 minutes.

Add the tomatoes, fish and reserved water to the leek and potato mixture and bring to the boil. Simmer for about 15 minutes or until the potatoes are soft, then work to a purée by passing through a

Epaule d'agneau farcie

3½ lb shoulder of lamb (boned)
4 anchovy fillets (chopped)
1 clove garlic (crushed)
2 oz butter
2 shallots (finely chopped)
1 bayleaf
½ pint stock (see page 124)
1 orange (peeled and thinly sliced)

For stuffing
2 tablespoons fresh white breadcrumbs
2 tablespoons chopped parsley
5 oz seedless raisins
grated rind and juice of 1 large orange
salt and pepper
1 oz butter
2 shallots (peeled and finely chopped)
2 tablespoons shelled walnuts (chopped)
beaten egg (to bind)

To finish
1 teaspoon arrowroot
2½ fl oz single cream
1 tablespoon chopped parsley (to garnish)

Trussing needle and coarse thread, or fine string

> Choose a 4 lb joint of lamb if cooking for eight. Otherwise the ingredient quantities remain the same.

Method
First prepare the stuffing. Place the breadcrumbs, parsley, raisins and orange rind together in a bowl and season well. Heat butter in a small pan, add the chopped shallots, allow to soften slightly then add walnuts and allow to colour.

Cool shallot mixture a little, then add to the breadcrumb mixture. Bind with a little beaten egg and orange juice to make a good, moist stuffing.

Stuff the boned joint of lamb and sew up (see step-by-step pictures). Set the oven at 325°F or Mark 3.

Crush the chopped anchovies to a paste with the garlic, then with a sharp-pointed knife, make 6–8 incisions over the surface of the joint. Work the paste well into these small cuts.

Melt the butter in a flameproof casserole, put in the joint and brown well on all sides. Add the chopped shallots, bayleaf, stock and peeled and sliced orange. Bring to the boil. Cover and cook in moderate oven for 1½ hours.

To freeze Lift the joint from the casserole

Galette au chocolat Cordon Bleu

5 egg whites
10 oz caster sugar
1½ oz cocoa

For filling
¾ lb fresh black cherries or 1 can (14 oz) black pitted cherries
1 rounded tablespoon caster sugar (for fresh cherries)
1 teaspoon arrowroot slaked (mixed) with a tablespoon of cold water
a little kirsch liqueur (for canned cherries)
4 oz plain dessert chocolate
2½ fl oz water
1 rounded teaspoon gelatine dissolved in a tablespoon of water
1 pint double cream

For decoration
icing sugar (to dust)
a little whipped cream
chocolate caraque (see page 9)

3 baking sheets lined with non-stick (silicone) cooking paper; ½-inch plain pipe

Method
Pre-set oven to 290°F or Mark 1. Whisk the egg whites until stiff, add 1 tablespoon of the measured sugar and continue beating for about 30 seconds. Sift the cocoa with the remaining sugar and quickly cut and fold into the whipped egg whites. Spread or pipe the mixture into three 7-inch rounds on the prepared baking sheets and bake for 1–1¼ hours, or until dry and crisp.

If using fresh cherries, stone them, put into a pan, cover with a lid and set on a low heat to draw out the juice. Add 1 rounded tablespoon of caster sugar and allow to simmer for 3–4 minutes. Thicken with a little arrowroot slaked (mixed) with cold water, and add to cherries to thicken the juice. Leave until cold.

(If using canned cherries, drain and leave them to macerate in a little kirsch, reserving the juice.)

Break the chocolate into small pieces, put into a pan with the 2½ fl oz water and stir continually over a gentle heat until the chocolate has melted. Allow to cool.

Mouli sieve, or use a liquidiser for this.

When cold, pack and freeze in cartons.
Thawing and serving Thaw overnight in refrigerator, turn into a pan and thin purée with 1 pint of milk. Bring to boil and simmer for 5 minutes. Slake (mix) the arrowroot with 2–3 tablespoons cold milk; add this liaison to the soup, allow to reboil and adjust seasoning.

Pour $\frac{1}{4}$ pint cream into a warm soup tureen and tip in the hot soup. Stir well, add the chopped parsley and serve. ∎

Spooning tomatoes over leeks and potatoes before flaking and adding the fish

Passing cooked ingredients through a Mouli sieve to purée them before freezing

and strain the liquid. When both are cold, wrap and freeze the meat; skim the fat from the gravy, pot and freeze it.
Thawing and serving Remove meat and gravy from the freezer the day before the party, and allow to thaw for at least 24 hours in the refrigerator. Carefully remove all string from the lamb, place the joint in a flameproof casserole, pour over the gravy and cook in a moderate oven, pre-set at 350°F or Mark 4, for 40–45 minutes.

Just before serving, mix one level teaspoon arrowroot with $2\frac{1}{2}$ fluid ounces of cream and pour in round the sides of the casserole to thicken gravy. Shake casserole to blend and return to the oven for 5 minutes. Remove lamb to serving dish and pour over gravy.

Sprinkle with chopped parsley, slice and serve with plainly boiled new potatoes, mangetout peas and glazed carrots. ∎

Sewing up boned shoulder of lamb after filling the cavity with the savoury stuffing

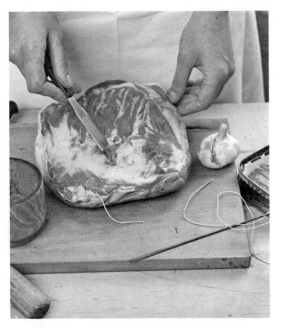

Working anchovy paste with a knife into small cuts on the surface of the meat

Dissolve the gelatine in the tablespoon of water by placing both in a bowl set in a pan of very hot water. Cool.

Start whisking the cream and, as it thickens, add the chocolate, then stir in the gelatine and continue whisking until the cream holds its shape.

Sandwich each meringue round with a layer of chocolate cream topped with a quarter of the cherries.
To freeze Slip the filled rounds into a freezer polythene bag, or set in a cake box and freeze.

Turn the rest of the cherries, with any juice, into a carton and freeze. (If using canned cherries, first thicken the reserved juice with a little arrowroot slaked (mixed) with a tablespoon of cold water.)
Thawing and serving Allow galette and sauce to thaw in the refrigerator for 24 hours before serving. Dust the top of the galette with icing sugar, decorate with a little extra plain whipped cream and chocolate caraque (see box overleaf).

Serve the cherry sauce separately. ∎

Pipe three 7-inch rounds of chocolate meringue on to lined baking sheets

Sandwich rounds with a thick layer of chocolate cream topped with cherries

Glazed carrots

1½ lb carrots
1 teaspoon sugar
1 oz butter
salt
mint (chopped)

Method
Peel carrots, leave whole, or quarter if small. If very large, cut them in thin slices. Put in a pan with water to cover, sugar, butter and a pinch of salt. Cover and cook steadily until tender, then remove lid and continue cooking until all the water has evaporated, when the butter and sugar will form a glaze round the carrots.

Add a little chopped mint just before serving. ■

Mangetout peas

1 lb mangetout peas
½ oz butter
salt and pepper

Method
Top and tail the pods and wash well. Boil gently with just enough salted water to cover. Allow 12–15 minutes cooking time – the pods should still be slightly firm. Drain thoroughly and return to pan with a good knob of butter, salt and pepper, before serving. ■

Above: the chocolate and cherry galette
Left: the stuffed shoulder of lamb, shown with its accompaniment of plain boiled potatoes tossed in butter, glazed carrots and mangetout peas

TIMETABLE

Day before (morning)
Take lamb and gravy from freezer. Leave in refrigerator to thaw.
Order cream for galette; make chocolate caraque, store in refrigerator.

Day before (evening)
Take fish purée, galette and cherry sauce from freezer. Leave to thaw in refrigerator.

Day of party (morning)
Tip fish purée into pan, blend in milk. Prepare arrowroot liaison, but do not add.
Remove string from lamb, place joint in casserole with the gravy, ready for further cooking. Set oven timer for 45 minutes, if oven is automatic.
Prepare vegetables, chop parsley and mint for garnish. Mix cream and arrowroot liaison ready for meat. Keep in refrigerator.

Day of party (afternoon)
Decorate galette and return to refrigerator in large covered container to prevent cream from picking up flavours from uncovered food.
Turn cherry sauce into bowl for serving.

Order of work

7.00 (Pre-set oven at 350°F or Mark 4.)

7.15 Check lamb is starting to cook.

7.30 Cook vegetables.

7.40 Stir soup until boiling, simmer 5 minutes. Add the liaison, adjust seasoning.
Turn out heat. Have cream ready to tip into warmed tureen.

7.55 Add cream and arrowroot liaison to lamb. Return to oven, on lowest setting. Dish up vegetables.

8.00 Serve first course.

Cooking times in individual recipes have sometimes been adjusted to help when cooking and serving this menu as a three-course meal.

Chocolate caraque
Melt 3 oz grated plain chocolate or chocolate couverture (cooking chocolate) on a plate over hot water and work with a palette knife until smooth. Spread thinly on a marble slab or laminated surface and leave until nearly set. With a sharp long knife, using a slight sawing movement and holding knife almost upright, shave off long scrolls or flakes. These will keep in an airtight tin, but look better when fresh.

ALTERNATIVE STARTER

Smoked mackerel pâté

2–3 smoked mackerel
a pinch of ground mace
3 oz butter (well-creamed)
½ lb curd cheese
pepper freshly ground from mill
a little lemon juice or 1–2 drops
   of Tabasco sauce
a little melted butter

Method
Remove the skin and all bones from the mackerel and pound well with the mace to a smooth paste. Work in the well-creamed butter and curd cheese and season with pepper and lemon juice or Tabasco. Fill into a container, cover with melted butter, wrap and freeze.

Thawing and serving Thaw for 24 hours in the refrigerator and serve with Melba toast and the following relish. ∎

This pâté freezes well. It is served with cucumber relish and wafer thin Melba toast

Cucumber relish

1 large cucumber

For dressing
2 tablespoons wine vinegar
1 teaspoon dry mustard
6 tablespoons salad oil
3 dessertspoons tomato ketchup, or fresh tomato pulp
1 tablespoon mixed chopped herbs (parsley, chives and mint)
salt and black pepper freshly ground from mill

Method
Slice the cucumber, salt lightly and leave pressed between two plates for about ½ hour, then rinse with ice-cold water and drain well. Combine the ingredients for the dressing, season with salt and pepper, and spoon over the cucumber. Chill well before serving. ∎

> **Melba toast:** cut thin slices of white bread, remove crusts, place on a baking sheet and dry out in a moderate oven, 350°F or Mark 4 until crisp.

ALTERNATIVE MAIN COURSE

Chicken paupiettes

6 chicken drumsticks
1½ oz butter
1 large onion (sliced)
2 carrots (sliced)
½ turnip (sliced)
a stick of celery (sliced)
½–¾ pint jellied stock
1 wine glass sherry
1 teaspoon tomato purée

For stuffing
4 oz cooked ham (shredded)
2–3 oz raw minced chicken
2–3 tablespoons fresh white breadcrumbs
pinch of dried herbs
pinch of ground mace
salt and pepper
1 shallot
1 oz butter
beaten egg (to bind)

Method
Bone out the drumsticks and prepare the stuffing. Place ham, chicken and breadcrumbs in a bowl with the herbs, mace and seasoning. Chop the shallot finely and cook in the butter until soft but not coloured, add to the ham mixture and bind with the beaten egg.

Fill into the drumsticks and sew or tie neatly with fine thread.

Melt the butter in a shallow pan and brown the paupiettes slowly on all sides; remove from the pan. Add the sliced, or diced, vegetables to the pan, cover, and cook slowly until they have absorbed the butter and begun to brown.

Replace paupiettes, pour over enough stock to cover the vegetables, season and cover with greaseproof paper and a lid. Cook for 15 minutes on top of the stove, then place in a moderate oven (350°F or Mark 4) for about 45 minutes. Take up paupiettes and place in a container; strain and reserve the contents of the pan. Tip the sherry into the pan and reduce by half, work in the tomato purée and the strained stock. Simmer until syrupy, adjust the seasoning and spoon over the paupiettes. Cover with foil and polythene and freeze.

Thawing and serving Thaw for 12 hours at refrigerator temperature, then heat at 380°F or Mark 5, for 40–45 minutes. Serve with a crisp green salad, or a fresh green vegetable of your choice. ∎

If serving eight, allow 12 chicken drumsticks. Other quantities remain the same.

> **Important:** since the freezer life of different types of food varies a good deal, we have included a chart of keeping times in this book on page 126. Uncooked meat, for example, has a long freezer life when compared with uncooked meat or poultry containing a stuffing.
>
> For perfect safety, we recommend freezing cooked dinner party dishes eg, côte de porc polonaise or chicken paupiettes for one month only. It is a good general rule to have a regular turn-round of dishes.

COMPLIMENTS TO THE COOK

For our second dinner party meal, two courses are taken from the freezer and the starter — tomatoes stuffed with a rich curd cheese and cods roe filling — can be quickly and simply put together on the day. The main course of pork chops, stuffed with a savoury celery and onion mixture and set on a bed of thinly sliced potato, can be cooked, then frozen. With this, Rosemary Hume and Muriel Downes suggest you serve braised cabbage from the freezer, or French beans.

And for pudding, why not try the apricot and hazelnut upside-down cake shown above? The sponge mixture is lightly flavoured with coffee. It's a freezer recipe, so turn to page 16, make a batch of mixture as we suggest and experiment with four different variations.

Tomates Farcies à la Grecque
★ *Côte de Porc Polonaise*
★ *Braised White Cabbage or French Beans*

★ *Apricot and Hazelnut Upside-down Cake with Soured Cream Sauce*

Red wine – Hermitage (Côtes du Rhone)

Tomates farcies à la grecque

6 even-size tomatoes
6 small rounds of brown bread (buttered)
watercress (to garnish)

For filling
6 oz curd cheese
1 tablespoon hot milk (see method)
6 oz jar smoked cods roe
pepper
squeeze of lemon juice

For dressing
1 tablespoon lemon juice
salt and black pepper freshly ground from mill
good pinch of sugar
4 tablespoons salad oil
1 dessertspoon mixed herbs (chopped)

Forcing bag and plain round pipe

If serving eight, you will need 8 tomatoes, 8 rounds of bread, 8 oz curd cheese and 5 tablespoons salad oil. Other quantities remain the same.

Method
Scald and skin tomatoes by placing in a bowl, pouring boiling water over, counting to 12 before pouring off the hot water and replacing it with cold. The skins should then come off easily. Slice off the flower ends (*not* the stalk ends), scoop out the seeds and discard, reserving any liquid from inside the tomatoes. Turn the tomatoes upside down to drain.

Prepare filling by working the curd cheese with the juice drained from the seeds and, if the mixture is too solid, add a tablespoon of hot milk. Gradually work in the cods roe and season to taste with pepper and a squeeze of lemon juice. Pipe this mixture into the tomatoes, or use a teaspoon to fill them, replace the caps and set each on a round of bread and butter, cut out with a 2-inch pastry cutter. Arrange on a dish.

To make dressing, mix the lemon juice

Côte de porc polonaise

3 lb loin of pork (chined)
½ oz butter
1½ lb potatoes
½ pint milk
1 oz dry cheese (grated)

For stuffing
2 shallots or 1 small onion
2 sticks celery
1 oz butter
2 tablespoons fresh white breadcrumbs
salt and pepper

Trussing needle and fine string

If serving eight, you will need a 3½ lb loin of pork, 2 lb potatoes, ¾ pint milk and 3 tablespoons breadcrumbs. Other quantities remain the same.

Method
Bone out the loin of pork, or ask the butcher to do this for you, and cut in thick even slices at least ¾ in wide. Anything narrower will make it difficult to stuff.

Peel and finely chop shallots or onion, chop celery very finely and cook for 2–3 minutes in the butter. Stir in breadcrumbs and season with salt and pepper. Allow to cool.

Set the oven at 375°F or Mark 5. Make a slit in the lean side of each pork slice and fill with the stuffing, keeping it in place with a stitch made with fine string and a trussing needle. Brown joint quickly on each side in the ½ oz butter.

Peel and slice the potatoes thinly (use a mandoline grater) and arrange in a flame-proof dish, seasoning between the layers. Cut string, pull out carefully and slide the

Apricot & hazelnut upside-down cake

(see page 16 for variations)

9 oz plain flour
4 teaspoons baking powder
½ teaspoon salt
2 oz butter, margarine or shortening
5 oz caster sugar
1 large egg
1 teaspoon instant coffee
4–5 fl oz milk

For topping
2½ oz butter
2½ oz soft light brown sugar
12–15 lightly browned hazelnuts
½ lb fresh apricots (poached and drained)
or 1 (14 oz) can whole apricots

8–9 inch moule à manqué

Method
First prepare the topping. Work the butter and sugar together and, when thoroughly mixed, spread it over the bottom and sides of the dry cake tin. Place hazelnuts on the mixture and over each, arrange half an apricot.

Set oven at 350°F or Mark 4. Now sift the flour in a bowl with the baking powder and salt and set aside.

Soften the butter, margarine or shortening, and beat in the sugar. Whisk the egg well, and beat in until the mixture is light and fluffy. Dissolve the coffee in the milk. Stir the flour into the butter, sugar and egg mixture alternately with the coffee-flavoured milk. Spoon into the prepared tin over the topping and bake at once in the pre-set oven for 50–60 minutes.

Test by piercing with a skewer. If it comes out clean the cake is ready. If serving immediately, invert tin on to a serving

with the seasonings, add the oil and whisk until the dressing thickens. Sprinkle herbs over, taste for seasoning and adjust if necessary. (If the dressing tastes sharp, yet oily, add more salt.) Spoon dressing over the tomatoes and garnish the dish with watercress.

Note: If you find curd cheese difficult to obtain, Philadelphia cream cheese may be substituted. The filling will be even richer. ■

meat on to the potatoes; the lean side should be almost covered, but the fat exposed. Pour over the milk and dust with the cheese.

Bake in a moderate oven, as pre-set, for 45–50 minutes. The actual time taken may vary a little according to your oven.

To freeze When cold, wrap and freeze.

Thawing and serving Take out the day before the party and thaw for 12 hours in a cool larder, or 24 hours in the refrigerator. Reheat for 20–30 minutes at 375°F or Mark 5. Serve with braised white cabbage – see recipe on page 14, or French beans – from the freezer if not in season. ■

After slitting chops, fill each with stuffing. Sew up each one with string, as shown

Placing chops, fat side uppermost, on to the layer of potato slices before baking

plate. Leave for a few minutes, while the brown sugar mixture runs down over the cake, then carefully remove the tin.

To freeze Allow the cake to cool in the tin then wrap and freeze.

Thawing and serving Allow to thaw for 3 hours at room temperature, then warm gently for 10–15 minutes in a pre-set oven, 325°F or Mark 3. Turn on to a serving plate as described above and serve with a soured cream sauce (see page 14). ■

To brown hazelnuts
The best way to brown hazelnuts thoroughly and evenly is to bake them in a hot oven for 5–6 minutes. Turn them on to a rough cloth, such as an oven cloth, and rub briskly to remove the dry skins.

Add flour to creamed butter mixture alternately with coffee-flavoured milk

Pouring cake mixture over prepared topping on the base and sides of cake tin

Rich and creamy stuffed tomatoes, finished with a sharp French dressing. Allow one per person as a starter

Braised white cabbage

1 medium-size Dutch cabbage
2 oz butter
2 tablespoons wine vinegar
1 tablespoon caster sugar
salt and pepper
1 tablespoon chopped parsley

Method
Wash and shred cabbage finely. Well rub a thick pan with butter and pack in the cabbage, adding the vinegar, sugar and seasoning. Cover with buttered paper and the pan lid and cook slowly for 20–25 minutes until the cabbage is just tender. Fork in chopped parsley just before serving.

If using the dish frozen, thaw and reheat for 20–25 minutes at 360°F or Mark 4, until thoroughly hot and sprinkle over parsley just before serving. ■

Soured cream sauce
(for upside-down cake)

¼ pint double cream
½ pint natural unsweetened yoghourt, or
¼ pint soured cream and ¼ pint yoghourt

Method
Whip the cream until just holding its shape, then stir in the yoghourt or soured cream. Turn into a dish for serving. ■

TIMETABLE

Day before (evening)
Take pork from freezer and transfer to refrigerator to thaw.

Day of party (morning)
Remove cake from freezer. Leave in refrigerator to thaw.
Take braised cabbage from freezer (if frozen). Place in the refrigerator to thaw.

Day of party (afternoon)
Prepare tomatoes, wash and pick over watercress and place it upside down in a small basin of cold water. Store in refrigerator.
Prepare dressing for tomatoes. Cut bread and butter rounds.
Wash and shred cabbage (if using fresh).

Order of work

7.00   Arrange tomatoes on serving dish, coat with dressing and garnish with watercress.

7.30   Set oven at 375°F or Mark 5. Start to cook French beans (if serving). Start to cook braised cabbage (if using fresh).

7.40   Place braised cabbage in oven to reheat (if from freezer). Put pork in oven to reheat.

7.55   Place cake to warm in plate-warming drawer or bottom of oven.
Dish up beans (if serving).
Finish cabbage (if using fresh).

8.00   Serve first course.

Cooking times in individual recipes have sometimes been adjusted to help when cooking and serving this menu as a three-course meal.

The stuffed pork chops are served with braised white cabbage, or French beans

Top left: pear and walnut. Right: the pineapple version, both served with soured cream sauce

Mark 4) for 50–60 minutes. When cake tests done, invert it immediately on to a serving plate. Leave in tin for a few minutes. When quite cold, remove tin, wrap cake and freeze. Thaw for 3–4 hours at room temperature.

Cherry and almond

1 lb black cherries
1 tablespoon caster sugar
pinch of ground cinnamon
1 oz flaked almonds (lightly toasted)

Method
Stone the cherries and place in a small pan with the sugar and cinnamon and cook gently until the juices run freely. Cover the bottom of a third prepared tin with the cherries, add the almonds and spoon one portion of chocolate cake mixture into the tin and bake as above. Allow an extra 5–10 minutes cooking time for this cake. Thaw for 3–4 hours at room temperature.

Pear and walnut

4 small ripe dessert pears, or 8 canned pear halves
a little sugar syrup
16 walnut halves

Method
Peel, halve, core and poach fresh pears in a light sugar syrup, or drain the juices from the canned variety. Arrange the pears and walnuts over the topping of the fourth and last tin. Spoon over the remaining chocolate cake mixture and bake as for cherry and almond cake. Thaw for 3–4 hours at room temperature.

Upside-down cakes

quantity for 4 cakes:

2¼ lb plain flour
4 level tablespoons baking powder
1 teaspoon salt
8 oz butter, margarine or shortening
1¼ lb caster sugar
4 eggs
about ¾ pint milk

For sugar topping
10 oz butter
10 oz soft light brown sugar

Four 8–9-inch diameter layer cake tins, or moules à manqué

Method
Prepare the topping: cream the butter and sugar together and spread it over the bottom and sides of the four cake tins.

Sift the flour with the baking powder and salt and set aside.

Soften the butter, margarine, or shortening and beat in the caster sugar and well-whisked eggs until the mixture is light and fluffy. Stir in the flour alternately with the milk and divide mixture into four portions.

Leave one portion plain, flavour a second portion with 1 teaspoon instant coffee.

Cook 6 oz dessert chocolate to a cream with about 5 tablespoons water, allow to cool and stir into the remaining two portions of cake mixture.

Apricot and hazelnut
Follow the instructions given on page 12 for this version, using the coffee-flavoured portion of basic mixture.

Pineapple, cherry and walnut
Cover the bottom of a second prepared tin with slices of canned pineapple, glacé cherries and walnut halves.

Spoon over the plain portion of cake mixture and bake in a moderate oven (350°F or

Sugar syrup: for every 1 lb fruit, dissolve 3–4 tablespoons granulated sugar in ½ pint water. Then boil rapidly for 2 minutes. Flavour with a strip of lemon rind or a piece of vanilla pod.

As an alternative to soured cream sauce, try **brandy butter**. Cream 4 oz unsalted butter, beat in 4 oz caster sugar, continue beating until white, then gradually add 2–3 tablespoons brandy. Chill well before serving.

A TRADITIONAL TOUCH

Start our third dinner menu with sole, either fresh, or from your freezer. Poach it, team it with tangy, pink-fleshed Texas grapefruit and make a rich hollandaise sauce in your liquidiser. The beef for the main course is marinated in wine, cooked slowly in the oven with vegetables and herbs, then cooled and frozen, with its gravy, until required. When thawed, it is cut into slices for serving. With it, serve deep-fried croquettes of polenta, or semolina, flavoured with onion, ham and just a touch of Dijon mustard.

To finish the meal, we couldn't resist one of Cordon Bleu's justly famous soufflés, to be made on the day.

As an alternative main course, try caneton rouennaise. Cold roast ducklings are filled with a rich pâté mixture, coated with aspic and served with a cherry compote. The recipe is on page 22.

Filets de Sole Florida

★ *Boeuf en Daube*
★ *Croquettes Romana*

Soufflé Moka au Gingembre

Red wine – Nuits St. Georges (Burgundy)

Filets de sole Florida

6 large fillets of lemon or Dover sole
(each approx. 5 oz)
½ pint court bouillon (see box)
2 Texan or Jaffa grapefruit

For hollandaise sauce
½ lb unsalted butter
6 egg yolks
2 tablespoons lemon juice
a few grains of cayenne pepper
pinch of salt

If serving eight, you will need 8 fillets of sole and ¾ lb unsalted butter; 9 egg yolks and 3 tablespoons lemon juice for hollandaise. Other quantities remain the same.

Method
Set the oven at 325°F or Mark 3.
Trim the fish, place the fillets unfolded in a lightly-buttered gratin dish. The gratin dish should be just large enough to hold the fish and suitable to take to the table. (If the soles are small and the fishmonger sells double fillets, fold them in two lengthwise.)
Cover with the cold court bouillon and set aside.
Remove the sections from the grapefruit and place between two ovenproof plates ready for heating in the plate-warmer, or at the very bottom of the oven.
Place the butter for hollandaise in a small pan and stand in a warm place to soften. Mix the yolks, lemon juice and seasoning in a small basin, cover and keep on one side.
Poach the fish in the pre-set oven for 8–10 minutes (or 10–12 minutes if the fillets are folded). Heat the grapefruit at the same time.
Now prepare the sauce. Put the egg yolk mixture in the liquidiser and blend for 15 seconds at maximum speed. Heat the butter until it bubbles but do not let it

Boeuf en daube

4 lb joint of beef cut from the aitchbone
½ pint red wine
3 cloves garlic (peeled and sliced)
2 tablespoons dripping, or oil
2 onions (sliced)
2 carrots (sliced)
2–3 sticks celery (sliced)
1½ pints jellied brown stock (see page 124)
1 tablespoon tomato purée
bouquet garni
salt and pepper

For serving
arrowroot (see method)
extra brown stock

If serving eight, you will need a 5 lb joint of beef. Other quantities remain the same.

Method
Place the joint in a deep dish, pour over the wine and add the garlic. Cover and leave overnight, or longer if possible, to marinate.
Then take up meat and wipe it dry, reserving marinade. Brown on all sides in the hot dripping or oil, in a thick flame-proof casserole. Lift out meat, reduce heat, and add the sliced vegetables. Cover and cook gently for 7–10 minutes. Strain the marinade into the casserole and allow to simmer until the liquid is reduced to half quantity. Then place the joint on the vegetables, add the stock, purée and bouquet garni. Season, cover and cook in a moderate oven at 325°F or Mark 3, for 3 hours.

Soufflé moka au gingembre

6 large eggs
10 oz caster sugar
1 tablespoon instant coffee granules, dissolved in ¼ pint freshly-boiled water
¾ oz gelatine
¼ pint water
¾ pint whipping, or double, cream
2–3 tablespoons preserved ginger (finely sliced)

For decoration
¼ pint double cream
coffee dragées or slices of preserved ginger

7-inch diameter top (No. 1 size) soufflé dish

Method
Prepare soufflé dish by tying a double-thickness band of greaseproof paper round the outside to stand 3 inches above top of dish.
Separate the eggs, place the yolks, sugar and coffee mixture in a basin and whisk at high speed until thick and mousse-like (or place basin over a pan of hot water and whisk by hand). Soak the gelatine in the water and dissolve over gentle heat. Partially whip the cream and whisk the egg whites until stiff.
Stir the cream very carefully into the yolk mixture, add dissolved gelatine and stand the bowl in a dish of cold water containing a few ice cubes. Fold the egg whites and ginger into the mixture and when it begins to thicken creamily, turn

brown. Turn down the speed of the liquidiser, remove the centre of the liquidiser lid and pour in the hot butter in a steady stream; cover and blend for a further 5 seconds. If you do not have a liquidiser, cream egg yolks in a bowl, add the lemon juice and seasoning and set the bowl over a pan of boiling water. Gradually add butter in small pieces, stirring vigorously until the sauce thickens. It should have the consistency of thick cream. Remove bowl from heat and taste for seasoning.

To serve Carefully tip the court bouillon from the fish and place 1–2 segments of grapefruit on each fillet. Blend the sauce for 2–3 seconds before turning into a bowl which should be just warm, not hot. Hand the sauce separately at table. ■

> **Court bouillon**
> Place a sliced carrot, a peeled onion, a bouquet garni, 4 peppercorns and 1½ tablespoons vinegar in 1½ pints water. Salt lightly, and bring to boil. Cover pan and simmer for 15–20 minutes. Strain before using.

After segmenting grapefruit, pour the court bouillon over fish, and poach

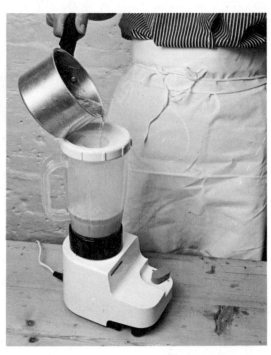

For sauce: turn down speed and pour in melted butter in a steady stream

To freeze Take up the joint, strain the gravy and set both aside to get cold. Wrap and freeze joint. Skim fat from gravy, pack into a carton and freeze.

Thawing and serving Thaw the joint for 24 hours and the gravy for 12 hours in the refrigerator. Slice the meat and arrange on a serving dish. Heat the gravy to boiling point and thicken lightly with arrowroot. (Allow 1 level tablespoon slaked (mixed) with a tablespoon of stock for every ½ pint of gravy.) Adjust seasoning. Spoon a little over the dish, cover with foil and heat for 20 minutes in a pre-set oven at 350°F or Mark 4. Serve meat separately from the croquettes romana, and hand the gravy in a sauceboat. Serve with courgettes. ■

After the cooked joint is thawed, it is cut into slices and arranged on a serving dish *for reheating. The croquettes, too, are now thawed and ready to be heated up*

into the prepared soufflé dish. Leave in the refrigerator to set. Allow 2 hours.

To serve Peel away the paper around the soufflé dish and decorate the top of the soufflé with whipped cream and coffee dragées, or sliced preserved ginger. ■

Tie a double-thickness band of grease-proof paper to stand 3 inches above rim

Whisk the egg yolks, sugar and dissolved coffee until thick and mousse-like

Croquettes romana

¾ pint milk and water (mixed)
1 bayleaf
1 small onion (peeled)
5 tablespoons (3 oz) polenta, or
  coarse semolina
¼ oz butter
3 oz cooked ham (finely chopped)
1 small egg
salt and pepper
Dijon mustard

For coating
flour seasoned with salt and pepper
beaten egg
pinch of salt
dry white breadcrumbs
deep fat for frying

If serving eight, you will need 1 pint milk and water, 6 tablespoons (4 oz) polenta, or coarse semolina and 4 oz cooked ham. All other quantities remain the same.

Method
Bring the ¾ pint of milk and water slowly to the boil with the bayleaf and whole onion. Draw aside, take out bayleaf and onion and sift in the polenta, or semolina. Simmer for 6–7 minutes, stirring frequently. Draw aside, beat in the butter, chopped ham and the egg. Season well with salt, pepper and mustard, and turn into a bowl to cool. When cold, scoop out in even-size pieces and roll each on a floured board to form a ball.

For coating: add salt to egg, brush the balls with this and roll in the breadcrumbs on a board sprinkled with seasoned flour. Fry in deep fat (350–375°F) until golden brown.

To freeze When cold, pack and freeze in a foil container.

Thawing and serving Take out and thaw at room temperature for 2–3 hours. Place on a baking sheet, uncovered, and heat on the shelf under the meat. Serve on a separate dish. ∎

TIMETABLE

Day before (evening)
Transfer beef and gravy from freezer to refrigerator to thaw. (Remove sole fillets from freezer, if using frozen fish.)

Day of party (morning)
Prepare soufflé, but do not decorate.
Section grapefruit; place between two plates ready for heating.
Wash and dry fish fillets (if using fresh). Arrange in dish ready for poaching. Store in refrigerator.
Make court bouillon, if none in freezer.
Prepare and wash vegetables.
Take croquettes out of freezer and leave to thaw.

Order of work

6.30	Whip cream and decorate soufflé.
7.00	Slice beef and arrange in serving dish. Thicken gravy and pour a little over beef.
7.30	Set oven at 350°F or Mark 4.
7.40	Put on vegetables to cook. Place beef and croquettes in oven to heat. Put the grapefruit segments to warm through. Make hollandaise.
7.50	Put on sole to poach.
7.55	Tip hollandaise into a warmed basin.
8.00	Strain court bouillon from fish, garnish. Serve first course.

Cooking times in individual recipes have sometimes been adjusted to help you when cooking and serving this menu as a three-course meal.

Left: the filets de sole Florida are ready to serve. The creamy hollandaise sauce is handed round separately to each guest. Above: the finished soufflé moka au gingembre, decorated with swirls of whipped cream, and slices of preserved ginger from the jar on the right

Unlike a hot soufflé, which has to be taken straight from oven to table, a cold soufflé can be made in advance. The eggs are always separated, and it is the stiffly-beaten egg whites that give it that characteristic soufflé texture. The mixture is poured into the dish to come about 1½ inches above the rim and, when the soufflé is set, it appears to have risen, like a hot soufflé traditionally would.

TYPES OF CHERRIES

There are three easily recognisable types of cherry which follow one another throughout the season:

1 The rich red **Duke or May Duke,** whose name is said to be a corruption of Médoc, the region of France where it was first cultivated.

2 The **Bigarreau,** whose firm flesh may be white, deep red or black. The best known type, the whitehearts, (of which Naps or Napoleons are one variety) loses its colour and flavour when cooked, so should always be eaten raw.

3 Deep red **Morellos,** which have a translucent, soft flesh. Though they look beautiful enough to eat, Morellos are not dessert cherries; their flavour is acid and astringent. When the stalk is gently pulled, the pit or stone comes with it, which is why they are cut off the tree and not pulled like the other varieties. These cherries are the very best for compotes, brandied cherries or cherry brandy, or conserves.

In addition to these main types, there are several varieties of red cherry which cook well and are used principally for compotes, sauces and sweets.

ALTERNATIVE MAIN COURSE

Caneton rouennaise

2 ducklings
¼ pint stock (see page 124)
1 wine glass red wine

For pâté
½ lb chicken livers and the livers from the ducks
1 medium-size onion (chopped)
1 clove garlic (finely chopped)
4–6 oz butter
small bouquet garni
salt and pepper
1–2 tablespoons brandy

For cherry compote
1 lb red cherries
2 tablespoons caster sugar
a pinch of powdered cinnamon
1 wine glass port, or red wine
grated rind and juice of 1 orange
½ lb redcurrant jelly

To finish
1 pint aspic jelly
bunch of watercress

Method
Set the ducklings in a roasting tin with the giblets, stock and wine, but reserve livers for pâté. Roast in a moderately hot oven at 400°F or Mark 6, for 15 minutes per lb and 15 minutes over. Baste duck regularly and turn during cooking.

To prepare pâté: soften onion and garlic over heat in 1 oz of the butter until just turning colour. Add the livers, bouquet garni, and seasoning and fry together for 3 minutes. Cool, discarding bouquet garni, and chop liver very finely, or mince, if the quantity is large, then pass mixture through a fine sieve. Cream the remaining butter well and work it into the sieved mixture with the brandy.

When the ducklings are quite cold, lift off the breast meat and cut away the bone. Fill the cavity with the pâté, cut the breast meat in long thin fillets and replace in position on the pâté. Chill for about 10 minutes to firm the pâté, then wrap carefully in foil and freeze.

To make the cherry compote: stone the cherries and place in a pan with sugar and cinnamon, cover and cook slowly for 5 minutes. Cool.

Meanwhile, reduce wine by half, adding orange rind and juice and juice from the cooked cherries. Then add redcurrant jelly. When mixture has melted, add to the cherries. When cold pot and freeze.

Thawing and serving Thaw for 24 hours in refrigerator then unwrap carefully and wipe off any moisture or fat. Line a silver dish with cold liquid aspic and brush or baste the ducks with aspic on the point of setting.

Arrange the ducks on the aspic-lined dish, garnish with watercress and serve the cherry compote separately. ■

The liqueurs kirsch and noyau are made from cherries and their stones. The stones when cracked, have a distinct almond flavour. That is why cherries are often cooked with almonds for desserts as the two flavours blend particularly well

THAT PROFESSIONAL LOOK

To show your professional skill, why not start this dinner party with eggs, gently poached, trimmed and set on a base of chicken liver cream flavoured with port and brandy.

Then serve baby chickens, flamed with sherry and cooked with a sauce of herbs and tomatoes, subtly flavoured with orange. This dish, and its accompaniment of spinach-filled pancakes topped with cheese, comes from the freezer. You can also freeze the almond French flan pastry from which the tart is made (timetable is on page 27).

As an alternative starter, there's a creamy artichoke and prawn bisque which can be served hot or chilled. And to follow — turkey suprêmes from the freezer.

Œufs Pochés au Porto

★ *Poussins en Cocotte*
★ *Crépinettes d'Épinards*

Tarte au Citron

White wine – Pouilly Fumé (Loire)

Oeufs pochés au porto

6 large eggs

1 pint commercially-prepared aspic
2 fl oz port
2 oz button mushroom (sliced – allow 2
   slices for each egg) or 6 thin slices of
   truffle
squeeze of lemon juice

For liver cream
6 oz chicken livers
1 small onion
1 clove garlic
1 oz butter
1 teaspoon fresh thyme (chopped)
salt and pepper
1 tablespoon brandy
3 fl oz double cream
2 tablespoons port

6 ramekins

If serving eight, you will need 8 large eggs, 1½ pints aspic, 2½ fl oz port, 8 slices truffle (if used) and for liver cream: 8 oz chicken livers, 1½ oz butter, 1½ tablespoons brandy, 4 fl oz double cream and 2½ tablespoons port. Other quantities remain the same. You will, of course, need 8 ramekins.

Method

Poach the eggs in a saucepan or deep frying pan filled with boiling water – add about 1 tablespoon vinegar to 1 quart of water. Do not add salt as this tends to toughen the white.

Keep heat low and water gently simmering, then break eggs into pan, stirring the water gently immediately beforehand. The action of the water brings the white up, over and round the yolk. Poach for about 3½–4½ minutes until firm. Lift out with a draining spoon or fish slice and drain thoroughly. Slip into a bowl of cold water until wanted.

Prepare aspic as directed on the packet, replacing the 2 fl oz of water with the port.

Cook mushrooms in 2 tablespoons of water and a squeeze of lemon juice for 1–2 minutes. Draw aside to cool.

Now prepare the liver cream. Peel and

Poussins en cocotte

3 double poussins
1½ oz butter
1 wine glass sherry

For tomato sauce
1 shallot (finely chopped)
½ oz butter
8 fl oz canned tomatoes
bunch of herbs containing parsley stalks,
   bayleaf and thyme
2-in stick of celery
pared rind of ½ orange
salt and pepper

To finish
1 teaspoon arrowroot slaked with 1
   tablespoon stock, or water
2 fresh tomatoes (skinned and roughly
   chopped)
1 tablespoon freshly chopped parsley
   (optional)

If serving eight, you will need 4 double poussins and 2 oz butter, and for sauce: 12 fl oz canned tomatoes. Other quantities remain the same.

Method

First prepare the tomato sauce (if using sauce you have frozen, remember to remove it from the freezer to a cool larder or refrigerator for 3–4 hours before wanted. Also, add the bunch of herbs to the casserole with the poussins).

Cook shallot in the butter until soft but not coloured. Add the tomatoes, herbs, celery, orange rind and seasoning. Stir well with a wooden spoon to bruise and break down the tomatoes while bringing the mixture to boiling point. Then cover and simmer for 15–20 minutes. Remove the herbs and pass the sauce through a nylon strainer.

Heat 1 oz of the butter in a deep flame-proof casserole and brown the poussins, two at a time, very slowly on all sides, adding the extra butter as necessary. Arrange poussins in the casserole, pour

---

Tarte au citron

For 1 lb lemon curd
8 oz caster sugar
4 oz unsalted butter
2 large lemons
3 eggs

For almond pastry
9 oz plain flour
4½ oz ground almonds
6 oz butter
4½ oz caster sugar
1 egg
2 egg yolks
2 drops vanilla, or almond essence, or
   the grated rind of ½ lemon
pinch of salt

To finish
beaten egg white
caster sugar (for dusting)

9-inch diameter flan ring, and baking sheet

Method

If you have no home-made lemon curd at hand, here is the method. Place the sugar, butter, grated rind and strained juice of the lemons, together with the well-beaten eggs into an enamel pan (or stone jam jar) standing in a large pan of boiling water.

Stir gently over a low heat until the mixture is thick.

Watchpoint Do not let it boil, or the mixture will curdle.

Pour immediately into clean dry jars, and cover tightly. Lemon curd will keep for several weeks if stored in a cool place.

To prepare the pastry, sift the flour with a pinch of salt on to a pastry board, make a well in the centre and sprinkle the almonds on the flour. Place the butter, sugar, egg, egg yolks and flavouring in the middle of the flour and work these ingredients together with the fingertips of one hand. When thoroughly blended, draw in the

chop onion and garlic very finely and sauté in the butter until barely coloured. Remove any ducts from livers (if using fresh), add to onion mixture and sauté briskly for 2–3 minutes. Draw aside, add thyme, seasoning and brandy. Cool, then finely chop, sieve, or reduce to a purée in a liquidiser. Adjust seasoning, whip cream and fold into the mixture with the port. Half-fill the ramekins with this and chill.

Drain each egg carefully, trimming white if necessary, and place one in each ramekin. Have aspic ready at setting point and coat each egg with one tablespoon. (If aspic has already set, warm gently, but not too much, as aspic must be on the point of setting, otherwise it will soak into the liver cream instead of coating the egg.) Garnish each with the well drained slices of mushroom or truffle. Coat again with the cool aspic and leave to set. ■

Left: adding whipped cream to liver purée. The eggs are already poached. Above:

cooling port-flavoured aspic over ice until just on the point of setting to coat eggs

the sherry over the browned birds and set alight. Shake casserole gently over a low heat until the flames subside then pour the prepared tomato sauce over the poussins.

Cover the casserole, bring sauce to boiling point, place in moderate oven at 350°F or Mark 4, for 30–35 minutes.

To freeze Remove the poussins, split each in two, cut away the backbone with kitchen scissors and place each half in a foil container. Cover, wrap, and freeze. Pot and freeze the sauce separately.

Thawing and serving Remove poussins and sauce the day before they are required and transfer to the refrigerator. Reheat in the foil dishes or a flameproof casserole at 350°F or Mark 4, for 30–35 minutes. Bring the sauce to the boil in a saucepan, bind with 1 teaspoon arrowroot mixed with 1 tablespoon stock or water. Adjust the seasoning and add the tomatoes.

Place the poussins on a serving dish and spoon the sauce over, then sprinkle with chopped parsley. Serve with crêpinettes d'épinards. ■

Left: pour sherry over browned birds, set alight, then add the tomato sauce. Above: when completely cooked, cut away backbone; pack and freeze the poussins

flour and almonds and knead lightly until smooth. Chill for at least an hour. Wrap and freeze.

Thawing and serving Thaw overnight in refrigerator if using frozen pastry. Pre-set oven at 375°F or Mark 5. Take two-thirds of the pastry, roll out into a round about ¼ in thick, line into the flan ring taking the pastry up the sides of the ring. Prick base lightly with a fork and chill for 5–10 minutes. Fill about three-quarters full with lemon curd. Roll out the remaining pastry into a round to fit the top of the flan. Seal the edges and mark the top in a spiral with the point of a knife.

Bake for about 40 minutes, covering the flan with a sheet of greaseproof paper after 30 minutes to prevent the crust browning. Take flan from the oven, remove greaseproof paper, brush with lightly beaten egg white and dust with caster sugar. Return to the oven for 8–10 minutes to 'frost' the top. Serve when cold. ■

To make the classic French flan pastry, work eggs, sugar and butter together with fingertips until blended

Draw in flour and ground almonds with a knife before kneading pastry lightly and chilling or freezing before rolling out

The poussins, with their tomato garnish, are ready to serve. Top right: the finished spinach-filled crêpinettes

Crêpinettes d'épinards

For pancake batter
3 oz plain flour
1 egg
1 egg yolk
7–8 fl oz milk
1 tablespoon melted butter, or salad oil

For filling
2 lb fresh leaf spinach
½ oz butter
½ oz flour
3 fl oz creamy milk
salt and pepper
a little grated nutmeg

To finish
1 oz melted butter
1–2 oz grated cheese

If serving eight, you will need 3 lb spinach, ¾ oz butter, ¾ oz flour and 5 fl oz milk to fill the pancakes. The same quantity of basic batter will suffice if you fry the pancakes nicely thin.

Method

To make pancakes, sift the flour with the salt into a bowl, make a well in the centre, add the egg and yolk and begin to add the milk slowly, stirring all the time. When half the milk has been added, stir in the melted butter or oil and beat well until smooth.

Add the remaining milk and leave to stand for 30 minutes before using. The batter should have the consistency of thin cream – if too thick, add a little extra milk.

Fry thin pancakes, no larger than five inches in diameter, allowing 2 per person. Set aside to cool, stacking one on top of the other, with a piece of greaseproof paper between each.

Cook the spinach, drain thoroughly, press between two plates to remove all the water and chop finely. (If using frozen spinach, allow to thaw, press between 2 plates to drain). Heat the spinach in a pan until all the moisture is driven off, then add the butter and the flour and blend in the milk. Stir until boiling, then season well, adding a very little grated nutmeg.

Fill the pancakes with the spinach mixture and roll up.

To freeze Place crêpinettes side by side in a foil container. Brush with melted butter and scatter over the cheese. When cold, wrap and freeze.

Thawing and serving Thaw for 2–3 hours at room temperature. When thawed, lift carefully into a well-buttered gratin dish and bake in a moderately hot oven, 375°F or Mark 5, for 20 minutes – or until golden-brown. ■

TIMETABLE

Day before (evening)
Remove livers from freezer and leave on bottom shelf of refrigerator to thaw. Remove poussins, sauce and almond pastry from freezer and leave in refrigerator to thaw.
Check store cupboard for lemon curd.

Day of party (morning)
Make liver cream, fill into ramekins. Press a round of foil on to each and leave in refrigerator.
Cook mushrooms and leave in liquid. Poach eggs and leave in a bowl of cold water.

Day of party (afternoon)
Remove crêpinettes from freezer (if frozen filled). Otherwise, take out number of pancakes required and leave to thaw.
Cook spinach and drain (or thaw frozen spinach).
Roll out almond pastry and fill and bake tarte au citron. Leave to cool.
Complete crêpinettes; leave in refrigerator.

Order of work

6.00	Make up aspic and complete oeufs pochés. Chill to set.
7.15	Set oven at 350°F or Mark 4.
7.30	Place poussins in oven to reheat.
7.40	Place crêpinettes in oven to reheat.
7.45	Reheat and finish sauce for poussins. Add to dish just before serving.
8.00	Serve first course.

Cooking times in individual recipes have sometimes been adjusted to help you when cooking and serving this menu as a three-course meal.

The finished tarte au citron straight from the oven; it is served cold

ALTERNATIVE STARTER

Artichoke and prawn bisque

1 lb Jerusalem artichokes
  (weighed when peeled)
½ lb potatoes (peeled)
1 medium-sized onion (peeled)
2 oz butter
1 level teaspoon paprika
1¼ pints milk
½ pint water
salt and pepper
4–6 oz fresh or frozen prawns
a few drops Tabasco

For liaison
1–2 egg yolks or 1 rounded
  teaspoon arrowroot
2½ fl oz cream

Method
Slice the vegetables thinly and sweat slowly in the butter in a covered pan for about 7–8 minutes without allowing them to colour. Stir in the paprika, milk and water. Season lightly and bring to the boil. Simmer until the vegetables are really tender, about 15–20 minutes.

Make sure the prawns are well thawed (if from the freezer). Dry them with a paper towel and chop finely. Work the soup in a liquidiser until very smooth. Return it to a clean pan; add prawns and Tabasco sauce.

Combine the egg yolks, or arrowroot, and cream for the liaison, and blend into the soup. Stir over gentle heat until it reaches scalding point. Draw aside and serve in a tureen with croûtons. ■

To make croûtons
Fry small cubes of stale white bread in shallow or deep fat until golden brown. After draining on absorbent paper, salt lightly.

Jerusalem artichokes are not to be confused with green globe artichokes. A Jerusalem artichoke is the root of a type of sunflower, looks rather like a very knobbly new potato and has a subtle and unusual flavour.

ALTERNATIVE MAIN COURSE

Turkey suprêmes

3–4 turkey breasts
2 oz butter (for frying)
1 wine glass white wine
salt and pepper
1 teaspoon tomato purée
6 fl oz jellied stock

For salpicon
8 oz mushrooms (sliced)
2 shallots or 1 small onion
  (finely chopped)
¾ oz butter
½ oz flour
3–4 fl oz stock
4 oz cooked tongue (shredded)
4 oz cooked ham (shredded)

For mornay sauce
1 oz butter
1 oz flour
¾ pint milk
3 oz cheese (grated)

To finish
1 teaspoon arrowroot slaked
  (mixed) with a little cold water

Method
Split the turkey breasts, place each suprême between two pieces of waxed, or heavy greaseproof, paper, and bat both out thinly, using a cutlet bat or the base of a heavy pan. Set aside.

To prepare salpicon: soften shallots, or onion, in ½ oz of the butter, add mushrooms and sauté briskly for 2–3 minutes. Draw aside, add the rest of the butter and stir in the flour. Moisten with stock and bring to the boil. Simmer for 1 minute, then draw aside and add the tongue and ham.

Cut the turkey meat into escalopes and sauté them in the 1 oz of butter, allowing them to colour slightly. Add the wine, season and cover. Simmer for 10–15 minutes. Take out and pack in a shallow foil container. To the gravy in the sauté pan, add 3–4 fl oz jellied stock and the teaspoon of tomato purée. Boil up well and, when cool, pour into a container for freezing.

Prepare mornay sauce: melt butter in a small pan, remove from heat and stir in flour. Blend in half the milk, then stir in rest. Stir over moderate heat until boiling; remove from heat and stir in half the cheese. Do not allow to reboil. Place a spoonful of the salpicon on the top of each escalope, coat with the mornay sauce and sprinkle with the rest of the cheese. Wrap and freeze.

Thawing and serving Allow to thaw out overnight in refrigerator. Bake for 30 minutes in a moderately hot oven, 375°F or Mark 5, to brown and reheat.

Bring the gravy to boiling point in a small pan, thicken slightly with 1 teaspoon arrowroot slaked with stock or water. Pour round suprêmes just before serving. ■

Maître d'hôtel potatoes

2 lb even-size potatoes
1½ oz butter
2 shallots (chopped)
2 tablespoons parsley (chopped)
salt and pepper

Method
Scrub potatoes and boil or steam in their skins until tender but firm. Drain and dry. Peel potatoes, slice and arrange in a hot dish and keep warm.

Melt butter in a small pan, add shallot, cover pan and set on low heat for 2–3 minutes. Then draw aside, add parsley and plenty of seasoning and pour over the potatoes. Slide into the oven for 2–3 minutes before serving. ■

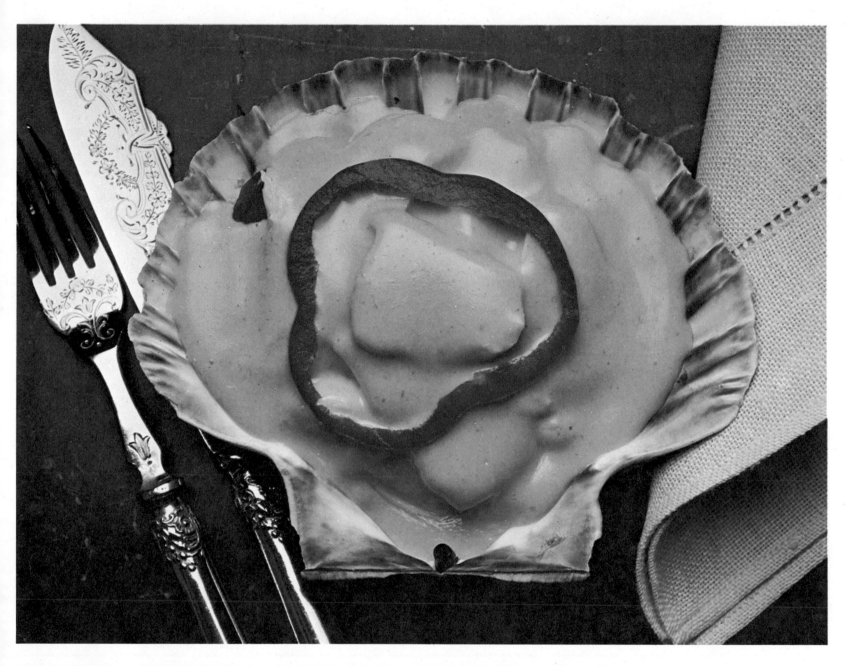

FOR SOPHISTICATED TASTES

For the first course of this three-course dinner party menu, there's a simple to prepare, but delicious dish of white fish, coated with pimiento-flavoured mayonnaise and served in shells (see the individual portion shown above). This can be made on the day of the party.

Follow it with an unusual savoury cream made with ham and chicken, with a madeira sauce. A julienne of celery makes a suitable accompaniment.

For dessert, try a light almond-flavoured sponge roll, filled with lemon cream and served with a rich, slightly tart, blackberry and apple sauce. Both the main course and the dessert, with their accompanying sauces, are from the freezer. Use the timetable on page 33 to plan your cooking.

Another freezer main course dish — a rich ballotine of pheasant — is on page 34.

Coquilles de Poisson Cordon-Bleu

★ *Pain de Jambon et Volaille*
★ *Haricots Verts or Julienne of Celery*

★ *Biscuit Roulé aux Amandes*
with Blackberry and Apple Sauce

White wine - Piesporter (Moselle)

Coquilles de poisson Cordon Bleu

1¼ lb steak of firm white fish (cod, turbot or halibut)
½ pint court bouillon (see page 19)
3 large ripe tomatoes
1 fresh red pepper (for decoration)

For sauce
½ pint thick mayonnaise (see page 125)
1 clove garlic, crushed with a little salt
1 teaspoon tomato purée
salt and pepper

6 scallop shells or ramekins

> **If serving eight,** you will need 1¾ lb fish, 4 tomatoes, ¾ pint mayonnaise (see page 125) and 8 scallop shells. Other quantities remain the same.

Method
Place the fish in a pan, cover with the court bouillon and poach gently for 35—40 minutes. Allow to cool in the liquid. When cold, drain off the cooking liquid, remove skin and bone from the fish and divide carefully into large flakes.

Scald, skin and quarter the tomatoes, scoop out the seeds and slice tomatoes again. Rub the tomato seeds in a nylon sieve and reserve the juice for the sauce. Slice the red pepper in thin rounds, remove the centre core and seeds, blanch, refresh and drain well.

Add the crushed garlic to the mayonnaise with the tomato purée. Adjust the seasoning and work in a little of the reserved tomato juice.

Pain de jambon et volaille

4 lb roasting chicken
½ lb cooked ham (this could be the end of a home-cooked corner or slipper of bacon, and a proportion of fat should be included)
salt and pepper
3 eggs (beaten)
4 fl oz cream

For panade
2 oz butter
2 oz flour
½ pint strong chicken stock (make this from the chicken carcase, giblets, 1 onion, 1 carrot, 1 stick celery, bouquet garni, salt and pepper and 2 pints water – see method)

For sauce madère
3 level tablespoons tomato purée
1 pint demi-glace sauce (see page 124)
small wineglass Madeira
¾ oz butter

Size 1 (3-pint capacity) soufflé dish

Method
Remove the skin from the chicken and, using a small sharp knife, cut every scrap of flesh from the carcase and pass through a mincer with the ham.

Now prepare the chicken stock. Cover the chicken carcase and giblets with the water. Add the onion, carrot, celery and bouquet garni, and season. Bring to the boil and simmer gently for 2 hours, then strain. Reserve ½ pint of this strong chicken stock.

Prepare the panade: melt the butter, blend in the flour and measured chicken stock, and bring to the boil. Turn on to a plate to cool. Beat the cooled panade into the minced meats and season well. Work in the beaten eggs, then the cream and turn into a large well-buttered soufflé dish. Smooth over the top, cover with foil and cook 'au bain-marie' for about 45 minutes at 350°F or Mark 4, until top is firm to the touch.

Allow to cool in the dish, and when

Biscuit roulé aux amandes

3½ oz flour, less 1 tablespoon to be replaced by 1 tablespoon cornflour
1½ teaspoons baking powder
6½ oz caster sugar
4 eggs (separated)
a pinch of salt
1 tablespoon cold water
1 teaspoon orange flower water

For filling
7 oz blanched almonds
2 oz caster sugar
3 egg whites
grated rind and juice of 1 lemon
7½ fl oz double cream

Paper case or swiss roll tin 13 inches by 10½ inches (for instructions on how to make a paper case, see page 77)

Method
Set the oven at 350°F or Mark 4.

Sift the mixed flours and baking powder four times. Sift the sugar and set aside 4 tablespoons to beat with the four egg whites. Beat the egg whites with a pinch of salt until stiff. Whisk in 3 tablespoons of the sugar then fold in the fourth.

Place the egg yolks, liquid and remaining sugar in a bowl. Beat until, when a little of the batter is lifted on the whisk, it falls in a thick ribbon on the mixture in the bowl and holds its shape. Fold the egg white mixture into the yolk mixture and finally fold in the flour. Pour into the greased and floured paper case or swiss roll tin. Spread mixture evenly and bake in the pre-set oven for 12 minutes.

Turn on to a greaseproof paper sprinkled with a little caster sugar, quickly remove the paper case or swiss roll tin, and roll the sponge up carefully with another piece of

Divide the shredded tomato among the scallop shells, spoon the flaked fish on top and coat with the mayonnaise. Garnish each 'coquille' with a red pepper ring. ■

Ingredients for making coquilles de poisson Cordon Bleu

quite cold, wrap in foil and slip into a polythene bag to freeze.

Meanwhile prepare the sauce madère. Add tomato purée to the prepared demiglace sauce and simmer, skimming often, until well reduced. Then add Madeira and beat in the butter. When the sauce is cold, turn into a carton, cover and freeze.

Thawing and serving Thaw out the chicken cream and the sauce in the refrigerator overnight. Reheat the cream by steaming gently on top of the stove for 20–25 minutes. Draw aside and leave for 5 minutes before turning out. Reheat sauce slowly just to boiling point.

Turn out cream carefully on to a serving dish, spoon over enough sauce to cover the dish and hand the rest of the sauce separately. Serve with haricots verts or julienne of celery (recipe overleaf). ■

Beat the cooled panade into the minced meats before adding the eggs and cream

Lower the covered ham and chicken cream into a bain-marie for cooking

greaseproof paper on the inside.

To prepare the filling: grind the nuts and then pound with the sugar using a pestle and mortar, adding the lightly-beaten egg whites a little at a time. Flavour with the lemon juice and rind. Alternatively, use your liquidiser to grate the almonds coarsely. Then add the sugar to the almonds by degrees, work in the egg whites, finishing with lemon juice and rind. The mixture should be creamy and not too soft.

Lightly whip the cream and fold into the almond mixture. Unroll the sponge, removing inside paper and spread with the cream. Roll up again and wrap in foil.

Slip into a polythene bag and freeze.

Thawing and serving Leave at room temperature for 3–4 hours then unwrap carefully and dust the roll with icing sugar. Serve with a fruit sauce – plum (see page 85), or blackberry and apple. ■

Turn cooked sponge on to greaseproof paper and quickly remove the paper case

Spread the cooled sponge thickly with the cream filling and carefully roll up again

The finished pain de jambon et volaille, coated with sauce madère, is served with a julienne of celery

Julienne of celery

1 large head of celery
1 oz butter
1 shallot or small onion (finely chopped)
salt
black pepper (ground from the mill)
chopped parsley (to garnish)

Method
Cut the celery into julienne strips ($\frac{1}{8}$-inch thick by $1\frac{1}{2}$-2 inches long). Melt the butter in a flameproof dish, add the celery and shallot, cover and shake over the heat for 4–5 minutes, taking care that the vegetables do not colour. Season to taste.

Then cover the dish with greaseproof paper and a lid and cook on top of the stove for a further 8 minutes. Sprinkle with chopped parsley and serve. ∎

Blackberry and apple sauce goes well with the biscuit roulé aux amandes

Blackberry and apple sauce

1 small cooking apple
½ lb fresh blackberries or 1 (14 oz) can
3–4 tablespoons granulated sugar (or half the quantity if using canned blackberries)
¼ pint water (see method)
1 rounded teaspoon arrowroot

Method
Peel and quarter the apple. Remove the core, cut the apple into slices and place in a pan with the blackberries. Add the sugar, cover and cook for 4–5 minutes, or until the juice begins to run. (If using canned blackberries, add a little juice, reserving the rest, cover and cook for 4–5 minutes).

Add the water, or if using canned blackberries, the reserved juice with 2½ fl oz water added. Simmer for 5–6 minutes then rub through a nylon strainer. Return purée to the pan, adjust sweetening and thicken with the arrowroot slaked (mixed) with a tablespoon of cold water.

Stir until boiling, then pour into a bowl and allow to cool. When cold, pour into a container and freeze.

Thawing and serving Remove from the freezer and thaw at room temperature for 3–4 hours, before serving.

TIMETABLE

Day before
Remove pain de jambon et volaille from the freezer and leave to thaw in the refrigerator. Place sauce madère to thaw in the refrigerator.
Make mayonnaise.

Day of party (morning)
Make up coquilles de poisson, cover and keep in refrigerator, but do not garnish with pepper rings.
Remove biscuit roulé aux amandes from the freezer and allow to thaw at room temperature.
Thaw blackberry and apple sauce at room temperature.

Day of party (afternoon)
Unwrap thawed biscuit roulé and dust with icing sugar.
Prepare julienne of celery (if serving).

Order of work
7.30   Reheat pain de jambon et volaille by steaming gently on top of the stove.
Cook julienne of celery (if serving).
Cook haricots verts straight from the freezer (if serving).
Reheat sauce madère gently to just below boiling point.

7.50   Dish up vegetables and keep hot.

7.55   Turn out pain de jambon et volaille on to a serving dish and pour a little sauce madère over. Keep hot.
Garnish each coquille with a red pepper ring.

8.00   Serve first course.

Cooking times in individual recipes have sometimes been adjusted to help you when cooking and serving this menu as a three-course meal.

Pheasant
(Season: 1 October– 1 February)

This handsome bird was originally a foreigner to Great Britain but for some time past has been a native of our woodlands. It is the only game bird which is bred for shooting. Hen birds are as a rule more tender and succulent than the cocks. Pheasants, like most game, are sold by the brace, ie. a cock and a hen. Young birds may be spit or oven roasted for approximately 45–55 minutes. Cocks and slightly older birds should be pot roasted to keep them as moist as possible. The flavour of a pheasant goes well with a sub-acid such as apple, or sometimes even grapes or raisins. A pheasant lends itself to a variety of dishes, but If served plainly roast it must be well hung otherwise it can be dull and tasteless. Serve with sprouts or braised celery, fried or browned crumbs, bread sauce and game chips. A good size bird serves 4–5 people.

ALTERNATIVE MAIN COURSE

Ballotine of pheasant

a brace of plump pheasants
salt and pepper ground from mill
1–2 oz butter
2 wine glasses red wine

For farce
8 oz veal or pork (minced)
6 oz cooked ham (minced)
¾ cup fresh white breadcrumbs
2 shallots, or 1 small onion (finely chopped)
¾ oz butter
1 dessertspoon freshly chopped herbs or 1 teaspoon chopped parsley
1–2 tablespoons sherry
pinch of ground mace, or nutmeg
1 egg (beaten)

For sauce
¾ pint demi-glace sauce (see page 124)
4 oz button mushrooms (finely sliced)
½ oz butter
3 shallots (chopped)
1 wine glass red wine
1 dessertspoon tomato purée

Trussing needle and fine string, or skewers

Method
Bone out the pheasant, spread out on a board, cut side uppermost, and season well.

To prepare the farce: mix the minced meats and breadcrumbs together. Soften shallots, or onion, in the butter without allowing to colour; add this to the meat mixture with the herbs, or parsley, and 1–2 tablespoons sherry. Add spice, salt and pepper and enough egg to moisten the farce but not to make it too wet. Spread farce over the pheasant, roll it up neatly, and sew or fasten it with small skewers.

Warm a thick flameproof casserole, drop in the 1 oz butter and brown the ballotine slowly on all sides. Add red wine, cover tightly and cook gently in a moderate oven, 350°F or Mark 4, for about 1 hour.

To finish: have ready the demi-glace sauce. Sauté the mushrooms in the ½ oz butter until just turning colour, add the shallots and continue to cook for 2–3 minutes. Pour on wine, allow to reduce to half quantity then blend in tomato purée and demi-glace sauce. Simmer 2–3 minutes, adjust seasoning and allow to cool, then pot and freeze.

When pheasant is cold, carve in slices and skim the fat from any liquid in the casserole. Pack the ballotine in a foil container, spoon the liquid over, then cover, wrap and freeze.

Thawing and serving Thaw pheasant and sauce 24 hours in refrigerator. Place pheasant in a flameproof serving dish, cover with foil and reheat at 350°F or Mark 4, about 35–40 minutes. Heat the sauce to boiling point, spoon half over the pheasant, and then serve rest in a gravy boat. ∎

Game chips

Choose large potatoes (1½ lb will be sufficient for up to 6 people). Peel and trim off the ends and cut in very thin slices. Soak slices in a large bowl of cold water for 1 hour, separating slices to prevent their sticking together. Drain well and leave wrapped in a clean teacloth for 20 minutes, again separating the slices so that they dry thoroughly.

Fry the slices a few at a time in a basket in deep fat heated to 350°F, and remove when bubbling subsides. When all slices have been cooked, reheat the fat to 400°F, put two or three batches of slices together in the basket and fry until golden-brown. Turn potato slices out of basket into pan to finish cooking. Drain well on crumpled, absorbent paper, pile on to a hot dish, sprinkle with salt and serve.

Watchpoint Never cover up game chips or they will lose all their crispness. ∎

A SUMMER MENU

This dinner party menu starts with a piquant soup of tomato and pimiento, delicately-flavoured with horseradish. It is a very simple soup to make, and comes from the freezer ready for reheating. The main course is a cold joint of veal, cooked, sliced and sandwiched with a mixture of cream cheese, bacon and spinach, and set in aspic. The meat can be cooked and frozen ready for slicing. The dish can then be put together on the day and served with new potatoes.

To finish, Rosemary Hume and Muriel Downes suggest a superb confection of rounds of puff pastry, glazed with red-currant, and filled with strawberries flavoured with orange and brandy (see above).

On page 40, there are two recipes using pork, which are more suitable for lunch, and an alternative main course of veal paupiettes with mushrooms and cream sauce.

★ *Potage Crème Créole*

Veau Farci en Gelée
New Potatoes

Tarte aux Fraises Cordon Bleu
with Whipped Cream

White wine - Mâcon (Burgundy)

Potage crème créole

2 tablespoons finely chopped onion
1 oz butter
4 tablespoons finely chopped canned
  pimiento
1½ oz flour
1 (14 oz) can Italian tomatoes
2 pints good chicken stock (see page 124)
salt and pepper
a very little cayenne pepper
1 dessertspoon freshly grated horseradish
  or 1 small teaspoon horseradish cream

To finish
2–3 fl oz cream

Method
Soften the onion in the butter without allowing it to colour. Add the pimiento and, after a few minutes, the flour. Add tomatoes and stock, bring to the boil, season, cover and simmer 20–25 minutes. Pass through a fine Mouli sieve, adjust seasoning, and add the grated horseradish or horseradish cream. Pack in cartons and freeze.
Thawing and serving Leave overnight in the refrigerator before pouring into a pan to reheat. Bring to the boil, then tip into a warmed tureen and 'streak' in the cream before serving. ■

Veau farci en gelée

1½ lb oyster of veal (weight without bone)
oil for browning
1 onion
1 carrot
bouquet garni
1 wine glass white wine or white stock
  (see page 124)
salt and pepper

For filling
1 lb leaf spinach or 1 (12 oz) packet frozen
  spinach
4 oz streaky bacon rashers (thinly cut)
1 shallot or 1 small onion (finely chopped)
a nut of butter
8 oz Philadelphia cream cheese
salt and pepper

To finish
1 pint commercially-prepared aspic, flavoured
  with sherry (see method)
watercress (to garnish)

2 lb loaf tin

If serving eight, you will need 2 lb veal, 1½ pints aspic, 2 shallots and 11 oz Philadelphia cream cheese. Other quantities remain the same.

Method
Set oven at 325°F or Mark 3.
Tie up the veal neatly. Brown all over in a little oil in a flameproof casserole. Add the onion and the carrot, peeled but left whole, the bouquet garni, wine or stock, and seasoning. Cover tightly and braise in the pre-set moderate oven for 45–50 minutes. Take out and allow to cool in the casserole.
When quite cold, remove joint, wrap in foil and freeze. Reserve the cooking liquid and freeze separately for future use.
Thawing and serving Leave in the refrigerator for 24 hours before slicing and filling.
To fill: boil the spinach 4–5 minutes and drain. Refresh with cold water and press well between 2 plates to remove all the water. (If using frozen spinach, blanch in boiling water 1–2 minutes before draining). Cut bacon into small strips and fry with the shallot, or onion, and nut of butter until crisp. Draw aside and allow to cool. Work into the cheese with the spinach and season.

Tarte aux fraises Cordon Bleu

8 oz quantity puff pastry (see page 125)
beaten egg (to glaze)
redcurrant jelly glaze (preferably made with
  home-made preserve – see method)

For pâte sucrée
2 oz flour
pinch of salt
1 oz butter
1 oz caster sugar
a little vanilla essence
1 egg yolk

For filling
1½ lb strawberries
1–2 tablespoons redcurrant jelly
grated rind and juice of 1 orange
1–2 tablespoons brandy
5 fl oz double cream (for serving)

Method
Remove puff pastry from the freezer and allow to thaw overnight.
Make up the pâte sucrée: sieve the flour with a pinch of salt on to a marble slab or pastry board, make a well in the centre and in it place the butter, sugar, a drop of vanilla essence and the egg yolk. Using the fingertips of one hand only, pinch and work these last ingredients together until well-blended. Then draw in the flour, knead lightly until smooth. Chill for 1–2 hours before using.
Set oven at 375°F or Mark 5.
Roll out the pâte sucrée to an 8-inch round, (use a flan ring as a guide) and slip on to a dampened baking sheet. Prick with a fork and bake in the pre-set oven.
Meanwhile roll out the thawed puff pastry to about $\frac{1}{10}$ inch thick. Again using the flan ring as a guide, cut out two 8-inch rounds of pastry and fold up the trimmings. With a plain cutter, cut a

These simple ingredients are made into a delicately flavoured tomato and pimiento soup. See the finished dish on page 39

Slice veal — the slices should not be more than $\frac{1}{4}$-inch thick — spread the slices with the cheese mixture and reshape into a joint. Chill for about 1 hour.

Have ready the aspic, made up as directed on the packet, replacing 3 tablespoons of water with sherry. Run about 1-inch of aspic into the loaf tin. When set, put in the veal joint and run cool aspic round the sides to come level with the veal. Allow to set, then fill to the top of the tin with aspic.

Watchpoint Make sure the veal is just below the top of the tin, otherwise it is difficult to turn out.

To turn out: dip tin in hot water for 2–3 seconds, lift out and dry. Turn out on to a chilled serving dish and garnish with watercress. Serve with hot small new potatoes, tossed in butter and parsley. ■

Tie veal up firmly to keep it in shape while braising with vegetables and wine or stock

Spread the slices of cooked veal with filling then reshape them into a joint

---

smaller round, about $3\frac{1}{2}$-inches in diameter, from the centre of each of the two larger puff pastry rounds and slip the 2 rings thus formed on to dampened baking sheets. Prick and chill. Meanwhile add the smaller rounds to the trimmings, roll out and cut a third 8-inch round. Brush this with beaten egg and then stamp out the centre as before. Chill the third ring.

From the centre round, cut out 6 crescents for decoration and set on a baking sheet. Bake these and the three puff pastry rings in a pre-set oven, 425°F or Mark 7, for 8 minutes and 12–15 minutes respectively. When well-browned, lift on to a rack to cool.

Meanwhile prepare the redcurrant glaze. Beat the redcurrant jelly preserve with a fork or small whisk until it liquefies, then rub through a strainer into a small saucepan. Heat it gently without stirring until it has become quite clear.

Do not allow it to boil as this will spoil

recipe continued on page 39

Using the fingertips of one hand, blend together ingredients for pâte sucrée base

Glaze and layer each puff pastry ring before decorating and filling the tarte

The rich, cold stuffed veal is garnished with watercress and ready to serve with hot new potatoes

The finished potage crème créole, shown in the tureen, streaked with cream

Day before

Remove cooked veal from the freezer and allow to thaw in the refrigerator. Thaw uncooked puff pastry in the refrigerator.

Take potage crème créole from the freezer and put in the refrigerator to thaw.

Day of party

Prepare and cook pastry case for tarte aux fraises but do not fill.

Make up aspic and leave to chill.

Prepare spinach filling for veal.

Fill, reshape into a joint and chill.

Coat veal with aspic and leave to set in the refrigerator.

Hull strawberries and leave to macerate in orange juice and brandy.

	Order of work
7.25	Whip cream for tarte. Wash and dry watercress.
7.40	Put new potatoes to boil, tossing before serving in butter and parsley.
7.45	Put soup to reheat. Remove veal from refrigerator, turn out of tin and garnish ready for serving.
8.00	Turn soup into a heated tureen. Streak with cream and serve first course. Between courses, turn strawberry filling into pastry case and serve immediately with cream.

Cooking times in individual recipes have sometimes been adjusted to help you when cooking and serving this menu as a three-course meal.

Tarte aux fraises Cordon Bleu

continued from page 37

both the colour and the flavour.

When both the pâte sucrée and the puff pastry are cooked and quite cold, brush the pâte sucrée round with redcurrant glaze, and place one puff pastry ring on top. Brush this with glaze and add the second puff pastry ring. Again brush this with glaze and place the egg-glazed ring on top. Decorate this with the crescents, securing them in place with a little redcurrant glaze.

Hull the strawberries. Put 2–3 tablespoons of redcurrant jelly (not glaze) into a bowl. Add the finely-grated rind of the orange, the orange juice and the brandy. Mix well. Add the strawberries and turn them over gently until well-coated. Just before serving, pile into the pastry case. Serve with lightly whipped cream. ∎

ALTERNATIVE MAIN COURSE

Paupiettes de veau aux champignons

8 escalopes of veal

For farce
1 small chicken
¼ pint milk
2 oz butter
2 oz flour (sifted)
4 oz flat mushrooms
1 large egg (beaten)
2½ fl oz cream
salt and white pepper
chicken stock (see page 124)

For velouté sauce
1½ oz butter
1¼ oz flour
¾ pint strong chicken stock

For garnish
4 oz button mushrooms
½ oz butter
a squeeze of lemon juice

For liaison
2 egg yolks
3–4 fl oz single cream

Method
Bat out the escalopes and, if large, cut each in two.

To prepare farce: cut the flesh from the chicken, skin it and pass it through the mincer – there should be at least 8 oz. Bring the milk to the boil with 1½ oz of the butter, then add the flour off the heat and beat until smooth. Turn this panade on to a plate and leave until cold.

Meanwhile, chop the mushrooms very finely, and cook in the remaining ½ oz butter until all the moisture has been driven off.

Pound the raw chicken meat well, add the panade gradually, then work in the beaten egg, mushroom mixture and cream. Season well with salt and ground white pepper.

Spread the veal escalopes with the chicken farce, roll up and secure each with a cocktail stick, or tie with thread. Poach in chicken stock about 20–30 minutes.

Prepare the velouté sauce. Melt the butter, add flour and allow to cook for 5 seconds until pale straw-coloured. Draw pan off heat, allow to cool slightly and blend in the stock. Stir over heat until sauce thickens, add seasoning, then bring to the boil and cook until syrupy. Remove from heat and allow to cool.

Now prepare the garnish. Slice or quarter the mushrooms, depending on size, and cook briskly for one minute in the butter and lemon juice: pot and freeze sauce, and pack and freeze mushroom garnish when cold.

To freeze Drain paupiettes when cool, wrap and freeze.

Thawing and serving Allow paupiettes to thaw for 24 hours in the refrigerator, and thaw sauce and garnish for 12 hours. Place the paupiettes in a buttered ovenproof dish, cover and heat in a moderate oven at 350°F, Mark 4, for 30–40 minutes.

Add mushroom garnish to the sauce and heat to boiling point, meanwhile beating the egg yolks into the cream.

Carefully add this liaison to the sauce, adjust seasoning, reheat and spoon over the paupiettes before serving.

Serve with a salad or green vegetable of your choice. ■

> **To prepare escalopes:** lay the slices of veal fillet between waxed or grease-proof paper and, using a cutlet bat, beat well to make them thin and flat.
>
> If the veal is properly prepared by the butcher, it should not be necessary for you to beat them.

DISHES FOR LUNCHEON

Kee's barbecued spare ribs

3 lb spare ribs
2 tablespoons flour, seasoned with salt and pepper and ¼ teaspoon ground ginger
1 onion
1 clove of garlic
4 tablespoons tomato ketchup
1 tablespoon Worcestershire sauce
1 pint jellied stock
1 bayleaf
4 carrots
1 small head celery
2 tablespoons white wine vinegar
2 tablespoons soft brown sugar
2 teaspoons cornflour
2 green peppers

Method
Cut the meat into even 3-inch lengths, roll in the seasoned flour and place in a baking tin. Chop the onion and garlic very finely and mix with the sauces, brush this over the meat and place in a moderate oven, 375°F or Mark 5, for about 35 minutes until brown. Remove the meat with a draining spoon and place in a pan with the stock, bayleaf and vegetables cut in bâtons; simmer for about 40 minutes, or until tender.

Mix the vinegar and brown sugar, add to the pan, cook for a few minutes, then thicken with the cornflour slaked with a little water. Allow to cool. Meanwhile, cut the peppers into squares, removing the core and seeds; blanch, drain and refresh.

To freeze Mix the peppers with the pork and tip into a container for freezing with the sauce.

Thawing and serving Thaw for 24 hours in refrigerator and bake for 45–50 minutes at 350°F or Mark 4. Serve with a dish of plainly boiled rice. ■

Sweet and sour pork

2½ lb shoulder cut of pork
1 tablespoon dark soy sauce
2 tablespoons light soy sauce
2 medium-size onions
2 oz soft brown sugar
2 fl oz cider vinegar or white wine vinegar
2 tablespoons sesame oil
¾ pint stock
1 green pepper
2 carrots
1 tablespoon cornflour

Method
Cut the meat into cubes and marinate in the mixed soy sauces for about an hour. Quarter the onions and cut again in half across; mix the sugar with the vinegar.

Cook the onion until soft but not coloured in the sesame oil, add meat a few pieces at a time and colour briskly on all sides. Moisten with the stock, add the vinegar and sugar, and simmer gently until tender, about 30–35 minutes. Meanwhile, cut the green pepper in squares, remove seeds, blanch, drain and refresh. Cut the carrots in bâtons, cook for about 10 minutes and drain well.

Mix the cornflour to a paste with a little cold water, add to the pork and simmer a further 5 minutes.

To freeze Allow to cool, then add the pepper and carrots. Wrap and freeze.

Thawing and serving Allow to thaw 12 hours in a cool larder, then reheat slowly in a sauté pan to boiling point. Serve with plain boiled or fried rice. ■

CHICKEN COOKED IN ALE

We start our next dinner party menu with individual cold salmon mousses flavoured with orange. Make these up on the day of the party so the mousse has no time to 'break' and will be creamier as a result. The salmon can be cooked beforehand and stored in the freezer.

The main course comes straight from the freezer. It is a savoury casserole of chicken cooked in brown ale (see above), served with petits pois à la française.

To finish, there's hazelnut meringue gâteau, filled with coffee-flavoured cream, and served with a sauce of coffee, caramel and rum. Both the meringue and the accompanying sauce can be made in advance and the gâteau can be decorated on the day. Refer to the timetable on page 45.

And for good measure, there's a rich pork pâté for luncheon and a summer iced pudding on page 46.

Petites Cocottes de Saumon Sevillienne

★ *Casserole de Poulet Brabançonne*
★ *Petits Pois à la Française*

★ *Vacherin Moka aux Noisettes*

Red wine - Côtes du Rhône

Petites cocottes de saumon sevillienne

10 oz salmon steak
1 small onion (sliced)
½ teaspoon salt
6 peppercorns
2 blades of mace

To finish
grated rind and juice of 1 orange
6 fl oz mayonnaise (see page 125)
salt and pepper
2 caps canned pimiento
1 pint commercially-prepared aspic

Melba toast (for serving)

6 ramekins or cocottes

If serving eight, you will need 12 oz salmon, 7½ fl oz mayonnaise (using 3 egg yolks), 1½ pints aspic, 3 pimiento caps and 8 ramekins or cocottes. Other quantities remain the same.

Method
Cover salmon with cold water, add onion, salt, peppercorns and mace. Cover pan and bring slowly to the boil. (This will take 10–15 minutes). Remove from heat and allow to get quite cold. Drain well, remove skin and bone and wrap the salmon in foil to freeze.

Thawing and serving Thaw in the refrigerator overnight, then flake and pound the fish using a pestle and mortar, or work in the mixer on the paddle attachment, with the finely-grated rind of the orange. Add mayonnaise and, when thoroughly mixed, season well. Add a little orange juice to taste. Half-fill each of the cocottes with the salmon mixture, smooth tops and chill for about 15 minutes. Shred pimiento and place a tea-

Casserole de poulet brabançonne

3½ lb roasting chicken
½ lb salt belly pork
2 tablespoons oil
1 oz butter
4 medium-size onions (peeled and sliced)
salt and white pepper
½ pint brown ale
½ pint good brown stock (see page 124)
1 sugar lump
1–2 French rolls (bâtons)
a little extra butter
1 dessertspoon Dijon mustard

If serving eight, you will need two 3 lb chickens – this will allow plenty. Other quantities remain the same.

Method
First, blanch and simmer pork for 35–40 minutes. Set oven at 325°F or Mark 3.

Heat the oil in a deep flameproof casserole. Add 1 oz butter and put in the chicken at once. Lower the heat and brown bird slowly all over for about 20 minutes, turning frequently. Strip skin off pork, remove any bones and cut pork into cubes. Remove chicken from the casserole, put in pork and onions, and fry gently until brown. Draw aside and lift out pork and onions with a draining spoon. Joint the chicken and trim away any pieces of bone. Place the joints in the casserole with the onions and pork, and season. Pour ale and half the stock over, adjust seasoning, and add the sugar lump. Cover and place in the pre-set oven for 15 minutes.

Meanwhile, slice the rolls, mix about 1 oz butter with the mustard and spread the bread with this. Take out the casserole, arrange the bread on top and spoon over the remaining stock. Return to the oven,

Vacherin moka aux noisettes

4 egg whites
8 oz caster sugar
½ teaspoon ground cinnamon
3 oz ground hazelnuts

For filling
½ teaspoon instant coffee
1 tablespoon soft dark brown sugar
½ pint double cream

For decoration
icing sugar (for dusting)
¼ pint double cream (whipped)
coffee dragées, or whole hazelnuts

2 baking sheets lined with non-stick (silicone) cooking paper

Method
Set oven at 290°F or Mark 1.

Whisk the egg whites until stiff, add 1 tablespoon of the measured caster sugar and continue beating for about 30 seconds. Sift the remaining sugar with the cinnamon and fold into the egg whites with the nuts. Pipe or spread into two 8-inch rounds on the prepared baking sheets. Bake in the pre-set oven for about 1–1¼ hours.

Mix the coffee and brown sugar with 1 tablespoon of hot water and allow to cool. Whip the ½ pint of cream and, as it begins to thicken, add the coffee syrup and continue beating until thick. Sandwich the two meringue rounds with the coffee cream.

Place in a cake box or wrap in foil, and freeze.

spoon on salmon mixture in each cocotte.
 Make up the aspic as directed on the packet. Set it over a bowl of ice cubes to cool, and when it is just at setting point, spoon a little over each cocotte. Replace in the refrigerator until aspic is set. Serve with Melba toast (see page 10). ∎

Pounding the cooked salmon before adding the mayonnaise and orange juice and rind

Spooning the shredded pimiento on to the cocottes before covering with cool aspic

uncovered, and increase the heat to 375°F or Mark 5 for 30 minutes, or until top is brown and crisp. Leave until cold, then wrap and pack in freezer.

Thawing and serving Allow to thaw for 24 hours in the refrigerator, then heat uncovered in a moderate oven, 350°F or Mark 4, for 35–40 minutes until at boiling point. Serve with petits pois à la française or plainly boiled peas, fresh or frozen, finished with a knob of butter and seasoned to taste. ∎

> **To blanch** means to whiten meats by bringing to the boil from cold water and draining before further cooking.

After browning the chicken well on all sides, strip the skin off the salt belly pork, remove any bones and cut it into cubes, then fry gently with the chopped onion

Thawing and serving Allow to thaw at room temperature for 4 hours, then dust the centre with sifted icing sugar and pipe rosettes of the plain whipped cream round the edge. Decorate with the dragées or nuts and serve with a caramel coffee sauce (sauce moka – see the recipe on page 45). ∎

Right: whisk the egg whites to a firm snow with a balloon whisk. Far right: pipe rosettes of whipped cream on the thawed vacherin, and decorate it with hazelnuts

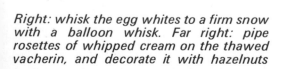

The finished vacherin moka aux noisettes, ready to serve with a coffee caramel sauce

Petits pois à la française

5 lb green peas (2½ pints shelled)
1 Cos lettuce (shredded)
12–24 small spring onions (cut in 2-inch lengths)
1 dessertspoon sugar
bouquet garni
1 oz butter
¼ pint water
salt

To finish
1 oz kneaded butter (see page 125)

Method
Put the peas in a pan with the shredded lettuce, spring onions, sugar, bouquet garni and butter; add the salted water. Instead of a lid, cover the pan with a deep plate filled with cold water and cook quickly for 25 minutes.

Note: the purpose of this plate of cold water is to condense the steam as it rises from the peas while they cook. As the water in the plate evaporates, add more cold water.

When the peas are cooked, remove the bouquet garni, and when quite cold, pack into cartons and freeze.

Thawing and serving Allow to thaw for 4 hours at room temperature. Reheat, thicken with the kneaded butter and adjust the seasoning. ■

The little cocottes of salmon sevillienne accompanied by Melba toast

Day before
Remove chicken casserole from the freezer and place in the refrigerator to thaw.
Take cooked salmon from the freezer, if using, and thaw overnight in the refrigerator.
Prepare mayonnaise, and keep in a cool place.
Make Melba toast and store in airtight tin.

Day of party (morning)
Make up salmon cocottes. Chill in the refrigerator.
Remove vacherin from the freezer and keep in the refrigerator.
Make sauce moka.

Day of party (afternoon)
Whip cream for vacherin and decorate. Keep in a cool place.
Remove petits pois à la française from the freezer and allow to thaw at room temperature.

Order of work
7.00	Set the oven at 360°F or Mark 4.
7.20	Place poulet brabanconne in oven to reheat.
7.40	Reheat petits pois, or boil garden peas straight from the freezer. Finish with butter. Remove salmon cocottes from the refrigerator.
8.00	Serve first course.

Cooking times in individual recipes have sometimes been adjusted to help you when cooking and serving this menu as a three-course meal.

Sauce moka

(for vacherin moka aux noisettes)

8 oz lump, or granulated sugar
6 fl oz water
1 tablespoon instant coffee dissolved in 2 tablespoons freshly boiled water
1 tablespoon rum

Method
Melt the sugar slowly in half the measured water, then boil hard until a good brown colour. Draw pan off heat and add the rest of the water. Return to heat and stir gently until dissolved. Pour off and allow to cool. As it thickens, stir in the dissolved coffee and rum. When cold, the sauce should be thick and syrupy.

Adding spring onions to peas to make a classic petits pois à la française

A LUNCHEON DISH

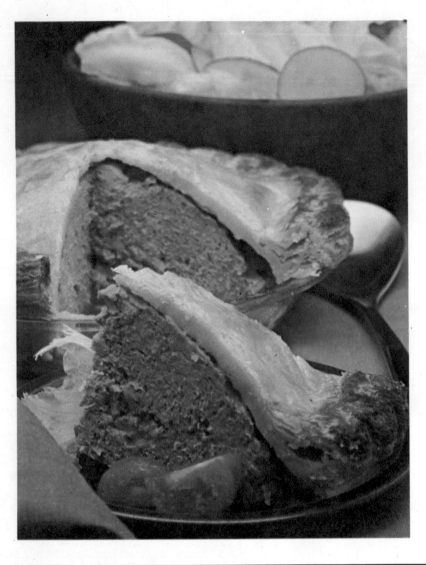

Pâté de porc sous croûte

Pâté de porc sous croûte

¾ lb shoulder meat
1½–2 lb fresh belly pork
1 large onion
2 dessert apples (Pippin variety)
2 oz cooked rice
salt and pepper
1 tablespoon chopped sage and
   parsley
¾ lb puff pastry (see page 125)

Two 7–8 inch pie plates

Method
Mince the shoulder meat, onion, peeled apples and rice through the finest blade, and the belly pork rather more coarsely. Season with salt and pepper and add herbs.

Fill the mixture into shallow pie plates, roll out puff pastry into rounds and cover. Bake for ½ hour at 425°F or Mark 7, then cover with a double thickness of damp grease-proof paper, reduce the oven temperature to 350°F or Mark 4, and continue cooking 45–50 minutes. When cold, wrap and freeze. Thaw for 24 hours in the refrigerator. ■

When serving this pâté for luncheon, a crisp green salad makes the perfect accompaniment. To save time, why not dress the salad in the bowl, instead if making the French dressing separately?

First, to crisp lettuce (Webbs or Iceberg), cucumber or white cabbage, add oil in the proportion of four parts oil to one of vinegar. Toss the ingredients in the oil, add seasoning, then lastly, the vinegar, making just enough dressing to coat the tossed salad and not to drown it.

ALTERNATIVE SWEET

Melon and orange sorbet

1 honeydew melon
1–2 tablespoons orange
   flavoured liqueur (Curaçaô,
   Cointreau or Grand Marnier)
2 pints (40 fl oz) orange water
   ice

Method
Cut melon in half and scoop out the seeds. Carefully remove the flesh of the melon and cut it in dice; sprinkle with the liqueur.

Turn the orange water ice into a chilled basin and beat until soft. Fold the diced and macerated melon into the water ice and quickly spoon the mixture into the melon skins. Reshape the melon, wrap in foil and tie securely in a polythene bag.

Chill for 1½ hours in the freezer or 2 hours in the ice box of the refrigerator.

To serve, unwrap the melon and ease the halves apart. Serve on a chilled plate and hand separately a small biscuit or petits fours such as miroirs or soleils on page 51, or orangines. ■

Note: Ogen melons are also suitable for this recipe but, if using, you will need two.

Orangines

1½ oz plain flour
2 oz butter
2 oz caster sugar
2 oz almonds (finely chopped)
2 oz candied orange peel (finely
   chopped)
1–2 drops of carmine colouring
1 dessertspoon milk

Method
Set oven at 350°F or Mark 4 and grease baking sheet.

Sift the flour. Soften the butter, add sugar to it and beat until white. Add the prepared almonds and candied peel, the flour, carmine and milk, and mix together.

Put the mixture, ½ teaspoon at a time, on the baking sheet. Flatten the shapes with a wet fork and bake in the pre-set oven until tinged with brown (7–8 minutes). Bake ½ teaspoon of mixture only at first, to test for size. Orangines for petits fours should be no more than 2 inches across.

Leave for 2–3 minutes before removing from the sheet.
Watchpoint The mixture must be coloured very delicately. The easiest way to do it is to dip a skewer into the carmine bottle and then just touch the mixture with it. ■

MORE FROM YOUR FREEZER

Start this last dinner party with poached fillets of brill or plaice covered with a salpicon of mixed vegetables and coated with a cream sauce (see the photograph above). The main course is a rich mixture of beefsteak, kidney and mushrooms, baked inside a pastry case (also shown above). Serve this with a seasonal salad — see page 50.

The dessert is a pineapple cream ice served with slices of fresh pineapple. Pour kirsch liqueur over each portion just before serving and accompany with a choice of petits fours.

With the exception of the petits fours and the fresh salads, all dishes for this dinner party menu can be made in advance and frozen until required. Refer to the timetable on page 51.

★ *Filets de Barbue Durand*

★ *Tourtière de Boeuf*
Salade de Saison

★ *Coupes d'Ananas with Petits Fours*

Red wine - Côtes de Bourg (Claret)

Filets de barbue Durand

6 large brill, or plaice, fillets
½ pint dry cider
juice of ½ lemon
¼ pint water
salt
white pepper (ground from the mill)
4 carrots (approx ¾ lb)
1 small turnip (approx ½ lb)
2 small onions
½ oz butter
bouquet garni

To finish
2–3 tomatoes
1 oz butter
1 oz flour
¼ pint single cream
1 tablespoon chopped parsley

If serving 8, you will need 8 fish fillets and 3–4 tomatoes. The other quantities remain the same.

This recipe, while originally prepared with brill, is just as good with large fillets of plaice or, indeed, any firm-fleshed white fish available. Allow 5 oz fish, weight without skin or bone, per head.

Method
Set the oven at 350°F or Mark 4.

Wash, trim and dry fish fillets, place in an ovenproof dish with ¼ pint of the cider, lemon juice, measured water and seasoning. Cover with a buttered paper and poach in the pre-set oven for 8 minutes.

Meanwhile, peel and slice the carrots in thin rounds. Peel the turnip thickly, cut into quarters, pare off the sharp edges and slice into thin rounds to match the carrots. Peel and slice the onions in thin rounds. Melt the butter in a small flameproof casserole, then add all the vegetables and stir carefully in the melted butter. Season with salt and pepper. Pour over the rest of the cider and tuck the bouquet garni in the middle. Cover and cook gently on top of the stove until tender and dry, taking care

Tourtière de boeuf

2 lb chuck steak
½ lb ox kidney
a little seasoned flour
¾ pint jellied brown stock (see page 124)
4 oz mushrooms

For pastry
12 oz plain flour
a pinch of salt
2 oz lard or shortening
6 oz butter
2 egg yolks mixed with 2 fl oz water

7-inch diameter spring-form mould

If serving eight, you will need 2½ lb chuck steak, ¾ lb kidney, ½ pint stock, and 6 oz mushrooms; for pastry, use 1 lb flour, 3 oz lard, 8 oz butter, and 3 egg yolks mixed with 3 fl oz water. Use a 9-inch mould. Other quantities remain the same.

Method
Set oven at 350°F or Mark 4.

Cut the steak and kidney into bite-size pieces and roll in the seasoned flour. Pack into an ovenproof casserole, add the stock, cover tightly and cook in the moderate pre-set oven for 1¼–1½ hours. Allow to cool.

Now make up the shortcrust pastry, if not from the freezer. Sift the flour with a pinch of salt into a mixing bowl. Drop in the lard and butter and cut into the flour until you have small pieces which are well-coated, then rub them in with the fingertips until the mixture looks like fine breadcrumbs. Tip the egg yolk and water mixture into the fat and flour and mix quickly with a palette knife to form a firm dough.

Turn on to a floured board and knead lightly until smooth. Chill in the refrigera-

Coupes d'ananas

1 large pineapple
sugar syrup or caster sugar (see method)
a little kirsch liqueur

For parfait mixture
¾ pint double cream
3 egg whites
6 oz caster sugar

6 coupe glasses

Method
Cut the skin carefully from the pineapple. Split pineapple in half lengthways and slice one half into six slices, each about ¼-inch thick. With a small plain round cutter, stamp out the core, and put pineapple pieces into a container. Spoon over 4–5 tablespoons thick sugar syrup (made by boiling sugar in a little water) or dust well with caster sugar. Cover and freeze.

With a fork, shred away the flesh of the other half pineapple from the core and turn this crushed pineapple into a pudding basin. Press any remaining pieces of pineapple with the core to extract any juice and add this to the crushed pineapple. Half whip the cream and set aside. Whisk the egg whites and, when stiff, add the

to see that the vegetables do not brown.

Remove fish from the oven, and allow to cool before placing it in a container for freezing. Tip the fish liquid into a separate container and freeze. Remove the bouquet garni from the vegetables and spoon them carefully over the fish. When cold, wrap and freeze.

Thawing and serving Remove fish and cooking liquid from the freezer and leave in a cool larder for 6 hours to thaw, then lift fish into an ovenproof gratin dish.

Set oven at 350°F or Mark 4. Skin and roughly chop the tomatoes, discarding the seeds, and scatter tomatoes over the fish and vegetables. Reheat uncovered, in the moderate oven for 20 minutes.

Melt the butter in a pan, remove from heat and stir in the flour. Cook until marbled in appearance, then blend in the cooking liquid from the fish and bring to the boil. Adjust the seasoning, add the cream and simmer sauce gently until syrupy. Add the parsley, spoon the sauce over the fish and vegetables and serve. ■

Placing the trimmed fillets of brill in an ovenproof dish before poaching in cider

Scattering chopped tomatoes over the thawed cooked fish and vegetables

tor for 30–40 minutes before using.

Wash, trim and quarter the mushrooms. Roll out the pastry, line into the spring-form mould, reserving a third for the lid. Turn the steak and kidney mixture, and the mushrooms into the mould. Roll out remaining pastry for the lid, cover mould and seal round the edge. Decorate with pastry trimmings and brush with beaten egg. Bake in a moderately hot oven, 400°F or Mark 6, for about 40 minutes.

When cold, remove from the tin, wrap and freeze.

Thawing and serving Thaw for 24 hours in the refrigerator, then reheat on a baking sheet or an ovenproof serving dish at 350°F or Mark 4 for 40–50 minutes. Serve with a seasonal salad (see page 50 for suggestions). ■

Line the spring-form mould with short-crust pastry, fill with the steak and kidney mixture, then cover with the pastry lid

caster sugar, a tablespoon at a time. Whisk again until the mixture stands in peaks; then, with a metal spoon, fold in the cream. Add the crushed pineapple, about a third at a time, turn at once into a container. Cover and freeze.

Thawing and serving Take out pineapple slices 3–4 hours before serving. Keep at room temperature, or in the refrigerator. Transfer parfait mixture from freezer to refrigerator one hour before serving. Spoon the parfait mixture into 6 chilled coupe glasses with an ice-cream scoop. Top each with a slice of pineapple and pour 1–2 tablespoons kirsch over and around each portion.

Serve immediately with petits fours (see page 51). ■

Shredding flesh from one pineapple half. The other half is sliced, ready to freeze

Adding the lightly whipped cream to the whisked egg whites and sugar mixture

The finished steak and kidney tourtière (serve with a choice of salads below) shown with the dessert — a kirsch flavoured pineapple cream ice, and a choice of two sorts of petits fours (see recipes opposite)

Beetroot, potato and apple salad

2 beetroots (cooked)
1 lb waxy potatoes (cooked)
2 dessert apples
French dressing (see page 125)

Method
Dice the beetroots and potatoes and peel and chop the apples. Mix together just before serving; toss in French dressing. ■

Chicory and orange salad

1 lb chicory
3 oranges
2 large carrots
French dressing (see page 125)

Method
Wash chicory, trim away stalk, separate leaves and cut into pieces. Remove skin and pith from the oranges with a sharp knife, then cut into segments and discard any pips. Peel and shred carrots into fine julienne strips (about 1½–2 inches long). Mix ingredients together and toss in French dressing. ■

A choice of petits fours

Miroirs

4 oz ground almonds
4 oz caster sugar
1 tablespoon thick well-reduced apricot glaze
1 vanilla pod
1 large egg white
a little beaten egg
a good pinch of salt
2 oz blanched almonds (well-chopped)

To finish
a little extra apricot glaze
2 oz pistachio nuts
a little vanilla sugar

Method
Set oven at 350°F or Mark 4.

Pound and bruise the ground almonds well, adding the sugar by degrees (see watchpoint). Add the apricot glaze and a pinch of vanilla scraped from the pod. Break the egg white with a fork and add it gradually to the almond mixture, working it in well. Take care to add only enough egg white to make a firm paste that can be rolled in the hand.

Roll the dough into small balls, each the size of a walnut. Roll these in beaten egg with a pinch of salt added, then in the chopped almonds and set each on a baking sheet lined with non-stick (silicone) cooking paper. Make an indentation in the centre of each with your finger. Bake in the pre-set moderate oven for 8–10 minutes, or until golden brown.

When cold, pipe a little apricot glaze in the centre of each and surround this with halved pistachio nuts. Sprinkle with a little vanilla sugar.

Watchpoint A much better result, when making petits fours and cakes, both in flavour and handling, is obtained if blanched almonds are used in place of ground almonds. Either grind the blanched almonds through a Mouli grater, then pound with the sugar until smooth, or use your liquidiser to grind almonds before pounding with sugar as above. ■

Soleils

For first mixture
2½ oz ground almonds
2½ oz caster sugar
1 rounded teaspoon plain flour
¾ oz butter
1 egg yolk
½ teaspoon rum
a little egg white (if necessary)
finely chopped almonds (to sprinkle)

For second mixture
2 small egg whites
2 oz ground almonds
2 oz caster sugar

To finish
apricot glaze
a little glacé icing, flavoured with rum (optional)

Forcing bag and ¼-inch plain pipe

Method
Set oven at 350°F or Mark 4.

Prepare the first mixture. Pound the almonds with the sugar, flour, butter, egg yolk and rum. Work well to a pliable paste.
Watchpoint If the mixture is a little dry, add a small quantity of egg white to moisten.

Prepare the second mixture. Whip the egg whites until stiff, then stir in the almonds and the sugar.

Fill first mixture into forcing bag and pipe small ovals, about 2½-inches long on to a well-buttered, floured baking sheet. Sprinkle with chopped almonds. Refill bag with second mixture and pipe to fill the centre of each small oval with this. Bake in the pre-set oven for 8–10 minutes, or until lightly coloured. Remove from the baking sheet and brush the centres with apricot glaze. When cool, brush again with a little light glacé icing, flavoured with rum if wished. ■

Apricot glaze
Turn 1 lb apricot jam into a pan, add the juice of ½ a lemon and 4 table-spoons water. Bring slowly to the boil, then simmer for 5 minutes. Strain, and return to the pan. Boil for a further 5 minutes and turn into a jam jar for keeping. If for immediate use, continue boiling until thick, then brush generously over the cake or petits fours. If using a smooth jam (with no lumps of fruit), water is not needed.

Glacé icing
Make a sugar syrup by dissolving 2½ tablespoons granulated sugar in 2½ fl oz water in a small saucepan. Bring to the boil, and boil steadily for 10 minutes. Remove from the heat and when quite cold, add 4–5 oz sifted icing sugar, 1 tablespoon at a time, and beat thoroughly with a wooden spatula.

TIMETABLE

Day before
Make petits fours and store in an airtight tin.
Remove tourtière de boeuf from the freezer and allow to thaw in the refrigerator. Make French dressing for salad.

Day of party (afternoon)
Remove fish and stock from freezer and place in a cool larder to thaw.
Take pineapple slices from freezer. Allow to thaw at room temperature or in the refrigerator.
Prepare salad ingredients, cover and keep in the refrigerator.
Skin tomatoes for fish and leave in a bowl of cold water until needed.

Order of work
7.00	Set oven at 350°F or Mark 4. Assemble salad and toss in dressing. Arrange petits fours on a serving dish.
7.20	Place tourtière in the pre-set oven to reheat. Place fish in an ovenproof gratin dish and spoon over vegetables and the chopped tomatoes.
7.40	Reheat fish in the oven on the shelf below the tourtière. Take pineapple cream ice from freezer and place in the refrigerator. Make the sauce to finish the fish.
8.00	Add chopped parsley to sauce for fish and spoon this sauce over the barbue durand. Serve immediately. Between courses, spoon parfait mixture into coupe glasses, top each with a pineapple slice and pour kirsch over.

Cooking times in individual recipes have sometimes been adjusted to help you when cooking and serving this menu as a three-course meal.

MAIN COURSES: BEEF

The recipes in this section are for hearty main course dishes, most of which can be cooked, then frozen. We start with meat, then poultry and finally, fish.

On this page — beef, starting with two ways of using ready-cooked mince from the freezer, each serving 4. The basic recipe is on page 126.

Hungarian mince

¾–1 lb mince (cooked)
1 small young marrow
1–2 oz butter
1 dessertspoon paprika
1 small onion (finely chopped)
2–3 tablespoons wine vinegar
dill, or caraway, seeds (to taste)
1 teaspoon caster sugar
kneaded butter made with ¾ oz
  butter and scant ½ oz flour

Method
Spread the thawed mince thickly on the bottom of a pie plate or dish, cover with foil and put into a moderate oven (350°F or Mark 4) to heat for about 10–12 minutes.

Peel marrow, cut into quarters, scoop out seeds and slice thinly. Melt 1½ oz butter in a large pan. Put in the marrow and fry quickly for 4–5 minutes, shaking the pan well. Add the paprika. Then take out the marrow and put in the onion, with more butter, if necessary, turning down heat.

Cover the pan for 1–2 minutes to cook the onion, then add the vinegar, dill (or caraway) seeds and the sugar. Thicken slightly with the kneaded butter, replace the marrow, cover and simmer for 5 minutes, when it should be just tender. Spoon marrow over the mince and serve.

Italian mince

¾ lb mince (cooked)
1 medium-size onion (chopped)
½ oz butter
¼ pint strong tomato sauce or
  1 (8 oz) can Italian tomatoes
1 clove garlic (crushed)
salt and pepper
6 oz short macaroni
dry cheese (grated)

Method
Soften the onion in the butter, then add the tomato sauce or the can of tomatoes, well crushed, and the garlic. Season, and cook to a thick pulp. Meanwhile, simmer the macaroni in boiling salted water for 12–15 minutes, until just tender. Drain, rinse under hot water and drain well a second time. Return to the pan and add the tomato pulp.

Turn the thawed mince into an ovenproof dish and spread the macaroni mixture on top. Sprinkle well with grated cheese and brown in a hot oven (425°F or Mark 7).

Alouettes sans têtes

6–8 thin slices of buttock steak,
  or slices from the 'leg of
  mutton' cut

For braising
1 tablespoon dripping
1 large onion (finely sliced)
1 large carrot (finely sliced)
1 stick celery (sliced)
1 wine glass sherry
½–¾ pint jellied brown stock
a little cornflour, or arrowroot
  (see method)
1 tablespoon chopped parsley

For stuffing
½ lb minced veal
1 small onion
½ oz butter
2 tablespoons dry white
  breadcrumbs
salt and pepper
½ teaspoon chopped thyme
grated rind and juice of one
  small orange

For garnish
2 sticks celery (cut into julienne
  strips)
2 carrots (cut into fine julienne
  strips)
½ oz butter
1 tablespoon sherry
2 slices lean ham
1 teaspoon shredded orange
  rind (blanched)

Method
Prepare the stuffing. Finely chop the onion and cook in the butter until soft but not coloured; cool. Mix the veal with the breadcrumbs, seasoning and thyme; add the onion. Work in the orange rind and add the juice a little at a time, beating well.

Bat out the slices of beef between two pieces of waxed paper and cut each slice in half. Spread the stuffing on each slice of meat, roll up and tie with thread.

Set the oven at 325°F or Mark 3. Brown the meat in the hot dripping in a flame-proof casserole, take out meat and put in the vegetables. Reduce the heat, cover the pan and cook until the fat has been absorbed and the vegetables are russet brown. Pour on the sherry and cook until mixture is reduced to half quantity; place the 'beef olives' on the vegetable mirepoix, pour over the stock and bring to the boil. Cover the casserole and simmer gently on top of the stove for ½ hour, then place in the pre-set oven for a further 1½ hours, or until tender.

Meanwhile, place the julienne of celery and carrot in a small, covered flameproof casserole with the butter and sherry, cook slowly on top of the stove for about 3–5 minutes, then put in the oven for 10–15 minutes, or until the carrot is tender. Add the ham, cut in julienne strips to match the vegetables.

To freeze When cold, add the prepared orange rind, wrap and freeze.

Take up the beef, remove the thread and place in a suitable container. Strain the liquid in the braising pan, reduce a little (there should be enough just to cover the meat) and then thicken lightly with 1 teaspoon cornflour or arrowroot, mixed to a paste with a little stock or water, and pour over the meat. Wrap and freeze.

Thawing and serving Allow to thaw for 24 hours in the refrigerator, then place the alouettes in an ovenproof casserole and spoon the julienne garnish on the top; cover and reheat at 350°F or Mark 4, for 35–40 minutes. Dust with chopped parsley just before serving.

Sauté de boeuf en pipérade

5 sirloin steaks, or a 2 lb piece
  of sirloin without bone
1 tablespoon oil
½ oz butter
¾ oz flour
½ pint jellied brown stock
1 dessertspoon tomato purée
salt and pepper
1 wine glass red wine

For tomato and pepper salpicon
½ lb ripe tomatoes
1 clove garlic
½ oz butter
1 red pepper
1 green pepper

Method
Cut each steak into three or the joint into 1½-inch cubes, brown quickly in the hot oil and butter and remove from the pan. Dust in the flour, brown slowly and then blend in the stock and tomato purée. Put the meat back in the sauté pan, season and add the flamed wine; cover and simmer gently for 25–30 minutes.

Meanwhile prepare the salpicon. Skin the tomatoes, remove the seeds, chop the flesh and reserve any liquid.

Peel and crush the clove of garlic with a little salt. Melt the butter, add the tomatoes and garlic and any juice strained from the tomato seeds, and cook gently to a rich pulp. Shred, blanch and refresh the peppers, removing seeds, add to the pan and continue cooking 3–5 minutes.

To freeze Lift the meat from the sauté pan into a container ready for freezing; boil the remaining sauce hard until thick and syrupy and pour over the beef. Spoon the salpicon on top of the meat. Wrap and freeze.

Thawing and serving Thaw for 24 hours in refrigerator, reheat at 375°F or Mark 5, for 35–40 minutes. Serve with small new potatoes tossed in butter and chopped parsley.

Top: sauté de boeuf en pipérade, with its salpicon of tomatoes and peppers. Below: the alouettes sans têtes

Boeuf braisé au vin rouge

2–2½ lb joint of 'leg of mutton'
  cut of beef
1 tablespoon beef dripping or oil
bouquet garni
salt and pepper
about ½ pint jellied brown stock
½ pint demi-glace sauce (see
  page 124)

For marinade
2 onions (sliced)
2 carrots (sliced)
2 sticks celery (sliced)
2 wine glasses red wine
6 peppercorns
1 clove garlic (chopped)

Method
Put all the ingredients for the
marinade in a small pan, bring
to the boil and simmer for 1
minute; allow to cool. Lay the
meat in a deep dish, pour over
the marinade and leave 12–24
hours, turning occasionally.

When ready to cook, take
up the meat, pat dry and
strain and reserve the marinade
and vegetables.

Heat the dripping in a
braising pan, brown the meat
on all sides, then take it out,
lower the heat and put in the
vegetables from the marinade.
Fry until turning colour, replace the beef, add the bouquet garni, a little seasoning
and the wine, and just enough
jellied brown stock to cover
the mirepoix of vegetables
but not the meat. Cover tightly
and bring to the boil. Place in a
very moderate oven, 350°F or
Mark 4 for 1 hour. Reduce
heat to 325°F or Mark 3, and
continue cooking for about 1½
hours, (exact length of time
depends on size of joint.)
Baste and turn from time to
time. Take up meat when
tender, reduce the liquor to
half quantity, strain, add the
demi-glace sauce and adjust
the seasoning.
To freeze Allow the meat to
cool then slice, moisten with a
little of the sauce, wrap and
freeze. Freeze the rest of the
sauce in a separate container.
Thawing and serving Thaw
12 hours at room temperature
and reheat at 375°F or Mark 5,
for 30 minutes. Heat the sauce
slowly to boiling point in a
saucepan, stirring occasionally to make sure it is smooth.
Serve the beef with a salpicon
of celery and walnut.

Celery and walnut salpicon

1 large head celery
1 oz butter
salt and pepper
2 oz walnuts (broken into
  quarters)
1 tablespoon chopped parsley

Method
Cut the celery in thick
julienne strips. Cook in a
covered sauté pan with the
butter and seasoning for 5–8
minutes. Meanwhile, place the
walnuts in baking tin, brush
with butter and toast in the
oven; add to the celery with
the parsley and turn into a
serving dish.

Estouffade de boeuf

4 lb back rib
3–4 tablespoons olive oil
2½ fl oz brandy
7½ fl oz red wine
1 dessertspoon tomato purée
½–¾ pint jellied brown stock
large bouquet of herbs (parsley,
  thyme, bayleaf and a strip of
  orange rind tied together)
1–2 cloves garlic (crushed)
salt and pepper
6–8 oz black olives (stoned)
kneaded butter (see page 125)

Method
Heat the oil in a thick, deep
cast iron flameproof casserole.
Put in the beef and brown
well on all sides. Pour off any
surplus fat and flame with the
brandy. Add wine, purée,
stock, herbs and garlic; season. Cover casserole tightly to
braise in the oven at 325°F or
Mark 3, for 2½–3 hours, turning the meat occasionally.
To freeze Remove herbs, turn
contents of casserole into a
bowl and, when cold, place in
refrigerator for 2–3 hours.
Then take off the fat and pack
down and freeze both beef
and gravy.
Thawing and serving Thaw
out in refrigerator overnight,
then heat gently on top of the
stove. Take out beef, slice and
arrange in a flameproof dish.
Thicken gravy slightly with
kneaded butter, add the olives,
bring to boiling point, draw
aside and adjust seasoning.
Spoon a little over the meat
and serve the rest separately.

LAMB

Lamb is a rich-tasting meat, and these recipes make good luncheon dishes for family or friends. All except the noisettes d'agneau napolitana can be cooked in advance and frozen, and each will serve 4, with some for 'seconds'.

Breast of lamb menagère

whole breast of lamb (2 pieces, one from each side of the carcase)
1 tablespoon dripping
2 medium-size onions
2 carrots
2 sticks celery
bouquet garni
1 clove of garlic (crushed with ½ teaspoon salt)
1 pint stock
a little arrowroot, or cornflour (to thicken)

For farce
1 large onion
1 oz butter
½ lb sausagemeat
1 dessertspoon chopped mixed herbs
salt and pepper

Method
Bone out the lamb, or ask the butcher to do it for you, and prepare the farce. Chop the onion finely, cook in the butter until soft but not coloured, then add to the sausagemeat with the herbs and season with salt and pepper. Spread this farce on the inside of each piece of breast, roll up and tie with fine string.

Heat the dripping in a heavy flameproof casserole and brown the meat on all sides; remove from the pan and lower the heat. Cut the vegetables into large dice, add to the pan, cover and cook slowly until beginning to colour, then drain off as much fat as possible. Replace the meat, add the bouquet garni and garlic and pour over the stock. Cover the pan, bring to the boil and then braise in a very moderate oven, 325°F or Mark 3, for 1½–2 hours. Take up the meat and set on one side. Strain the stock in the pan, allow to get quite cold, then remove all fat; reheat and thicken with a little arrowroot or cornflour.

To freeze Remove string from the meat, slice and arrange in a container ready for freezing; spoon over a little of the gravy. Cover and wrap when cold to freeze; pack the remaining gravy separately.

Thawing and serving Thaw for 24 hours in the refrigerator and reheat at 350°F or Mark 4, for about 35–45 minutes. Serve with vegetables in season.

Carré d'agneau à la grecque

2 lb best end of neck
1 tablespoon oil
a little arrowroot (to thicken sauce)

For sauce
½ oz butter
½ oz flour
7½ fl oz stock
1 (15 oz) can tomatoes
bouquet garni
salt and pepper
a pinch or two of sugar
1 teaspoon tomato purée

To finish
1 dozen black olives (halved and and stoned)
4 tomatoes (skinned and quartered)
1 tablespoon mixed chopped herbs

Method
Have the lamb boned out and tie securely. Prepare the sauce. Melt the butter, blend in the flour and stock and bring to the boil. Add the tomatoes, bouquet garni, seasoning and purée and stir well to partly crush the tomatoes. Cover and simmer for ½ hour. Strain.

Brown the lamb on all sides in the hot oil in a casserole, tip away any surplus fat and pour the tomato sauce over. Cover and cook in a moderate oven, 355°F or Mark 4, for 1–1¼ hours.

Take up the meat and set on one side to cool. Skim the sauce well, thicken lightly with arrowroot and cover with a piece of greaseproof paper to prevent a skin forming.

To freeze When the sauce is cold, pour half into a carton for freezing; add the olives, tomatoes and herbs to the remainder of the sauce.

Carve the meat in thick slices, place in a container and spoon over remainder of sauce. Wrap and freeze.

Thawing and serving Thaw overnight in refrigerator and reheat at 350°F or Mark 4, for 35–45 minutes. The sauce from the carton should be heated to boiling point and served separately.

Dundee lamb

2–2½ lb breast of lamb or trimmings from best end
1 onion (stuck with a clove)
1 carrot (peeled)
salt
6 peppercorns
bouquet garni (containing 1 stick of celery)
2 tablespoons wine vinegar
1 lb onions (sliced and blanched)
2 oz butter
1½ oz fresh white breadcrumbs
2 oz dry cheese (grated)

Method
Put meat in a pan of cold water to cover, bring slowly to boil, then skim well. Add whole onion and carrot, seasoning, bouquet garni and wine vinegar and simmer gently for 1½ hours, or until tender. Lift out of pan, remove all bones and then press meat between two plates until cold. Keep cooking liquid.

Cook the onion slices slowly in butter until golden-brown. Place lamb in a shallow, ovenproof dish, cover with onions and then top with the crumbs and cheese mixed together. Spoon any butter left over from the onions on top and pour round about ¼ pint of the cooking liquid. Bake at 400°F or Mark 6 for 30 minutes or until brown and crisp.

To freeze Allow to cool before wrapping and freezing.

Thawing and serving Thaw overnight in refrigerator. Reheat at 350°F or Mark 4 for 30–40 minutes.

Spiced lamb

1 lb slice from leg of lamb
2 green chillies (finely chopped) or ½ teaspoon chilli powder
½ teaspoon garam masala
1 teaspoon ground cumin
1 clove garlic (crushed)
5 fl oz natural yoghourt
3 medium-size onions (thinly sliced)
2½ oz butter
salt
1 oz shredded or flaked almonds
1½ oz sultanas

To finish
8 oz long grain rice
3–4 fl oz hot milk
a pinch of saffron

Method
Cut the meat into 1-inch squares. Mix the spices and garlic with the yoghourt and add to the meat. Marinate for 30 minutes to 1 hour. Meanwhile, fry the onions in 2 oz of the butter until turning colour, lift out with a draining spoon and add the meat.

Fry for about 5 minutes, turning the meat frequently to prevent sticking. Then replace the onions, add a little salt, and water barely to cover – ½ to ¾ pint. Cover and simmer until the meat is tender, about 40–45 minutes.

Meanwhile fry the almonds in the rest of the butter and when turning colour, add the sultanas. Fry for a minute, then cool.

When both the lamb mixture and the almond and sultana mixture are cold, pot them separately and freeze.

Thawing and serving Thaw lamb and almonds and sultanas overnight. Infuse the saffron in the hot milk. Warm the lamb slightly. Boil the rice for 10 minutes, then drain.

Layer the rice and lamb in a casserole finishing with rice, spoon over the saffron-flavoured milk. Cover with foil and then with the lid. Place in a moderate oven, 350°F or Mark 4, for 15–20 minutes or until very hot. Sprinkle top with almonds and sultanas 5 minutes before serving.

Noisettes d'agneau napolitana

2–2½ lb small loin of lamb
salt and pepper
1 dessertspoon mixed chopped herbs
2 oz butter
1 wine glass white wine
1 wine glass stock
6 oz spaghetti
6–8 large flat mushrooms
2 tablespoons sherry
½ pint stock
a little arrowroot
2 oz cooked ham (shredded)

For spaghetti sauce
1 lb ripe tomatoes
¾ oz butter
1 medium-size onion (finely chopped)
1 clove garlic (finely chopped)
½ oz flour
¼ pint stock
1 dessertspoon tomato purée
1 bayleaf

Method

Set the oven at 380°F or Mark 6. Bone out the loin, or ask your butcher to do it for you and give you the bones for stock. Season the inside, dust with mixed herbs, roll up and tie securely with fine string. Make a good stock from the bones with vegetables (an onion, carrot, a stick of celery, a few peppercorns and a bouquet garni) to flavour. Spread the meat with 1 oz butter, pour round the wine and wine glass of stock, and cook in the pre-set oven from about 1 hour. Baste and turn meat from time to time.

Meanwhile, cook the spaghetti and keep in hand hot water while preparing the sauce. Skin the tomatoes and cut in four, scoop out the seeds and rub these in a strainer, reserving the juice. Coarsely chop the tomato flesh and set aside.

Melt the butter, add the onion and garlic, finely chopped, and cook slowly until soft, then blend in the flour and cook to a pale straw colour. Draw the pan aside, add the tomato flesh, the juice from the seeds, stock and tomato purée, season, add the bayleaf and stir until boiling. Simmer to a thick pulp, then adjust seasoning.

Noisettes of lamb are served with spaghetti coated in a rich tomato sauce

Wash and trim the mushrooms, place in a buttered ovenproof dish, season and cover with foil. Cook on a shelf above the meat for about 10 minutes and keep warm. Drain the spaghetti, heat in ½ oz butter, mix with the sauce and keep hot.

Tip off the fat from the roasting tin into a pan leaving any sediment, add the sherry and ½ pint stock. Boil up well, reduce and strain. Thicken lightly with arrowroot and add the remaining butter and the ham.

Cut lamb into 'noisettes', arrange in a circle interlaced with the mushrooms on a large round dish, and spoon over the gravy and ham (see photo above). Pile the spaghetti in the middle and serve while still piping hot.

Variation: for a quicker way of preparing noisettes, instead of first braising the boned out loin of lamb, when it is securely tied, cut it into noisettes and set aside. Cook the spaghetti ahead of time and drain, then keep in warm water until you are ready to start cooking.

Make the spaghetti sauce, trim the mushrooms and add the stalks and the peelings to the sauce.

Grill or pan fry the noisettes of meat and grill the mushrooms at the same time. Heat a little butter in a pan, drain the cooked spaghetti, turn it into the melted butter and reheat, tossing frequently to prevent sticking, until the steam stops rising and the pasta is thoroughly hot.

Add 1–2 oz Parmesan cheese and toss over a gentle heat until the cheese is melted and every strand of spaghetti is coated.

Arrange the noisettes on a bed of mushrooms and serve accompanied by the spaghetti with the sauce handed separately.

Mushroom stalks and peelings should not be thrown away. Chop them finely, cook in butter until dry and then store in an airtight jar. Use in soups and sauces to add flavour.

VEAL AND PORK

Buy veal when it is plentiful or on 'special offer' from your butcher. These two dishes can both be frozen; the party blanquette will serve 8–10 people, the veau à l'orange will serve 4.

Two rather different ways of presenting pork follow, each of which caters for 4. There are other main course pork dishes to be found, particularly in the dinner party menus in the first section.

Why not serve rice or noodles instead of potatoes with these dishes?

Blanquette de veau

3 lb shoulder cut or breast of
  veal (weight without bone)
1 large carrot (quartered)
1 large onion (quartered)
bouquet garni containing ½ stick
  of celery
a pinch of salt
6 white peppercorns
2 pints light stock (veal,
  chicken or vegetable) or water
2¼ oz butter
2 oz flour

To finish
3–4 egg yolks
½ pint single cream
a squeeze of lemon juice
a mixture of freshly cooked
  vegetables (see method)

Method
Cut the meat into chunks, soak overnight in lightly salted cold water, blanch, drain and refresh. Put the meat in a large pan with the vegetables, add bouquet garni, salt, peppercorns and stock. Cover and simmer gently for 1–1½ hours. Lift out meat with a draining spoon, strain off stock and measure. If more than 1½ pints, return it to the pan and boil rapidly to reduce the quantity to 1½ pints.

Melt 2 oz butter, stir in the flour and cook for 1–2 minutes until a pale straw colour. Draw the pan aside and pour on the remaining pint of stock in a thin, steady stream, beating all the time. Return to the heat,

stir until boiling and cook for a further 3 minutes. Dot the surface with the remaining ¼ oz butter, cover pan and leave to cool. (The butter will melt and cover the surface of the sauce and so prevent a skin forming.) When meat and sauce are cold, pack separately and freeze.

Thawing and serving After thawing for 24 hours in refrigerator, place the meat in a large, ovenproof casserole and heat in a moderate oven, 350°F or Mark 4. Cook a quantity of vegetables eg. ¼ lb button mushrooms, ½ lb young carrots, 1–2 bunches spring onions and ½ lb French or Bobby beans, or shelled peas.

Stir the sauce over gentle heat until quite smooth and bring just to boiling point. Mix the egg yolks with the cream in a small basin. Take the

casserole from the oven and, holding the lid to one side, carefully drain off any stock from the meat into the sauce. Add a little of the hot sauce to the egg and cream liaison, then pour the mixture slowly back into the rest of the sauce. Taste for seasoning, add the lemon juice and pour the sauce over the meat. Shake casserole to blend all together. Add the vegetables, freshly cooked and drained, cover and keep warm for 15 minutes before serving to allow the flavour of the sauce to penetrate the meat.

Note: The given quantity could be frozen in two batches and, with half the quantity of fresh vegetables added on reheating, each batch would serve 4–5 people.

Sauté de veau à l'orange

1½–2 lb shoulder cut of veal
  (weight without bone)
1 tablespoon oil
1 oz butter
1 tablespoon brandy
grated rind and juice of 1 orange
¼ pint jellied white stock

For sauce
1 (8 oz) can tomatoes
1 medium-size onion (chopped)
1 oz butter
2 cloves garlic (crushed with ½
  teaspoon salt)
½ bayleaf
sprig of thyme
salt and pepper

To finish
2 teaspoons arrowroot
2 tablespoons stock, or water

Method
First prepare the sauce. Sauté the onion a few minutes in the butter, then add the tomatoes, crushed garlic, herbs and seasoning. Simmer for 8–10 minutes, strain and set aside. Cut the veal in 1½-inch pieces, heat the oil in a sauté pan, add the butter and, when foaming, put in the veal. Brown on all sides. Flame with the brandy, add the orange rind and juice and reduce until brown and sticky. Add the stock and tomato sauce, bring to the boil and cook gently, stirring occasionally, for about 35–40 minutes. When cold, wrap and freeze.

Thawing and serving Allow to thaw 24 hours in refrigerator, turn into an ovenproof casserole and reheat for 30–40 minutes at 350°F or Mark 4. Mix 2 level teaspoons arrowroot with 2 tablespoons stock or water and pour carefully around the sides of the casserole. Shake the pan gently to blend it in with the meat. Replace in the oven for 5 minutes before serving.

This party blanquette de veau has extra vegetables added

Paupiettes de porc

2 large pork fillets (tenderloin – weighing 1½ – 2 lb)
2 tablespoons oil
1 oz butter
1 wine glass Madeira

For duxelles
6 oz flat mushrooms
1 oz butter
1 shallot (finely chopped)
3 oz raw chicken (minced)
1 egg white
2 tablespoons fresh white breadcrumbs
salt
3–4 tablespoons double cream

For sauce
8 oz can tomatoes
1 medium-size onion
1 oz butter
2 cloves garlic (peeled and crushed with ½ teaspoon salt)
½ bayleaf
sprig of thyme

To finish
3 tomatoes
1 teaspoon arrowroot

Method

Split the fillets (but not right through), bat out and cut each into four. Now prepare the stuffing: chop mushrooms finely, melt butter and add shallot. After a few seconds, add the mushrooms. Cook for 3–4 minutes, stirring frequently, until most of the moisture has evaporated. Turn out and allow to cool. Work the minced chicken with the lightly broken egg white, adding it by degrees. Season and beat in the crumbs, mushroom duxelles and cream. Spread the stuffing on each piece of pork, roll up and tie with fine string or thread.

For the sauce; slice the onion and sauté in the butter for a few minutes, then add all the other ingredients; season and simmer for 8–10 minutes before straining.

Brown the paupiettes in the hot oil and butter in a flameproof casserole, add the Madeira, flame it and continue cooking until the liquid is reduced to half quantity. Pour over the tomato sauce, cover and cook in a moderate oven at 350°F or Mark 4, for 45–50 minutes.

The paupiettes de porc are accompanied by plain boiled noodles, tossed in butter

To freeze Take out the paupiettes, remove the string and place in a container. Reduce the sauce a little, then rub through a nylon strainer and spoon over the paupiettes. When cold, cover and freeze.

Thawing and serving After thawing for 24 hours in the refrigerator, place the paupiettes in a deep flameproof casserole or dish, cover and reheat in a moderate oven, at 350°F or Mark 5, to boiling point – about 35–40 minutes.

Meanwhile, scald and skin the tomatoes (see page 12), quarter, and scoop out the seeds. If tomatoes are very large, cut each quarter again. Rub the tomato seeds in a nylon strainer and use the juice to mix with 1 teaspoon arrowroot.

Lift the dish of paupiettes from the oven, pour the arrowroot mixture round the dish and shake dish gently to blend it in. Spoon the tomatoes over the meat and return dish to the oven for a further 5–8 minutes. The tomatoes should be hot, but remain quite firm.

Serve with plain boiled noodles, tossed in butter and sprinkled with Parmesan.

Boulettes of pork italienne

1½ lb pork (minced)
6–8 oz fresh white breadcrumbs
1 clove of garlic (crushed with ½ teaspoon salt)
salt and pepper
pinch of dried sage
pinch of dried thyme
2 eggs
2½ fl oz milk
1 pint light stock (veal, chicken or vegetable)

For sauce
1½ oz butter
4 oz mushrooms (quartered)
1¼ oz flour
stock (from the boulettes)
1 dessertspoon tomato purée
4 tomatoes (peeled, quartered and coarsely shredded)

Method

Place the pork and crumbs in a basin, add the garlic, pepper from the mill and the herbs. Mix well with a fork or electric

beater. Whisk the eggs with the milk and add this gradually to the meat mixture, beating well between each addition. Divide into 24 equal portions and shape into croquettes on a lightly floured board; place in a shallow pan, pour over the stock and simmer very gently for about 20 minutes.

To prepare the sauce: melt ¾ oz butter in a pan, add mushrooms, sauté for 1 minute, then blend in the remainder of the butter and the flour. Draw off the heat. Carefully pour off the stock from the boulettes into a measuring jug, (there should

be ¾ pint). Pour this on to the roux in the pan, blend until smooth and then stir over gentle heat until boiling. Add tomato purée, allow to simmer 2–3 minutes, then cool.

To freeze Lift the boulettes from their pan, with a draining spoon, into a container for freezing. Add the shredded tomato to the cold sauce and spoon over the boulettes. Cover and freeze.

Thawing and serving Thaw for 24 hours in refrigerator and bake for 45–50 minutes at 350°F or Mark 4. Serve with a dish of plainly boiled rice.

POULTRY AND GAME PIES

These pies have one thing in common — they can all be made in advance and frozen, though you do not need to own a freezer in order to bake and enjoy them. Most are made to be served cold with salads — see the recipe index for suitable suggestions — and each recipe should serve at least 4–6 people, depending on appetite . . .

Chicken pie 1

8 oz quantity of puff pastry
(from the freezer)
3 lb roasting chicken
1½–2 oz butter
salt and pepper
1 wine glass sherry
6 rashers streaky bacon

For forcemeat balls
2 chicken livers
2 oz butter
1 medium-size onion (chopped)
1 cup dry white breadcrumbs
1 tablespoon chopped parsley
1 teaspoon mixed dried herbs
grated rind of ½ lemon
beaten egg (to bind)

To finish
jellied stock from carcase
1¾ oz butter
¾ oz flour
squeeze of lemon juice
1 tablespoon cream
1 egg yolk

Method
Rub the chicken with the butter, season inside, and set in a roasting tin with the giblets and ¼ pint water. Roast in a moderate oven (350°F or Mark 4), for about 1¼ hours until well-browned, basting and turning from time to time and adding 1–2 tablespoons of water if the butter shows signs of over-browning. Take up the bird and pour sherry into the pan to deglaze it.

Lightly sauté chicken livers in butter for 2–3 minutes, remove from pan; sauté onion until transparent. Mix the crumbs with the herbs and lemon rind and season well. Chop livers, add these with the onion and bind with the beaten egg. Roll this mixture into small balls.

Spread out the bacon rashers, trim off rind and cut each in half, roll up, place on a thin skewer; grill until crisp.

Cut the chicken into neat joints, removing the bones and place in a pie dish with the forcemeat balls and bacon rolls, and spoon over the juices from the roasting tin. Roll out the pastry to cover pie, decorate with pastry trimmings, wrap and freeze.

Make ¾ pint good jellied stock from the chicken carcase, remove all trace of fat when cold, then pack and freeze separately.

Thawing and serving Remove chicken stock from freezer the day before required. Remove pie from freezer and thaw at room temperature for 2 hours, brush the pastry with beaten egg and bake in a hot oven, 425°F or Mark 7, for 15 minutes, then reduce the heat to 375°F or Mark 5, and continue cooking for about 35 minutes.

Make a sauce to accompany the pie with the thawed-out chicken stock. Make a roux with ¾ oz each of butter and flour, add the stock and, when the sauce has boiled for 3 minutes, flavour with a little lemon juice and add a tablespoon of cream. Just before serving, beat in 1 egg yolk and an extra 1 oz of butter.

Chicken pie 1 with forcemeat balls and bacon rolls

Chicken pie 2

8 oz quantity of puff pastry
(from the freezer)
beaten egg (to glaze)
3 lb roasting chicken
1 onion (sliced)
1 carrot (sliced)
2 sticks celery (sliced)
bouquet garni
½ teaspoon salt
6 white peppercorns
½ bottle dry white wine
3 tablespoons chopped parsley

Method
Split the chicken in half, wash well, remove any fat from the inside and the giblets, and place chicken halves in a pan with the vegetables, bouquet garni, seasoning and the white wine. Simmer gently for 1¼ hours.

Strain off liquid, allow to cool and skim off any fat. Remove the skin from the chicken, shred the meat, mix with the chopped parsley and place in a deep pie plate — Pyrex or foil — and spoon over the wine jelly; chill well. Cover the pie with the rolled-out pastry, decorate with trimmings and brush with beaten egg; bake for 25–30 minutes in a hot oven at 425°F or Mark 7, until well risen, brown and crisp. When cold, wrap and freeze.

Thawing and serving Thaw for 5–6 hours at room temperature. Eat cold with potato mayonnaise and salads of your choice.

Chicken and ham pie

8 oz quantity of puff pastry
beaten egg (to glaze)
3½–4 lb chicken
1 onion (sliced)
1 carrot (sliced)
2 sticks celery (sliced)
mixed herbs
bouquet garni
salt
6 white peppercorns
½ pint white wine
2 shallots or 1 small onion
    (finely chopped)
1 oz butter
6 oz cooked ham (minced or
    finely chopped)
2 tablespoons dry white
    breadcrumbs
1 teaspoon chopped marjoram or
    sage
½ beaten egg

*9-inch diameter pie dish, 2-pint
capacity*

Method

Cut the backbone from the chicken, put in a pan with the giblets, vegetables and herbs, season with salt and peppercorns and cover with 1½ pints water. Simmer gently for 1 hour, then strain.

Add wine to this stock and poach the chicken in this until tender, about 1 hour; allow to cool in the liquid.

Cook the shallots in the butter until soft but not coloured. Mix the ham with the breadcrumbs, marjoram or sage and season; add the shallot and bind with the beaten egg. Shape into balls.

Shred the chicken, reserving the jelly, and place in the pie dish with the ham balls and just enough wine jelly to fill the dish. When quite cold, wrap and freeze. Make and freeze pastry separately.

Thawing and serving Thaw for 2 hours, then roll out the pastry and cover the dish; brush the top with beaten egg. Bake in a hot oven, 425°F or Mark 7, for about 20 minutes, until golden brown.

Serve the pie cold with potato mayonnaise.

Tourtière de gibier

To serve 8

For pastry
14 oz plain flour
2 oz lard
5 oz butter
2 small eggs (beaten)
1 teaspoon salt

For filling
2 grouse or 3 pigeons
3 tablespoons sherry, or brandy
salt and pepper ground from mill
a pinch of ground mace
1 lb pork (minced)
¼ lb streaky bacon (minced)
½ lb beef sausages
livers from the game birds
    (minced)
1 clove garlic (crushed with ½
    teaspoon salt)
1 teaspoon chopped marjoram,
    or oregano
1 tablespoon chopped parsley

To finish
½ pint jellied stock

8-inch spring-form mould

Method

First prepare the pastry: sift the flour on to a board, make a well in the centre and in this place the fats, beaten egg and salt, reserving a little of the egg to glaze the pie. Using the fingers of one hand, work up ingredients together until a smooth paste is formed. If necessary, add 1–2 tablespoons of cold water, but avoid getting the paste too wet. Chill the pastry in the refrigerator while preparing the filling.

Cut the meat from game birds into thin slices, place in a dish and pour over the sherry or brandy. Season well with salt, pepper and mace. Mix the pork, bacon, meat from the sausages and livers together, work in the garlic and then add the herbs.

Roll out the pastry and line two-thirds of it into the mould; fill with alternate layers of the farce mixture and game meat. Cover with pastry, making a small hole in the top; decorate with the pastry trimmings and brush lightly with beaten egg. Bake in a moderately hot oven, 375°F or Mark 5, for about 35 minutes until the pastry is well browned, then wrap it in a double sheet of dampened greaseproof paper. Lower the heat to 325°F or Mark 3, and continue to cook for a further 45–50 minutes. When cold, wrap and freeze.

Thawing and serving Allow to thaw for 36 hours in the refrigerator, then pour ½ pint jellied stock into the pie, through the hole in the centre of the crust. Serve cold with salads.

Potato mayonnaise. It might be nice to have a variation on the usual theme to serve with these rich-tasting pies.

Take 1 lb small new potatoes (or 1½ lb old ones), boil, peel and allow to cool. Cut up the old potatoes into neat pieces, or leave new ones whole, and mix well into 5 fl oz soured cream. Add salt and pepper and lots of snipped chives.

If you need rather more, but have no more potatoes to hand, or the sauce looks a little thin, hard boil an egg, sieve the yolk and beat this into the soured cream to thicken it. Shred the cooked egg white and mix it into the dressing before adding the potatoes.

Tartlettes Lucullus

4 oz quantity rich shortcrust
    pastry (see page 125)

For mousse
8 oz chicken livers
2 oz butter
1 small onion (finely chopped)
3½ fl oz double cream
salt and pepper
1 tablespoon brandy

To finish
4 oz cooked ham (sliced)
¼ pint commercially-prepared
    aspic
a little chopped truffle
½ bunch of watercress
    (to garnish)

*8 tartlet moulds; forcing bag and
½-inch plain pipe*

Method

Prepare pastry and chill. Roll out thinly and line into 8 tartlet moulds. Bake blind (see page 71). Meanwhile, sauté the livers in 1 oz of the butter with the onion for about 3 minutes. Turn out and cool. Chop, then put into the liquidiser with the cream and seasoning. Blend until smooth. Remove from liquidiser and add brandy by degrees.

Fill the mousse into a forcing bag with a plain pipe; pipe into the tartlets to fill. Cover each with a round of foil, pack down and freeze.

Thawing and serving Thaw out for 3 hours. Then stamp out 8 rounds of ham to fit tops of tartlets. Lay a slice of ham on top of each.

Chill for about 15 minutes. Have ready about ¼ pint aspic to which has been added about 1 teaspoon of chopped truffle. When cool and at setting point, brush the 'tartlettes' with this, giving 2 coats if necessary.

Serve cold, garnished with a little watercress.

Note: The term '4 oz quantity of pastry' refers to the amount obtained by using 4 oz flour in all cases, not 4 oz of prepared dough. For this recipe, halve the basic quantities given on page 125.

FISH AND SHELLFISH

Fish used to be considered a more economical alternative to meat, although salmon and sole have always been luxuries. You will find recipes for sole and salmon on this and the next two pages, but with budget-conscious cooks in mind, we have included some less formal but equally savoury recipes for herrings, haddock and plaice.

From experience, we find the freezer life of white fish is good, and dishes can be cooked, frozen, thawed out and often reheated without any 'finishing off' at the last minute. Remember that if the fish is coated with a sauce it must be protected with either grated cheese or breadcrumbs to prevent a skin forming, otherwise the appearance of the finished dish suffers.

The freezing of shellfish is best left to the professional, so buy it in the frozen state and use as advised on the packet. Each of these dishes will serve 4.

Herrings parame

4 even-size herrings
salt and pepper
1½ oz butter
4 oz flat mushrooms
4 shallots, or 2 small onions
1 tablespoon chopped parsley

For serving
bread croûtes (see method)
chopped parsley (to garnish)
a little grated lemon rind

4 sheets greaseproof paper or foil

Method
Cut ovals out of the paper, or foil, each large enough to fold round a herring, spread with half the butter and sprinkle with salt and pepper.

Wash the mushrooms in salted water, chop finely and set on one side. Melt the remaining butter, add the finely chopped shallots, or onions, and cook slowly until soft but not coloured; add the prepared mushrooms and cook briskly until all the moisture has evaporated; season and add the chopped parsley.

Split the herrings down the back, remove the bones, fill with the mushroom duxelles and reshape. Place each herring on a prepared paper, fold over and twist round the edge. Set in a flameproof dish and bake in a moderate oven, 350°F or Mark 4, for 20–30 minutes.

Cut a long croûte from the bread to fit each herring and fry in oil and butter to a pale golden brown.

Unwrap the fish and lay each one on a croûte and when cold rewrap in foil and freeze.

Thawing and serving Thaw and reheat as for herrings normande and serve dusted with chopped parsley and a little grated lemon rind.

Herrings normande

4 herrings
1 medium-size onion
2 sharp dessert apples
1 dessertspoon chopped mixed parsley, chives and thyme
salt and black pepper freshly ground from mill
1 oz butter
2 tablespoons mild cider vinegar

Method
Split and bone the herrings, wash, dry and lay flat. Chop the onion finely, peel and dice the apple and mix all together with the herbs. Season the inside of the herring with salt and pepper and cover each fish with onion mixture; roll up head to tail. Place the fish in a buttered flameproof dish, melt the remainder of the butter, mix with the cider and pour over the top. Bake in a very moderate oven at 350°F or Mark 4, for about 20–30 minutes. When cold, lift carefully into a container, wrap and freeze.

Thawing and serving Thaw for 4–5 hours at room temperature and bake for 20–25 minutes at 350°F or Mark 4.

Herrings normande, with a savoury filling of onion and apple, make a good dish for lunch or supper

Casserole of fish panaché

1 lb fresh haddock fillet
1½–2 lb finnan haddock
2 lb fresh spinach, or 1 large packet frozen leaf spinach
1 pint béchamel sauce (made with 1 pint flavoured milk, 2 oz flour and 2 oz butter) see page 124 for method
1½ lb potatoes
1 oz butter
8 oz mushrooms
1 small onion
2–3 tablespoons cream
2 oz grated cheese

3-pint capacity soufflé dish

Method
Cook the fresh haddock in a buttered ovenproof dish in a moderate oven, 350°F or Mark 4, for 10–15 minutes. Cover the finnan haddock with milk and water, cover with a lid and bring slowly to the boil. Turn off the heat and leave for 10 minutes.

Drain, lift away the bone and carefully remove the fish from the skin, in large flakes.

Cook the fresh spinach, or leave the frozen spinach to thaw, press between two plates to remove any excess water then dry over gentle heat in ½ oz of the butter. Now make the béchamel sauce. Cook the potatoes and prepare a light potato purée.

Chop the mushrooms coarsely and the onion finely, and cook in the remaining ½ oz butter until all the moisture has evaporated. Bind with about ¼ pint of the béchamel sauce and season to taste. Place the spinach at the bottom of the buttered soufflé dish and cover with the fresh haddock, bound with ½ pint béchamel sauce. Now make a third layer using half the potato purée.

Mix the finnan haddock with the remaining sauce and the cream, and spoon this mixture on top of the potato. Cover the finnan with the mushrooms and finish with the remaining potatoes. Scatter over the grated cheese. Wrap and freeze.

Thawing and serving Thaw for 12 hours in a cool larder, then bake in a moderately hot oven, 400°F or Mark 6, for 40–45 minutes, or until brown and crisp.

Carrelet aux oignons

6 plaice fillets
¼ pint water
a squeeze of lemon juice
6 peppercorns
grated cheese

For onion fondue
3 large onions (about 1 lb)
1–1½ oz butter
salt and pepper

For sauce
1¼ oz butter
1 oz flour
scant ½ pint light stock, or fish liquor
salt and pepper
2½ fl oz single cream
1 level dessertspoon Dijon mustard

Method
First prepare fondue. Peel and slice onions thinly, melt the butter in a stewpan, add onions, cover tightly and cook slowly until melted and tender, but not coloured — about 15–20 minutes. Season.

Meanwhile skin fish, wash and dry. Fold under the tips of the fillets and lay in a flame-proof dish. Add water, lemon juice and peppercorns. Cover with buttered paper and poach in a slow-to-moderate oven at 325°F or Mark 3 for 10–15 minutes.

To prepare sauce: melt butter, stir in flour and pour on liquid, blend, season and stir until boiling. Add cream and continue to boil gently for 2–3 minutes. Draw pan aside and beat in the mustard. Do not reboil. Lift the onion fondue on to an ovenproof serving dish with a draining spoon. Arrange the poached fillets on the top and spoon over the sauce. Scatter well with grated cheese.

When the dish is quite cold, wrap in foil and freeze.

Thawing and serving Thaw in refrigerator for 4–5 hours, then brown in a pre-heated oven, 350°F or Mark 4, for 20–25 minutes.

Shellfish italienne

Choose an assortment of shellfish, cockles, mussels and prawns. Cockles and mussels can be bought fresh or pickled in jars. The prawns can come from the freezer.

¾–1 pint shellfish (cooked and shelled)
8 oz (250 g) lasagne

For tomato sauce
3 ripe tomatoes
1 large clove garlic (chopped)
½ bayleaf
½ oz butter
1 level teaspoon tomato purée
salt and pepper

For mornay sauce
1 oz butter
scant 1 oz flour
12 fl oz milk
2 oz cheese (grated)

Method
First prepare the tomato sauce. Cut tomatoes in half and squeeze to remove seeds, put into a pan with the garlic, bayleaf, butter and purée. Cover and cook to a pulp, rub through a strainer, adjust seasoning and mix with the prepared shellfish; set aside.

Simmer the lasagne in plenty of boiling salted water until tender, about 20–25 minutes. Strain and rinse with hot water.

Prepare the mornay sauce: melt the butter, remove from the heat and stir in the flour. Blend in the milk and stir over a moderate heat until boiling. Boil gently for 1–2 minutes, then remove from heat and beat in 1½ oz grated cheese. Season well.

Layer the lasagne, shellfish mixture and mornay sauce in a shallow ovenproof dish. Finish with the mornay sauce and sprinkle with the remaining cheese. Put into a quick oven, 480°F or Mark 9 for 10–15 minutes, until well-browned and bubbling.

Filets de sole et langoustines

two 2 lb Dover, or lemon, sole (weighed with bone, then filleted)
a squeeze of lemon juice
a little seasoned flour
1 egg (beaten)
dried white breadcrumbs (for coating)
½ lb scampi or 8 Dublin Bay prawns
1 oz butter, plus a little oil (for frying)

For butter sauce
1 wine glass white wine
1 shallot or 1 small onion (finely chopped)
6 peppercorns
blade of mace
1 egg yolk (beaten)
2 oz butter

For roux
1¼ oz butter
1 oz flour
½ pint fish stock (see box)

Method
Skin the fillets, wash and dry them. Prepare stock from the bones (see box). Take 4 fillets, fold and place in a buttered dish, sprinkle with lemon juice and a little fish stock, cover with a buttered paper and leave ready for poaching. Cut the other 4 fillets into wide strips, dip them into the flour, egg and breadcrumbs.

Set the oven at 350°F or Mark 4.

Prepare the sauce: put the wine, shallot, peppercorns and mace in a pan and reduce the liquid to a teaspoonful. Strain on to the beaten yolk, thicken in a bain-marie, adding the 2 oz butter piece by piece.

Make a roux by melting the butter, stirring in the flour and cooking to a pale straw colour, then strain on the stock and stir until boiling. Draw aside, season and beat in butter sauce. Cover and keep warm.

Put the folded fillets to poach in the pre-set oven. Shallow fry the crumbed pieces and lightly sauté the scampi or prawns in the butter for 3–5 minutes, without allowing them to colour.

Arrange the poached fillets in the centre of a serving dish and place the scampi on the top, coat with the sauce and surround with the fried fillets. Serve with French beans.

Fish stock: Sole bones make the best stock, but plaice bones may be used. Discard heads, trim side fins. Place bones in a large pan with a few peppercorns, a bayleaf and a pinch of salt. Pour on about 1 pint water, bring to the boil and simmer very gently for 20–30 minutes. Strain stock before using.

Filets de sole Carmelite

two 1¼ lb Dover sole (filleted)
bones from sole
6 oz steak of fresh salmon
1 egg white
2½ fl oz double cream
salt and white pepper
1–2 tablespoons milk
2½ oz butter
1 large onion (blanched and sliced)
bouquet garni, containing a stick of celery
6 white peppercorns
extra ½ teaspoon salt
a slice of lemon
12 large cooked prawns (to garnish)

To finish
2 tablespoons white wine
1 oz butter
¾ oz flour
1 tablespoon double cream

Method
Wash, skin and trim the fillets of sole and dry well. Remove the skin and bone from the salmon and mince twice; there should be 4 oz. Put the minced salmon in a bowl set on ice and beat well with a wooden spoon to break down the fibres. Whisk the egg white with a fork until just frothy and beat into the salmon a little at a time. Rub through a fine wire sieve, or use a liquidiser. Beat in the cream, season, and add the milk.

Spread the skin side of each fillet with the salmon farce and fold in half. Pack and cover with foil and freeze immediately.

Drop ½ oz of the butter into a saucepan, place the onion on top, cover pan and set on gentle heat for 5 minutes. Then add the sole bones, a pint of cold water, the herbs, seasonings and lemon. Cover and simmer gently for 20–30 minutes. Strain and measure liquid. Reduce to 8 fluid ounces by rapid boiling. When cool, pot and freeze.

Shell prawns, leaving the heads on eight; set aside for garnish. Remove the black eyes from the shells and pound the shells with the remaining prawns and the 2 oz of butter. Rub through a wire sieve. Place prawn butter in a container, cover with foil and pack the eight prawns for the garnish on the top. Cover and freeze.

Thawing and serving Allow fish, stock and garnish to thaw in the refrigerator for 3–4 hours. Moisten fish with white wine, cover with a buttered paper and poach in the oven for 20–25 minutes at 325°F or Mark 3.

Meanwhile prepare the sauce: Melt the 1 oz butter, blend in flour and cook gently until straw-coloured and marbled in appearance. Draw pan aside, stir in fish stock. Return pan to heat and stir until boiling. Cook for 1–2 minutes. Take pan off heat and beat in the prawn butter a small piece at a time. Adjust seasoning and add the cream.

Place prawn garnish in a small buttered dish, cover with foil and warm in the oven for 5–8 minutes.

Arrange the fillets of sole on a hot serving dish, coat with the sauce and garnish with the prawns.

To skin and fillet sole
Trim away outside fins with scissors. Lay fish on a board and, starting at the head end, slip your thumb about 1 inch under the black skin at the cut where the fish was cleaned. Run your thumb right round the fish, then grasp tail end firmly and rip off skin.

Repeat on other side of the fish.

Sole may be skinned whole and the fishmonger will skin them on both sides, if asked.

Sole is usually cut into a double fillet – the flesh on both sides of the backbone, top and underside is taken off in one piece (two fillets from each fish). If filleting at home, it is easier to take the flesh off in four fillets. Run the point of your knife down the backbone and with short, sharp strokes keeping the knife on the bone, work from the head outwards until the tail is reached and the fillet is detached.

Turn the fish round and, starting from the tail, take off the other half of the fillet in the same way. Turn the fish over and repeat the process.

Quenelles de poisson à la crème

1¼ lb fresh haddock or codling fillets
4 oz fresh white breadcrumbs
3–4 fl oz water
2 egg whites
salt and pepper
3 fl oz double cream
7½ fl oz white wine and water (mixed)

For cream sauce
1 oz butter
1 oz flour
generous ½ pint milk
salt and pepper
2½ fl oz cream
dry grated cheese

Method
Set oven at 350°F or Mark 4. Skin and mince the fish; when minced, it should yield 1 lb. Soak the crumbs in a little cold water and squeeze dry in a piece of muslin. Work this panade into the fish, adding the measured water by degrees, and the egg whites, lightly broken with a fork. Season with salt and pepper and work in the cream. Shape this mixture into egg shapes, using two dessertspoons dipped into boiling water. Lay these quenelles in a buttered ovenproof dish, pour in the wine and water round the side of the fish and cover with foil.

Poach in the pre-set oven for about 20–25 minutes until firm to the touch.

Lift out carefully and drain well. Place in a foil container, cover with foil and pack down in the freezer.

Thawing and serving Thaw in the refrigerator for about 4 hours, transfer to an ovenproof dish and prepare the sauce.

Melt the butter, stir in flour and blend in the milk. Stir over heat until thickening, then season and continue to stir until boiling. Simmer a few minutes, then add the cream. Reboil and spoon sauce over the fish. Sprinkle well with grated cheese and slide into a pre-set oven, 350°F or Mark 4. Set on the top shelf and allow to brown and reheat thoroughly, about 15 minutes.

Salmon galette

12 oz rich shortcrust pastry
½–¾ lb salmon steak (cooked and flaked)
½ clove garlic
salt and pepper
1 teaspoon paprika
1 teaspoon tomato purée
¼–½ pint mayonnaise
6 oz firm mushrooms
1 tablespoon oil
1 shallot (finely chopped)
1 tablespoon chopped herbs (parsley, mint and thyme)
2 caps canned pimiento

8-inch diameter pie plate or spring-form mould

Method
Line pie plate, or mould, with the pastry, keeping back enough for a top and decoration.

Crush the garlic with a little salt, mix with the paprika and tomato purée and work this into the mayonnaise.

Trim the mushrooms, wash quickly in salted water and chop finely. Heat the oil in a pan, add the mushrooms and fry briskly until all the moisture has evaporated; reduce the heat; add the shallot and herbs and continue cooking for about 1 minute; turn on to a plate to cool. Cut the pimiento in small dice and mix with the mushrooms; season to taste.

Place a layer of the mushroom mixture on the pastry, carefully mix the salmon with the mayonnaise and place on top, spoon over the rest of the mushroom mixture, cover with a lid of pastry and decorate. Wrap in foil and polythene and freeze.

Thawing and serving Remove galette from the freezer 12 hours before baking at 375°F or Mark 5, for 30 minutes until golden, then cover with greaseproof paper or foil, and continue baking at 300°F or Mark 2, for about 25 minutes.

Salmon steaks with mushrooms

4 salmon steaks
1 wine glass white wine
8 fl oz warm water
6 peppercorns
sprig of parsley
1¼ oz butter
1 oz flour

For hollandaise sauce
2 tablespoons white wine
  vinegar
blade of mace
6 peppercorns
1 shallot (finely chopped) .
1 egg yolk
2 oz butter

For garnish
4 oz mushrooms
½ oz butter
1 tablespoon grated Parmesan

Method
Place the fish in a shallow pan with the seasonings and parsley, pour over the wine and water and poach for about 15 minutes.

Reduce the vinegar with the mace, peppercorns and shallot to 1 teaspoon. Cream the egg yolk with a small nut of the butter until thick, strain on the reduced vinegar, stand in a bain-marie and beat until thick. Then add the remaining butter, a small piece at a time, beating well between each addition. Cover and set aside.

Take up the fish, drain well and remove skin and bones. Strain and reserve liquid.

Melt the 1¼ oz butter, blend in the flour and cook gently until marbled, pour on the stock from the fish and stir until boiling. Simmer 2–3 minutes, remove from heat and beat in all but 1 tablespoon hollandaise.

Trim, wash and slice the mushrooms and sauté briskly for 1 minute in a nut of butter.

Place the salmon in a foil container, coat with the sauce and spoon the mushrooms over; spread the remaining hollandaise carefully over the top and dust with Parmesan cheese. When cold, cover with foil and a polythene bag, or freezer-wrap, and freeze.

Thawing and serving Remove from the freezer 5 hours before required. Heat in a moderate oven at 350°F or Mark 4, for 30 minutes and glaze under the grill.

Coat the salmon mousse with a little extra mayonnaise before serving, and garnish with watercress and cucumber — perfect for summer parties

Buy salmon in season and treat it for the freezer in this way: Cut a thick darne (steak), or the tail piece, weighing 3 lb, and cook this wrapped in foil and freeze ready to serve cold as a main course for a dinner party for six.

The meat that can be flaked after cooking, from the head and shoulder piece, will be perfect for kedgerees, or a luxurious fish pie.

Salmon mousse

1 lb salmon steak
court bouillon (see page 19)
béchamel sauce (made with ¾ oz
  butter, ¾ oz flour, ½ pint
  flavoured milk)
¼ pint mayonnaise
1 dessertspoon gelatine,
  dissolved in 3 tablespoons
  light stock or warm water
3½ fl oz double cream
1 egg white (stiffly whisked)

To garnish
extra mayonnaise
cucumber slices
bunch of watercress

2 pint capacity (No. 2 size) soufflé dish, or 6–7 inch diameter cake tin

Method
Poach the salmon and leave to cool in the court bouillon; prepare béchamel sauce, cover with buttered paper and leave until cold. Remove skin and bone from the fish and flake into a bowl, pound well with the sauce and work in the mayonnaise. Season well and add the warm gelatine.

Partially whip the cream and fold into the mixture with the stiffly-whisked egg white. Turn into a lightly-oiled soufflé dish or cake tin, cover with foil and polythene and freeze.

Thawing and serving Thaw for 24 hours at refrigerator temperature and serve mousse, turned out of the mould, coated with extra mayonnaise and garnished with cucumber slices and watercress.

QUICK, BATCH AND BUDGET DISHES

In this chapter, there are three sections. The first deals with dishes that can be speedily put together, enabling the busy cook-hostess to produce a Cordon Bleu meal — with a fresh fruit salad or cheese and fruit to follow — in a matter of minutes. Then there are recipes for main courses that have been adapted either for the freezer, or for cooking in batches, such as pizzas or savoury loaves.

We finish with a section of budget recipes for family meals. Dishes generally serve six, unless otherwise stated, and quantities can easily be adjusted up or down.

Thinly cut steaks

As steak is now so expensive, many supermarkets now sell thinly cut steaks. If frozen, they thaw out quickly. Dab each steak dry before cooking.

Plainly fry steaks in a very hot, thick frying pan in not more than a dessertspoon of oil. Allow one minute of 'fierce' cooking on one side before turning and giving the meat just half a minute on the other side. Place on a hot serving dish, pepper the steaks well and pour over any juices from the pan.

Steaks with mushroom salpicon

To serve 4

4 thinly cut steaks
½–¾ oz butter
1 medium-size onion (finely chopped)
8 oz mushrooms (washed and sliced)
a dash of anchovy essence
salt and pepper
2–3 tablespoons cream
1 dessertspoon fresh herbs (optional)

Method

Fry the steaks as above and dish them up flat. Add the butter and onion to the pan, cook slowly for 1–2 minutes, then add mushrooms and sauté briskly for 2 minutes. Add anchovy essence, seasoning and cream. Boil up for half a minute until the cream disappears, then spoon salpicon over the steaks.

When fresh herbs are available, add a dessertspoon, chopped, with the seasoning.

Steak paupiettes

6 thinly cut sirloin steaks
¾ lb sausagemeat
1 small egg (beaten)
1 dessertspoon chopped parsley
3–4 bacon rashers
1–2 tablespoons beef dripping
4 large onions (cut into rounds)
¼–½ pint brown jellied stock (see page 124)
salt and pepper
a little arrowroot or kneaded butter

Method

Work the sausagemeat with the beaten egg and a dessert-spoon freshly chopped parsley. Spread on to the steaks and roll up. Tie each with thread or fine string, or fasten with a cocktail stick. Remove rind from bacon rashers, cut into strips and blanch.

Heat a thick, flameproof casserole and drop in 1–2 tablespoons dripping. When the fat is smoking, put in the paupiettes and brown carefully all over. Lift out, lower heat and put in the bacon and onion rounds pushed out into rings. Cook slowly until coloured — a dusting of icing sugar will help this — and stir frequently.

Take out half the onion and pour off any surplus fat. Replace the paupiettes, pour in about three-quarters of the measured stock, add seasoning and the rest of the onion. Cover tightly and braise in the oven at 350°F or Mark 4 for 35–40 minutes, or until tender. Baste and turn the paupiettes once or twice.

To serve: pack into a warmed gratin dish and cover with the onions. Boil up the gravy, adding the rest of the stock and thicken lightly with a little arrowroot slaked with cold water, or kneaded butter. Spoon over the paupiettes and serve very hot.

Thinly cut steak, topped with a savoury mushroom salpicon

Steak with spiced marrow

To serve 4

4 thinly cut steaks
black pepper freshly ground from the mill
1 small marrow
2 shallots or small pickling onions
2 oz butter
½ teaspoon paprika
½ teaspoon cumin
salt and pepper
2 tablespoons wine vinegar

Method

Grind a little black pepper over each steak and set on one side.

Peel the marrow, scoop out the seeds and cut in pieces the size of your little finger. Chop the shallots or pickling onions finely. Melt half the butter in a frying pan. Add the shallots or pickling onions, cover the pan and cook slowly until soft but not coloured. Dust in the paprika and cumin, cook for 1 minute, then add the marrow and season.

Stir well to mix in the onion and spices, and sauté 4–5 minutes. Moisten with the vinegar, cover the pan first with a buttered paper and then a lid, and simmer 5–6 minutes. Adjust seasoning and turn into a serving dish and keep warm.

Wipe the pan with a piece of absorbent paper, drop in the remaining butter and when hot fry the steaks until brown on each side.

Arrange steaks on the marrow and pour over any juices in the pan. Serve immediately.

Côtelettes de veau paprika

6 veal cutlets
1½–2 oz butter
1 medium-size onion (finely
    chopped)
1 teaspoon paprika
4 large ripe tomatoes (scalded,
    skinned and de-seeded)
2–3 caps canned pimiento
    (chopped)
½ bayleaf
salt and pepper

For sauce:
1 oz butter
scant 1 oz flour
¾ pint milk
2 tablespoons cream

Method
Brown the cutlets on both sides in the butter on a very moderate heat in a sauté pan. Take out the cutlets and add the onion and paprika to the pan. Cook for 3–4 minutes, then add the tomatoes, coarsely chopped, the pimiento and the bayleaf. Season, replace the cutlets, cover tightly and cook in a moderate oven at 350°F or Mark 4, or simmer on top of the stove for 20–25 minutes.

Meanwhile, prepare the sauce. Melt the butter, stir in the flour and cook until marbled in appearance. Stir in the milk and cook over a moderate heat until boiling. Boil gently for 1–2 minutes. Season to taste.

Dish up the cutlets, add a little of the gravy to the sauce, blend, then return to the sauté pan. Boil up and add the cream. Spoon sauce over the dish and serve with plainly boiled pasta shells or noodles.

Cooking noodles
Noodles should be cooked in plenty of boiling salted water. When you can sever a piece with your thumbnail, it is done 'al donto'. Strain off and rinse under very hot water. If they must be kept hot before serving, pour ½ pint hand-hot water into the rinsed pan, put in the noodles, cover and keep on one side. When ready to serve, strain and toss in butter over a gentle heat for 2–3 minutes.

Truites au four

6 trout
a little seasoned flour
2 oz butter
½ pint natural yoghourt
1 tablespoon horseradish cream
salt and pepper

Method
Set the oven at 350°F or Mark 4. Trim, wash and dry trout and leave the heads on. Roll each in seasoned flour. Heat a flameproof dish, drop in the butter and, when foaming, lay in the trout. Fry on moderate heat for 4–5 minutes, then turn carefully and continue to cook for a further 4 minutes. Do not allow to colour too much, just a light brown to crisp the skin.

Slide the dish into the preset oven for 5 minutes, then mix the yoghourt with the horseradish cream and season.

Coat the trout with this and return to the oven for a further 5 minutes. Serve very hot with a beetroot and potato salad.
Note: the horseradish cream can be taken from the freezer or bought ready bottled. If using the latter, add 1–2 tablespoons of lightly-whipped fresh cream, then stir into the natural yoghourt.

Beetroot and potato salad

2 medium-size cooked beetroot
    (thinly sliced)
½–¾ lb small waxy potatoes
French dressing
1 tablespoon snipped chives

Method
Arrange the sliced beetroot overlapping round the edge of a serving dish. Boil potatoes, peel while hot and dress them straight away with French dressing. Leave them whole if really small, otherwise quarter them.

Add about a tablespoon of snipped chives and pile in the centre of the dish.

For truites au four, the trout is coated with a sauce of natural yoghourt flavoured with horseradish cream. A beetroot and potato salad makes the perfect accompaniment to this dish

Poussins farcis aux raisins

To serve 4

4 single poussins
4 oz seeded raisins
1 glass sherry
1 medium-size onion (finely chopped)
¾ oz butter
4 rashers streaky bacon

For pilaf
1 medium-size onion (chopped or sliced)
1 oz butter
6 oz Italian 'risotto' rice
1 dessertspoon tomato purée
1¼ pints stock
1 bayleaf
salt and pepper

Method
Macerate (soak) the raisins in the sherry for as long as possible.

Set the oven at 350°F or Mark 4.

Soften the onion in the butter, add the raisins, sauté for 1–2 minutes, then stuff the birds with this mixture. Wrap the breast of each in a bacon rasher.

Now prepare the pilaf. Choose a large flameproof casserole, melt the butter in this and add the onion. Cook gently until beginning to colour, add the rice, cook for half a minute, then add the tomato purée and ¼ pint of the stock. Stir over the heat to blend well, and season.

Set the poussins on the rice, and pour round remaining stock. Add bayleaf.

Cover the casserole and cook in the pre-set oven for 15 minutes, then remove the lid. Increase heat slightly to 380°–400°F, Mark 5–6, and continue to cook for a further 10–15 minutes, until bacon is crisp.

Risotto, or Italian, rice is a thick grain rice used in dishes where the maximum amount of liquid must be absorbed. It should not be washed before cooking.

Chicken mexicain, sautéed in butter with wine and onion, is then tucked into a mixture of sweetcorn and rice

CHICKEN JOINTS

The following five recipes show you different ways of preparing frozen chicken joints, now readily available in packs from your local supermarket or bulk-buy freezer centre. These dishes are quickly put together once the joints have thawed and are not refrozen, but eaten straight-away. Allow the chicken joints to thaw out for at least 12 hours before cooking. Basic quantities are for four servings — with second helpings allowed — or for six.

Chicken mexicain

4–6 chicken breasts
1½ oz butter
1 Spanish onion (sliced)
2 wine glasses white wine
1 dessertspoon tomato purée
3 oz rice (cooked, drained and dried)
1 (11½ oz) can sweetcorn kernels
salt and pepper

The chicken, tomato purée and cooked rice can all come from the freezer.

Method
Allow the chicken breasts to thaw completely, then dry well on kitchen paper. Melt 1 oz of the butter in a sauté pan, put in the chicken breasts, skin side down, and cook slowly until golden brown. Lift the chicken from the pan, put in the onion, cover and cook for 5 minutes. Pour on the white wine, simmer until reduced to half quantity, blend in the tomato purée and replace the chicken in the pan, flesh side down. Baste with the liquid, cover and cook gently for 20–30 minutes.

Take up the chicken breasts, trim, and reduce the juices in the pan until thick and syrupy. Drop in the remaining ½ oz of butter, add the cooked rice and stir with a fork over a moderate heat. Turn the hot rice and the well-drained sweetcorn into a lightly buttered ovenproof casserole, season well, then tuck the pieces of chicken in with the rice mixture. Cover and slip into a moderate oven, 350°F or Mark 4, for 10–15 minutes. Serve with a green salad.

Chicken sauté paprika

4–6 chicken joints
1 tablespoon flour
1 teaspoon paprika
1½ oz butter
½ pint tomato sauce
1 (7 oz) can pimientos
salt
1 (5 fl oz) carton single cream
1 teaspoon arrowroot

For serving
6–8 oz noodles
1 oz shredded almonds
1 oz butter

The chicken joints and tomato sauce are from the freezer.

Method
Allow the chicken joints to thaw completely, dry well on kitchen paper and roll in the flour sprinkled with paprika. Thaw out sauce.

Brown the chicken joints slowly in butter on the skin side only, turn and pour over the tomato sauce and the juice from the canned pimientos. Season lightly with salt, cover and simmer gently for 30–35 minutes. Shred and add the pimientos and the cream, reboil and thicken if necessary with a teaspoon of arrowroot mixed to a paste with a little water.

Serve with plainly boiled noodles mixed with 1 oz shredded almonds fried in the butter until golden brown.

Chicken en casserole dijonnaise

4–6 chicken joints
2 rashers unsmoked bacon
1 oz butter
1 shallot (finely chopped)
¾ oz flour
½ pint chicken stock
bouquet garni
salt and pepper ground from mill
2 tablespoons double cream
1 teaspoon Dijon mustard
1 tablespoon chopped parsley

Method
Dry the chicken joints on kitchen paper when completely thawed. Remove the rind from the bacon and cut each rasher across in ½-inch strips. Melt the butter in a flameproof casserole, put in

the chicken joints skin side down, and brown slowly on all sides. Remove from the pan, add the bacon strips and shallot and continue to cook until both are golden brown. Blend in the flour, cook for 2–3 minutes until the roux is straw-coloured and marbled in appearance, tip on the stock and stir until boiling. Replace the chicken in the casserole, add the herbs and season with salt and pepper from the mill. Cover and cook in a moderate oven, 350°F or Mark 4, for 30–35 minutes.

Remove the bouquet garni, skin any surplus fat from the gravy as some will have come from the bacon during cooking, add the cream, bring to the boil and adjust the seasoning. Blend in the mustard and parsley and serve the casserole with plainly cooked potatoes (a purée during the winter months and small new potatoes in the summer).

Watchpoint Do not allow the sauce to boil after the mustard has been added; it will spoil the delicate flavour.

Chicken Reginiello

4–6 chicken joints
½ oz butter
1 wine glass dry white vermouth
2 sprigs tarragon
salt and pepper

For sauce
1 oz butter
1 oz flour
½ pint milk
3 oz Reginiello cheese (grated) – or 2 oz Cheddar and 1 oz Parmesan (grated)
2 tablespoons double cream

To finish
1 tablespoon browned crumbs

Method
Melt the butter in a flameproof casserole, put in the chicken joints skin side down, and cook gently until the skin is golden-coloured but not brown. Turn the joints over, pour on the vermouth, add the tarragon and season with salt and white pepper. Cover tightly and place in a moderate oven, 350°F or Mark 5, for 30–35 minutes.

Meanwhile prepare a white sauce by melting the butter,

adding the flour and when cooked to a roux, gradually add milk. Cover with a well-buttered paper to prevent a skin forming and set aside.

Take up the chicken, trim the joints and arrange in an entrée dish. Add the white sauce to the casserole, stir until boiling then strain; return the sauce to the casserole, place over a low heat and beat in the cheese a little at a time. Adjust the seasoning and add the cream.

Spoon the sauce over the chicken, dust with the browned crumbs and brown lightly under the grill.

Chicken sauté chasseur

4–6 chicken joints
1 tablespoon seasoned flour
2 wine glasses white wine
1½ oz butter
4 oz button mushrooms (finely sliced)
1 shallot or ½ small onion (finely chopped)
1 tablespoon tomato purée
½ pint demi-glace sauce (see page 124)

Take the joints, tomato purée and demi-glace sauce from the freezer.

Method
Dry the chicken joints well; dust evenly with seasoned flour. Melt 1 oz of the butter in a sauté pan, put in the chicken skin side down, and brown slowly. Turn the joints over and pour over 1 glass of the wine. Cover tightly and cook very gently for 8–10 minutes.

Meanwhile, melt the remaining ½ oz butter in a small saucepan, add the mushrooms and sauté briskly until taking colour, then lower the heat, add the shallot, or onion, and cook for a further minute. Pour on 1 glass of white wine, simmer until sauce is reduced to half quantity, then blend in the tomato purée and demi-glace sauce. Simmer for 5 minutes.

Take out and trim the chicken joints, replace in pan, pour over the sauce and continue simmering gently for 15–20 minutes.

Serve garnished with croûtes of fried bread.

TURKEY

Turkey croquettes

¾ lb minced meat from the legs and left-over carcase meat
1 cup dry white breadcrumbs
1 oz grated Parmesan cheese
a pinch of chopped mixed herbs
salt and pepper
1 egg (beaten)
a little seasoned flour
oil (for frying)

For brown sauce
1 medium-size onion (finely chopped)
1 tablespoon dripping
1 level tablespoon flour
¾ pint jellied stock
1 teaspoon tomato purée
bayleaf

To finish
a pineapple slice, for each croquette
1 oz butter
sugar (for dusting)
sherry
a little pepper ground from mill

Method
First prepare the sauce. Brown the onion in the dripping, stir in the flour, add the stock and tomato purée. Add the bayleaf and simmer for 15–20 minutes until syrupy. Meanwhile, prepare the croquettes.

Add the crumbs, cheese and herbs to the minced meat, season and bind with the beaten egg. Shape into flat cakes, roll lightly in seasoned flour and fry in hot oil until nicely brown, turning once only. Arrange in an ovenproof dish and spoon sauce over.

Cover with a piece of foil or greaseproof paper and cook in a moderate oven (350°–360°F or Mark 4) for 5–7 minutes. Meanwhile, fry a slice of pineapple for each croquette in a little butter, dusting with caster sugar. When browned, sprinkle with sherry, and grind over a little pepper.

Top each croquette with a slice of pineapple and serve.

Barbecued turkey

This recipe is quick to prepare if you marinate the turkey joints overnight and finish the dish the following day. If serving with fried rice, this can be being prepared while the turkey is braising.

turkey legs (thighs or drumsticks)
2–3 tablespoons bacon fat, or butter
1 large onion (chopped)
$\frac{1}{4}$–$\frac{1}{3}$ pint jellied stock
3–4 ripe tomatoes

For marinade
1$\frac{1}{2}$ oz butter
3 tablespoons tomato ketchup
2 tablespoons soy sauce
2 tablespoons sharp fruit sauce
2 tablespoons Worcestershire sauce
salt and pepper
a little mustard
a little sugar

Method
First prepare the marinade. Melt the butter in a flameproof dish. Add the four sauces, and mix well, adding the seasonings to taste. Cut the turkey meat into pieces and put into the marinade, turning and basting well. Leave for a few hours. Then melt 2–3 tablespoons of bacon fat, or butter, in a flameproof casserole, add the onion and sauté until soft, but not coloured. Lift the pieces of turkey from the marinade and sauté gently until nicely browned. Add stock, cover and braise 35–40 minutes. Turn the pieces occasionally and after 30 minutes' cooking time, add the rest of the marinade. Continue cooking for a further 5–6 minutes.

Meanwhile scald, peel, quarter and seed the tomatoes. Add to the pan, bring sauce to the boil and spoon over the drained turkey. Serve with fried rice or a pilaf.

Note: this recipe can be made in advance and the turkey pieces frozen with the sauce spooned over. Thaw overnight in the refrigerator; reheat in a moderate oven, 350°F or Mark 4 for 30–35 minutes.

Salpicons for pilafs

The salpicons given here are intended for quickly prepared lunch or supper dishes. But you can make them in advance and freeze. Thaw overnight in the refrigerator; otherwise they can be made up and served with rice pilaf straight away.

The chicken for the chicken and pimiento salpicon should be poached and ready for use. So choose the haddock or kidney filling if in a hurry!

Alternatively, use left-over cooked turkey meat. You would need about 1$\frac{1}{2}$ lb shredded cooked meat.

Smoked haddock, bacon and mushroom

$\frac{3}{4}$ lb smoked haddock fillet
milk and water (see method)
6 oz unsmoked streaky bacon rashers
2 oz butter
1 medium-size onion (thinly sliced)
8 oz cup mushrooms (sliced)
white pepper from the mill

Method
Poach the fish in milk and water to cover for 12–15 minutes. Meanwhile cut rind from the bacon rashers and snip across into lardons (strips). Drain fish, remove skin and any bones. Break into flakes with a fork.

Melt two-thirds of the butter in a shallow pan, add onion and bacon and frizzle gently for 5–6 minutes, or until turning colour.

Add the rest of the butter and the mushrooms, and continue to cook for a further 3–4 minutes, stirring frequently with a fork. Season well with pepper and add the haddock.

Turn into a container to freeze when cold, or if for immediate use, fork into 8 oz plainly boiled rice or a pilaf, and serve very hot.

Chicken and pimiento

3 lb roasting chicken or boiling fowl
1 onion (peeled and quartered)
1 carrot (peeled and sliced)
1 stick of celery
bouquet garni
$\frac{1}{2}$ teaspoon salt
6 peppercorns

or 1$\frac{1}{2}$ lb cooked turkey meat (shredded)

For salpicon
1 large onion
1$\frac{1}{2}$ oz butter
1–2 red or green peppers
1 rounded tablespoon flour
$\frac{1}{4}$–$\frac{1}{2}$ pint chicken stock
salt and pepper

To finish
4 fl oz cream

Method
Put the chicken into a large pan, add the onion, carrot and celery with the bouquet garni, salt and peppercorns. Pour in enough cold water to come level with the top of the thighs. Cover pan and poach gently until chicken is tender, 1$\frac{1}{2}$–2 hours for a boiling fowl, 45–50 minutes for a roasting bird. Cool in the liquid.

Skin chicken and cut the meat from the carcase. Shred the meat not too finely and set aside.

For salpicon: peel and slice the onion thinly, and soften in butter. Shred peppers and blanch them. Stir flour into the onion and add $\frac{1}{2}$ pint of stock. Blend, bring to the boil and season. Add the peppers and the shredded chicken or turkey. Cook for 5–10 minutes to heat through, add the cream, then cook for a further 1–2 minutes. Serve with the pilaf.
If freezing, mix sauce, peppers and chicken or turkey, but do not add the cream. Turn into a container and freeze when cold.
Thawing and serving Allow salpicon to thaw in the refrigerator overnight, then place in the oven with the pilaf for 15–20 minutes to reheat. Add the cream and return to the oven for a few minutes. It is important that the salpicon be brought to boiling point when reheating before serving.

Kidney and tomato

6 lambs kidneys
1–1$\frac{1}{2}$ oz butter
2$\frac{1}{2}$ fl oz sweet sherry or Marsala
2 medium-size onions (finely sliced)
4–6 oz flat mushrooms (quartered)
1 tablespoon flour
1 dessertspoon tomato purée
8 fl oz stock
1 bayleaf
1 clove of garlic (crushed with a little salt)
salt and pepper
4 tomatoes

Method
Skin and split the kidneys. Sauté in the butter just long enough to 'seize' them. Flame with the sherry or Marsala. Take them out, add the onions and, after a few minutes, the mushrooms.

Sauté for a few more minutes, then stir in the flour, purée and stock. Add bayleaf, garlic and seasoning. Replace the kidneys and simmer gently for 15–20 minutes. Scald, skin, de-seed and slice the tomatoes. Add them to the pan just before serving with the pilaf.

Basic pilaf

8 oz long grain rice
1 medium-size onion
2 oz butter
1$\frac{1}{4}$ pints chicken stock
salt and pepper
1$\frac{1}{2}$ oz grated cheese

Method
Set oven at 350°F or Mark 4. Peel and slice or chop onion, soften in two-thirds of the butter. Add rice, fry gently for a minute or two, then pour on the stock. Season, bring to the boil, cover and put casserole into the pre-set oven, for 15–20 minutes, or until the rice is tender and the stock absorbed.

Dot the surface with the rest of the butter and scatter the cheese over. Cover and leave on one side for 6–7 minutes, then turn carefully with a fork before serving with the chosen salpicon.

Cheese crumb flans

For crumb crust
4 oz cheese flavoured biscuits
2½ oz butter (melted)
2 oz mild cheese (such as
    Jarlberg or Gruyère, grated)
salt and pepper
Dijon mustard to taste

8½-inch diameter ovenproof china flan dish

Method
Set the oven 350°F or Mark 4.
Crush the biscuits fairly finely, put into a bowl, stir in the melted butter, the grated cheese and seasonings. Turn into the flan dish and press mixture over the bottom and sides with the back of a spoon. Bake in the pre-set oven for 10 minutes, then allow to cool.

Fill the flan with either of the following fillings and serve cold with a 'salade de saison'.
Note: the crumb crust can be baked and then frozen.

Egg, pimiento and tomato

2½ oz butter
1 medium-size onion (finely chopped)
2 cloves garlic
4 large ripe tomatoes
salt and pepper
2–3 caps canned pimiento (shredded)
6 eggs (beaten)
2–3 tablespoons cream
freshly-chopped mixed herbs

Method
Melt half the butter in a shallow pan, add onion and the garlic cloves, peeled and finely chopped, and cook slowly until turning colour.

Scald tomatoes, peel, squeeze to remove seeds and coarsely chop. Add to pan. Season well and increase heat, cooking rapidly until thick and pulpy. Draw aside, add the rest of the butter, the shredded pimiento, eggs and cream.

Stir slowly with a metal spoon until the mixture thickens creamily — be careful not to allow the mixture to become too solid.

Cool slightly, then turn into the crumb crust. Sprinkle with the freshly-chopped herbs and serve cold.

Savoury ham and cheese

½ pint béchamel sauce (see page 124) made with:
    ¾ oz butter
    1 rounded teaspoon paprika pepper
    ¾ oz flour
    ½ pint flavoured milk
2 egg yolks
1 oz grated cheese
salt and pepper
1 level dessertspoon gelatine dissolved in 2–3 tablespoons water
4 fl oz double cream (lightly whipped)
1 egg white
2–3 fl oz commercially-prepared aspic
4 oz lean sliced ham (shredded)
1 dessertspoon chopped parsley

Method
Prepare béchamel sauce, but add paprika to the melted butter before stirring in the flour. When sauce is boiling, draw aside and beat in the yolks and cheese. Season and allow to cool.

Add gelatine and, when at setting point, fold in the cream. Whip the egg white until stiff and fold it into the mixture. Turn the filling into the crumb crust and place in the refrigerator for half an hour before serving.

Make up aspic and allow to cool.

Mix the ham and parsley with the cool aspic and coat the top of the flan with the mixture.

A cheese crumb flan with egg, pimiento and tomato filling

Use the back of a spoon to press crumb mixture down firmly before baking. Crumb crusts can be baked in a flan ring. (see above), or in an ovenproof serving dish

BATCH DISHES

Another variation on the quick-to-prepare theme is to cook ahead and freeze a batch of pizzas, flans or savoury loaves, making them together. Then all you have to do is remember to take them out of the freezer on the day of the party.

The pizzas would be enough for a sizeable supper party, or an impromptu family occasion. The savoury loaves make splendid centrepieces for buffet parties — freeze them decorated, but ungarnished. The quiches are the perfect answer for unexpected guests. Each serves 4–6 and, like the pizzas, are quickly reheated.

Pizzas

Basic dough for 3 pizzas
12 oz flour
1 teaspoon salt
scant ¾ oz yeast
1 teaspoon sugar
small half-teacup (approx. 2½
  fl oz) warm milk
2 eggs (beaten)
2 oz butter

Three 8-inch diameter flan rings

Method
Sift the flour and salt into a warmed basin. Cream the yeast with the sugar and add to the warmed milk with the beaten eggs. Add all the liquid to the flour and beat thoroughly. Cream the butter and work into the dough. Cover and leave to rise for 40 minutes in a warm place.

from heat, stir in the flour and blend in the milk. Bring to the boil, then remove pan from heat and beat in grated cheese.

Take a third of the dough and pat out with your fist on a floured baking sheet to fill a 10-inch diameter flan ring. Cover with the scampi and mushroom mixture and spoon over the cheese cream. Prove the pizza (leave in a warm place to rise) for a further 10 minutes, then bake in a hot oven (400°F or Mark 6) for 25–35 minutes.

When cold, wrap in foil and freeze.

Thawing and serving Thaw for 1–2 hours at room temperature, then reheat in a moderate oven (350°F or Mark 4) for 15–20 minutes.

Scampi and mushroom pizza

8 oz scampi
2 oz butter
8 oz firm white mushrooms
1 shallot
salt and pepper

For cheese cream
½ oz butter
½ oz flour
¼ pint milk
1½ oz grated cheese

Method
Drop half the butter into a sauté pan, add the scampi and cook gently for 2–3 minutes, then remove with a draining spoon.

Wash, trim and slice the mushrooms and finely chop the shallot, add to the pan with the remaining 1 oz butter and sauté briskly for 2–3 minutes. Mix with the scampi and season to taste.

Prepare the cheese cream: melt the butter, remove pan

Devilled ham pizza

6 oz cooked ham
2 tablespoons peach chutney
1 large onion (peeled)
2 oz butter
2 caps canned pimiento
  (shredded)
1–2 drops Tabasco sauce

Method
Shred the ham and moisten with the chutney. Slice the onion, cook slowly in the butter until soft and golden, then add the shredded pimiento. Mix the ham, onion and pimiento together and season with Tabasco sauce.

Place this mixture on another portion of the dough, prove for 10 minutes and bake as above. Wrap and freeze as for scampi and mushroom pizza.

Thawing and serving follow instructions for scampi and mushroom pizza above.

Pizza Espagnole

2 lb Spanish onions (finely sliced)
4 tablespoons olive oil
1 teaspoon tomato purée
1 dessertspoon anchovy essence
4 oz curd cheese
4 tablespoons double cream
black pepper ground from the
  mill

To finish
2 tablespoons each grated
  Cheddar and Parmesan cheese
  (mixed)

Method
Cook the onions very slowly in the oil until golden brown, using a large frying pan and turning them frequently with a basting spoon. Work in the tomato purée, anchovy essence, curd cheese and cream; season with the pepper.

Taste the mixture and add a little salt if necessary. Pat out the third portion of dough, cover with the onion mixture and scatter the grated cheeses over the top. Prove the pizza for 10 minutes, then bake as above.

When cold, wrap in foil and freeze.

Thawing and serving Thaw for 1–2 hours at room temperature, then reheat as for scampi and mushroom pizza.

Two of the pizzas made from a batch of dough and then frozen. Right: scampi and mushroom pizza, and below: pizza with devilled ham topping, served with chianti

Savoury loaves

Decorating one of the savoury loaves before it is frozen

Each will serve eight, and there are six different fillings. Use your choice of three in each loaf.

2 large white sandwich loaves (unsliced)
1 lb butter

For decoration
1 lb curd, or cream, cheese
salt and pepper

For garnish
2 bunches of radishes
bunch of watercress
1 jar cocktail gherkins
½ cucumber
4 hard boiled eggs
4 small round beetroot (cooked)

Forcing bag and vegetable rose pipe

Method
Wrap the loaves in foil or waxed paper and slip into freezer while preparing the fillings. This will make them easier to slice.

For filling 1
1 small carton frozen chopped spinach
1 oz butter
1 shallot or small onion
6 oz cream, or curd, cheese
salt and pepper

Allow the spinach to thaw completely and tip away the liquid. Melt the butter, add the finely chopped shallot, cook until soft and the butter is lightly browned, then add the spinach and continue cooking until quite dry. Allow to cool. Beat the spinach purée into the cheese and season to taste.

For filling 2
1 (7½ oz) can tuna fish
2–3 tablespoons mayonnaise
a squeeze of lemon juice

Pound the tuna with the mayonnaise and season with lemon juice.

For filling 3
½ lb shoulder ham (cooked)
2 tablespoons thick white sauce
1 tablespoon tomato chilli sauce
a little chutney

Mince ham and pound with the white sauce. Add tomato chilli sauce and a little chutney to taste.

For filling 4
6 oz liver sausage
1 oz butter
1–2 teaspoons Dijon mustard

Pound the liver sausage, work in the creamed butter and season with Dijon mustard.

For filling 5
6 oz flat mushrooms
3 oz butter
2–3 spring onions
4 hard boiled egg yolks (sieved)
1–2 teaspoons freshly chopped mint
salt and pepper

Wash the mushrooms, squeeze dry and chop finely. Place in a shallow pan with 1 oz of the butter and the finely chopped onions. Cook briskly until all the water has been driven off. Allow to cool, then mix in the egg yolks, remainder of the butter, mint and seasoning.

For filling 6
6 oz corned beef (sliced)
1–2 tablespoons chopped sweet dill pickles

Finely chop the corned beef and work in the pickles.

Remove the crusts from the loaves and cut each in ¼ inch slices along the length of the loaves. Butter the slices and sandwich together with the prepared fillings, using three types of filling alternately in each loaf. There should be about six layers of filling. Reshape into two loaves.

To decorate: season the curd, or cream, cheese with salt and pepper and add a little single cream if necessary to give a good spreading consistency. Spread the top and sides of the loaves with half the cheese, and smooth with a palette knife. Fill the forcing bag and pipe a little of the cheese to decorate the top. Decorate sides of each loaf, place in cake box and freeze.

Thawing and serving Thaw 8–12 hours, and decorate each with radish roses, watercress, gherkins etc. as desired.

Quiches variées

For three flans
1¼ lb rich shortcrust pastry, made with:
1¼ lb flour
pinch of salt
8 oz butter
5–6 oz shortening
2 egg yolks
approx. 4 tablespoons water to mix

For basic custard mixture
4 eggs
2 egg yolks
4 oz grated cheese
salt and pepper
¾ pint milk
1 oz butter
2 medium-size onions
¼ pint single cream

Three 8-inch diameter flan rings

Method
Sift the flour with a pinch of salt into a mixing bowl. Drop in the butter and shortening and cut it into the flour until the small pieces are well coated. Then rub them in with the fingertips until the mixture looks like fine breadcrumbs. Mix egg yolks with water, tip into the fat and flour and mix quickly with a palette knife to a firm dough.

Turn on to a floured board and knead lightly until smooth. If possible, chill in refrigerator (wrapped in greaseproof paper, a polythene bag or foil) for 30 minutes before using.

Beat the eggs and yolks in a basin with the cheese, seasoning and milk. Melt the butter in a small pan and add the onions, peeled and finely sliced. Cook until golden and transparent and add to the egg mixture with the cream.

Divide the basic custard mixture in three and to one third, add 3 oz streaky bacon rashers lightly fried, or grilled, and cut in small pieces.

To the second 'third', add a 4 oz salmon steak, poached and flaked, or 4 oz canned salmon (well drained).

For the last portion, cook an 8 oz can tomatoes, with 1 clove garlic, crushed with a little salt, until thick and pulpy and when cold, add to the custard with 2 oz extra grated cheese.

Place each flan ring on a baking sheet and line with the raw pastry (see page 89). Fill each with one portion of the mixture and bake in a moderately hot oven at 375°F—400°F or Mark 5–6, for about 30 minutes, or until cooked. When cold, wrap in foil and freeze.

Thawing and serving Thaw for 1–2 hours in refrigerator and reheat in a moderate oven (350°F or Mark 4) for 15–20 minutes.

BUDGET DISHES

It is often thought that in order to produce a luxury dish, one needs luxury ingredients. Now, while it is pleasant to have at one's elbow the juiciest asparagus, the freshest salmon and the rarest, most succulent beef, in these days of rising food prices more and more people are realising that tasty dishes can be made from humbler ingredients.

This is something that Rosemary Hume and Muriel Downes have always known, for the French are thrifty cooks. So, to demonstrate that Cordon Bleu food need not be reserved for that special occasion, here are some recipes that are not only economical but delicious to eat. They can be put together easily from ingredients in your store-cupboard and freezer.

The gratin alsacienne, for example, with its crisply cooked cabbage, fish, and savoury cheese topping, is a firm favourite at the London Cordon Bleu School, and gives new meaning to the words 'fish pie'. The savoury choux ring on page 75, with its choice of two fillings, is clever way of stretching small quantities of left-over chicken, or using up gammon rashers and onions. Top of the milk can always be substituted for the cream if you are cooking to a budget.

Presentation is all-important, too, and we can guarantee that these dishes look as tempting as they are delicious to eat. The quantities of the recipes in this section serve six, unless otherwise stated.

Tomates farcies piedmontaise

6–8 large tomatoes
4 oz firm button mushrooms (finely sliced)
squeeze of lemon juice
salt and pepper
3 oz rice (cooked)
½ head celery
1 rounded teaspoon gelatine dissolved in 1 large tablespoon water
¼ pint mayonnaise
small rounds of brown bread and butter
4 oz ham (cooked and shredded)
1 tablespoon chopped parsley
French dressing

Method

Scald and skin the tomatoes, cut in half and scoop out all the seeds. Turn upside down to drain. Cook the mushrooms briskly with a squeeze of lemon juice and seasoning, and when cold, mix with the rice. Meanwhile, finely shred the celery, leave in ice cold water to curl.

Dissolve the gelatine in the water, add to the mayonnaise and as it thickens, mix into the rice and mushrooms and season well. Fill the tomato halves with this mixture. Set each half tomato on a round of bread and butter round the sides of a serving dish. Drain the celery very well, mix with the ham, parsley and a little French dressing and pile in the centre of the dish surrounded with the tomatoes.

Gratin alsacienne

1 (2 lb) firm white cabbage
½ head celery
1 medium-size onion
1½ oz butter
salt and pepper
4 tablespoons chicken or veal stock

For topping
½ lb coley, cod or haddock fillet
1 lb potatoes
½ oz butter
4 fl oz hot milk
2 oz grated cheese

Method

Set the oven at 325°F or Mark 3. Trim the cabbage, cut it in four and then shred very finely. Cut the celery into bâtons.

Peel and slice the onion. Melt the butter in a flameproof casserole, add the onion and cook until soft but not coloured. Mix in the cabbage and celery, and season with salt and pepper. Moisten with the stock, press a piece of foil or buttered greaseproof paper over the cabbage, cover with the lid and cook in the pre-set oven for 1–1½ hours.

Meanwhile, oven poach the fish in water to cover for 12–15 minutes, or until it flakes easily, and boil the potatoes in salted water. When the potatoes are tender, drain off the water and dry them well, add the butter, crush with a potato masher and beat in the hot milk. Flake the fish and add to the potatoes.

Tip the cabbage into an entrée dish and cover with the fish and potato mixture. Smooth the top and sprinkle thickly with the cheese.

Raise the oven temperature to 400°F or Mark 6, and bake until the cheese topping melts and browns.

Kipper and mushroom flan

8 oz quantity of rich shortcrust pastry (see page 125)
4–6 kipper fillets (depending on size)
8 oz flat mushrooms
1 oz butter

For cheese custard
2 eggs
7½ fl oz milk
2½ fl oz single cream
2 oz grated cheese
salt and black pepper

9–10-inch diameter flan ring or flan dish

Method

Set the oven at 375°F or Mark 5.

Prepare the pastry. Line the ring or dish and bake blind in the pre-set oven for 10–12 minutes, or until the pastry is set.

Meanwhile, poach the fish fillets in water to cover, for 6–7 minutes and sauté the mushrooms whole in the butter.

Beat the eggs lightly with a fork, add the milk, cream and cheese. Season with a little salt and rather more black pepper.

Skin the fillets, arrange in the pastry case, pour over the cheese custard and set the mushrooms on top. Return the flan to the oven to brown and complete the cooking, about 20–25 minutes.

Eat hot or cold with a side salad of your choice.

To bake blind
Line a flan ring with pastry and chill for 30 minutes. Line the pastry with crumpled greaseproof paper, pressing it well into the dough at the bottom edge and sides. Three-parts fill the flan with uncooked rice, or beans (to hold the shape) and put into the oven to bake. An 8-inch diameter flan ring holding a 6–8 oz quantity of pastry should cook for about 25 minutes in an oven at 400°F or Mark 6.

After 20 minutes of cooking time, take flan out of the oven and carefully remove the paper and rice, or beans. Replace flan in the oven to complete cooking (see page 89).

Liver flan

For rich shortcrust pastry see page 125 for method, but use:
6 oz flour
3 oz butter
1 oz lard or shortening
1 egg yolk
2–3 tablespoons cold water

For filling
1¼–1½ lb lambs or ox liver (in one piece)
2–3 carrots or 1 large packet frozen chopped spinach
good pinch of salt
pinch of sugar
¼–½ oz butter
salt and pepper
2 dessertspoons freshly chopped parsley
2 oz dripping or butter
1 medium-size onion (thinly sliced)
2 tablespoons cider vinegar
¼ pint stock

8–9-inch diameter flan ring or flan dish

Method

Set oven at 400°F or Mark 6.

First make up the pastry, roll out and line into a dish or flan ring. Bake blind for 10 minutes, then remove the flan ring and the beans or rice and return the pastry case to the oven for long enough to ensure the flan is crisp and dry. Keep it warm.

Meanwhile, peel and slice carrots into rounds, put into a pan and barely cover with water. Add a good pinch of salt, sugar and the butter; cover and cook fairly rapidly until all the liquid has evaporated. Season, sprinkle with a dessertspoon of parsley, and keep warm.

If using spinach in place of carrots, put it into a pan, cover and set on gentle heat to draw out moisture, then remove lid and increase heat. Cook, stirring frequently until fairly dry, season and add a nut of butter.

Remove any skin and ducts from the liver, slice, then cut into strips. Heat a heavy iron or aluminium frying pan, drop in the fat and when hot add the sliced onion. Cook gently until a golden brown, then add the liver and sauté briskly for about 3 minutes, turning it frequently. Add the vinegar and seasoning and moisten with a little stock.

Turn the carrots (or spinach) into the flan case, add a dessertspoon of parsley to the liver, then lift out with a slice and arrange over the vegetables. Reduce any remaining gravy in the pan and spoon this over the liver.

Note: It is important that the liver is very quickly sautéed — for not more than 3 or 4 minutes — so that it remains tender.

If wished, a 'ruff' of puréed potato to which an egg yolk has been added may be piped round the edge of the flan. Brown lightly under the grill before serving.

more recipes overleaf

73

Eggs bonne femme

6 new-laid eggs
3 medium-size potatoes
1 medium-size onion
6 oz unsmoked streaky bacon
3 oz butter
2–3 tablespoons single cream
chopped parsley (to garnish)

Method
Set the oven at 375°F or Mark 5. Slice the potatoes and onion very thinly. Remove rind from the bacon and cut into strips. Blanch the bacon and onion, and drain. Melt 2 oz of the butter in a metal flameproof dish, put in the vegetables to make a flat layer and scatter bacon on the top. Cover and cook gently on the top of the cooker for about 6–10 minutes, or until tender.

Make 6 depressions on the surface and break an egg into each. Melt the remaining butter and spoon it over the eggs with the cream or milk. Bake the eggs in the pre-set oven until the whites are just set — about 6 minutes. Sprinkle with parsley and serve at once.
Note: Only a metal dish can conduct heat well enough to cook the vegetables through in a short time. This makes a good, light supper dish.

Potato galette with sausage filling

The idea of using potatoes as the means of presenting a small amount of meat in an attractive way is not new, but the following recipe is a tasty variation on the theme.

1½ lb potatoes
salt
1 oz butter
pepper ground from the mill
1 teaspoon Dijon mustard
1 oz dry Cheddar cheese (grated)
about 2 fl oz hot milk
2 tablespoons browned
    breadcrumbs

For filling
2 large onions (about ½ lb) —
    finely sliced
1½ oz butter
4–6 large pork or beef sausages

8–8½-inch diameter shallow cake tin

Potato galette with sausage filling, served with braised cabbage and spicy tomato sauce

Method
Cover the potatoes with cold water, add salt and boil gently until just tender; drain off the water. Return the potatoes, covered with the lid, to the stove over the lowest possible heat and leave for 2–3 minutes until dry and floury. Drop half the butter into the pan, crush the potatoes with a potato masher and season with pepper, Dijon mustard and the cheese. Beat in enough hot milk to make a fairly stiff purée. Rub the remaining butter round the cake tin and dust it out with the browned crumbs.

Set the oven at 375°F or Mark 5. Meanwhile prepare the filling. Cook the onions very slowly in the butter in a covered pan until soft and golden. Simmer the sausages in salted water, or stock if available, for 20 minutes; allow to cool a little, remove the skins and cut in slices.

Put a thick layer of the potato purée at the bottom of the prepared tin, cover with the onion fondue and the sliced sausages and fill the tin with the remaining potato. Smooth over with a palette knife and bake in the pre-set oven for about 45 minutes until well browned. Leave in the tin for a few moments before turning out.

Serve with braised or plainly cooked cabbage and spicy apple and tomato sauce. The next recipe is for an alternative filling.

Mushroom and bacon filling

14 oz flat mushrooms
½ oz butter
4 rashers streaky bacon (cut in strips)
½ small head celery (washed, dried and sliced)
1 shallot or small pickling onion (finely chopped)
1 teaspoon chopped mixed herbs
salt and pepper

Method
Wash and trim the mushrooms; cut the stalks level with the caps, remove the peel and chop both very finely. Cut the mushrooms caps in thick slices and set aside.

Melt the butter in a sauté pan, drop in the bacon and cook slowly until the fat begins to run, then add the celery, increase the heat and cook briskly until golden brown.

Lift bacon and celery from the pan with a draining spoon, add the mushroom stalks and peelings, shallot and herbs, and cook slowly until all the moisture is driven off. Add the sliced mushrooms and cook until tender, adding an extra nut of butter if necessary. Mix in the bacon and celery and season to taste.

Spread this filling on the layer of potato at the bottom of the prepared tin, cover and bake as before.

Spicy apple and tomato sauce

½ oz butter
1 medium-size onion (sliced)
1 large cooking apple (weight ½–¾ lb)
1 teaspoon paprika
1 tablespoon tomato purée
¼ pint stock or water
dash of Tabasco
1 tablespoon sugar
1 small clove of garlic (crushed with a little salt)
pepper
½ bayleaf

Method
Melt the butter, add onion and cook slowly for 3–4 minutes without allowing to colour. Peel, core and slice the apple, add to the pan with the paprika, and mix well with the butter and onion. Cook for 1 minute, then stir in the tomato purée, stock and all the other ingredients. Bring to the boil and simmer until the apple is soft and pulpy, about 15 minutes. Rub through a wire or nylon strainer, reheat and serve.

Savoury choux ring

For choux pastry
  (see page 101 for step-by-step
  pictures)
3¾ oz plain flour
a pinch of salt
3 oz butter
7½ fl oz water
3 eggs
1½ oz Parmesan cheese (grated)
salt and pepper
a little Dijon mustard
4–6 oz streaky bacon rashers

8½–9-inch diameter savarin or ring mould

Method
Set oven at 375°F or Mark 5. Sift the flour with a pinch of salt on to a sheet of stiff paper. Place the butter and water in a pan over gentle heat. When the butter has melted, bring the water to the boil, draw aside, and immediately tip in all the flour. Beat until smooth and the mixture leaves the side of the pan. Leave to cool.

Whisk the eggs lightly and add them by degrees to the mixture, beating thoroughly. The finished paste should be smooth and shiny and hold its shape.

Watchpoint If the eggs are exceptionally large, it is wise to keep back one white, adding it only if necessary.

Fold in about 1 oz of the cheese, season well and add mustard to taste. Turn into the well-greased mould and sprinkle the top with the remaining cheese. Cut rind from the rashers and cut across in thin strips. Blanch and drain. Sprinkle on top of the cheese.

Bake for about 1 hour or until very firm to the touch, increasing the oven temperature after 30 minutes to 400°F or Mark 6. Turn out on to a cake rack and fill with either of the following fillings.

To fill the ring, split in two whilst still hot, and place the bottom ring in an ovenproof serving dish. Have your chosen filling very hot, then spoon on to the ring and top with the other. Slide dish into a hot oven, 425°F or Mark 7, for 7–10 minutes then serve at once with a green salad or hot vegetable of your choice.

Chicken and mushroom filling

¾ lb cooked chicken (shredded)
1 small onion (finely chopped)
1 oz butter
8 oz flat mushrooms (quartered)
salt and pepper
1 tablespoon flour
½ pint chicken stock

Method
Fry the onion in butter for 2 minutes, then add the mushrooms. Shake over a brisk heat for 4–5 minutes, then season, draw aside, stir in the flour and add the stock. Stir until boiling. Add the shredded chicken and heat through.
Note: You can also make this recipe with chicken joints. Use 2–3 thighs and 2–3 drumsticks. Brown the joints slowly in butter, season, add 2½ fl oz stock, cover and simmer about 12 minutes or until tender. Take out the joints and reduce the liquid to 3–4 tablespoons. Cook the onion in the liquid and continue as above.

Bacon and egg filling

½ lb gammon rashers of bacon
  (cut into strips and blanched)
6 eggs
½–¾ pint béchamel sauce (see
  page 124) made with:
  1¼ oz butter
  1¼ oz flour
  ½ pint flavoured milk
2 medium-size onions (thinly
  sliced)
1 oz butter
2½ fl oz cream
salt and pepper

Method
Hard boil the eggs for 10 minutes and chop them not too finely. Prepare béchamel sauce and set aside. Soften the onions in butter, add the bacon and continue to fry until just turning colour. Lift the onions and bacon from the pan with a draining spoon to remove any surplus fat, and stir them into the sauce with the eggs. Add the cream. If the mixture is too solid, add a little milk. Season lightly.

Vegetable fritto misto

Choose 3–4 vegetables from this list:
parsnips and halved walnuts,
potatoes, spinach, cauliflower,
beetroot, brussels sprouts,
mushrooms, onions
herbs (parsley, marjoram,
  thyme, etc.)
lemons
½ oz butter
1 egg (separated)
French dressing (for marinade)
seasoned flour
tomato sauce (to serve)

For fritter batter
8 oz flour
large pinch of salt
1½ teaspoons yeast
about ½ pint warm water
5 teaspoons oil

Deep fat bath

Method
Prepare the fritter batter. Sift flour and salt into a warm basin. Mix yeast in about half the warm water, and stir into the flour with the oil. Add the rest of the water to make the consistency of thick cream. Beat well and cover, leave in a warm place for 15–20 minutes – by then the mixture should be well-risen.

Prepare the vegetables as follows:
Parsnips Peel and cut in slices. Cook until tender in boiling salted water. Drain well and then purée with ½ oz butter and an egg yolk. Allow to cool, then turn onto a floured board and divide into pieces about the size of a large walnut. Place a walnut half carefully on each side of each ball, then dip in the fritter batter and deep fry.
Spinach Branch the spinach (about ½–¾ lb), wash well, blanch and drain. Season well and spoon over a little French dressing, then leave to marinate. Take several leaves and roll in the seasoned flour in the shape of a cigar. Then dip into the fritter batter and fry.
Cauliflower Sprig the cauliflower, boil until just tender in salted water, then drain. Marinate in a little French dressing, then dip into the batter and fry.
Beetroot Boil in the skins for about 1½ hours, or until cooked, cool, peel and slice.

Marinate in French dressing. Dry before rolling in seasoned flour, dip in the fritter batter and fry in the deep fat.
Brussels sprouts Blanch the sprouts for 4–5 minutes, then drain. Roll in seasoned flour and dip in the batter and fry in the deep fat.
Mushrooms Do not cook these before frying. Merely wipe and marinate in French dressing. Dry and roll in seasoned flour, dip in fritter batter and fry.
Onions Choose Spanish onions and cut them into rings about ¼-inch thick. Mix onions thoroughly with a little raw egg white (about half an egg white), then sift in enough seasoned flour to coat the rings. Fry at once in deep fat.
Herbs Dip the sprigs in fritter batter and drop into deep fat.
Lemons Boil the whole lemon until really tender, about 45 minutes. Drain, cut into eighths and lay on absorbent paper for about 5 minutes to drain. Then dip in fritter batter and fry.

Pile the fried vegetables up on a hot dish and serve with tomato sauce.

Tomato sauce

2 oz butter
4 tablespoons flour
1 tablespoon tomato purée
1½ pints stock
1 large (15 oz) can Italian
  tomatoes
1 bayleaf
1 clove of garlic (crushed)

Method
Melt the butter in a pan, stir in the flour and cook until marbled in appearance. Blend in the tomato purée and stock, and stir until boiling. Add the canned tomatoes, bruising them well with a wooden spoon, and season. Add bayleaf and garlic.

Cover pan and simmer 20–30 minutes. Strain and serve.

Savoury 'pains perdus'

This is an interesting way of stretching small quantities of cooked chicken, meat or fish. Left-over meat from a roast joint, incorporating any remaining appropriate sauce, stuffing or vegetable, can be used to make an attractive, economical dish.

Basic 'pain'

Light milk bread or a sliced starch-reduced loaf such as Nimble or Slimcea gives the best results. Allow two slices per person and always have the filling ingredients ready before preparing the bread.

To serve 4

8 thin slices bread
4 fl oz creamy milk seasoned
    with salt and pepper
1 egg (lightly beaten)
1–2 oz melted butter

Method
Set the oven at 400°F or Mark 6. Remove the crust from the bread and roll each slice firmly with a rolling pin. Then dip each slice first in the seasoned milk and then in beaten egg.

Place a large spoonful of one of the following fillings on the bread and roll up carefully but firmly. Place in a well-buttered ovenproof dish, brush well with melted butter and bake in the pre-set oven until brown and crisp, about 20–30 minutes.

Watchpoint Make sure the slice of bread overlaps a little and put the join on the underside when placing the rolls in the dish for baking. This should prevent the rolls from uncurling while in the oven.

Ham filling

8 slices cooked ham
2 teaspoons made English
    mustard
black pepper ground from mill

Method
Spread the ham with the mustard, grind over a little black pepper and place the ham on the prepared bread. Roll and bake as above.

Lamb filling

left-over cold cooked lamb (cut from leg, loin or shoulder)
1 tablespoon bottled spicy sauce
1 dessertspoon bottled fruity
    sauce
1 dessertspoon tomato ketchup
2 courgettes (4 if very small)
2 tomatoes
1 medium-size onion (finely
    sliced)
½ oz butter
salt and pepper
1 tablespoon grated cheese

Method
Trim away any excess fat and cut the meat in small dice or shreds. Mix together the sauces, spoon over the meat and leave to marinate for 30 minutes.

Trim and slice the courgettes thinly, blanch them in boiling salted water for 2–3 minutes, and drain well. Scald and skin the tomatoes, remove the seeds and coarsely chop the flesh. Cook the sliced onion in the butter until soft and golden, add the courgettes and tomatoes, season and simmer until well reduced.

Now spread some marinated lamb with any of the sauce remaining over each slice of prepared bread. Place a good spoonful of the courgette mixture on top and curl each slice of bread round the filling. Lift carefully into the baking dish and sprinkle with grated cheese after brushing with melted butter.

Beef filling

left-over cold cooked beef
3 tablespoons grated beetroot
1 teaspoon horseradish cream
    sauce or 1 teaspoon bottled
    horseradish cream mixed with
    2 tablespoons whipped double
    cream
a little made English mustard

Method
Slice the cooked beef as thinly as possible. Mix the grated beetroot with the horseradish cream.

Spread the slices of prepared bread with a little made mustard, cover with the beef, and top with the beetroot and horseradish mixture. Roll up and bake as before.

Serve with a chicory, beetroot and grated carrot salad.

Pork filling

left-over cold cooked pork
left-over sage and onion stuffing
a little cream or milk
6 cocktail onions (finely sliced)
3 sweet cocktail gherkins
    (chopped)
1 tablespoon tomato and chilli
    chutney
3 tablespoons apple sauce

Method
Slice the cooked pork and work a little thin cream or milk into any left-over sage and onion stuffing to make a spreadable consistency. Spread the stuffing over the prepared bread and cover with thin slices of pork.

Mix the cocktail onions, gherkins and chutney with the apple sauce, and spoon this mixture on to the sliced pork. Roll up and bake as before.

Serve these pork rolls with a white cabbage salad.

Chicken filling

left-over cold cooked chicken
1 oz butter
1 medium-size onion (finely
    sliced)
½ teaspoon paprika
pinch of cayenne pepper
¼ teaspoon cumin
1 dessertspoon tomato purée
4 fl oz stock
salt and pepper
1 (7 oz) can Mexicorn

Method
Cut the cold chicken into 'finger-size' pieces. Melt the butter, add the onion and cook very slowly uncovered until just taking colour. Stir in the spices and cook 2–3 minutes. Put in the chicken pieces, turn until well-coated on all sides with the butter, spices and onion, and continue cooking a further 2–3 minutes.

Blend in the tomato purée and stock, season lightly with salt and pepper and allow to cook very gently until well reduced and sticky. Add the well drained Mexicorn and mix carefully. Fill into the prepared slices of bread and roll and slice as before.

IDEAS FOR PUDDINGS

Raspberry cremets

1 lb frozen raspberries, or
    1 (14 oz) can raspberries
1 dessertspoon gelatine
3 tablespoons custard powder
¾ pint milk
thinly pared rind of ½ orange
12 fl oz natural yoghourt
approx. 1 tablespoon sugar

Method
Allow frozen raspberries to defrost. Drain the raspberries and pour 2 tablespoons of the juice on to the gelatine and leave to soak. Mix the custard powder with 4 tablespoons of the milk and infuse the orange rind in the remaining milk over a gentle heat for about 5 minutes. Strain.

Blend the flavoured milk with the slaked custard powder, return to the pan and stir until boiling. Remove from the heat, stir in the soaked gelatine and tip into a bowl. Cover and allow to cool.

Whisk the custard carefully while it is cooling with either a wheel whisk or electric beater – this not only prevents a skin forming but makes the finished custard much lighter in texture.

When it is cold, add the yoghourt, then whisk again thoroughly and sweeten to taste. Fold in the drained raspberries and pour at once into a serving bowl. Cover and chill for at least 1 hour before serving.

Note: Other red fruit such as redcurrants, blackcurrants, loganberries and blackberries would be equally suitable for this recipe.

Two delicious budget puddings — raspberry cremets (left) and Swedish chocolate roll

Swedish chocolate roll

3 eggs
5½ oz caster sugar
2¼ oz fécule (potato flour) or arrowroot
2 teaspoons baking powder
2 tablespoons cocoa powder
icing sugar (for dredging)

For filling
3 fl oz milk
2½ oz caster sugar
1 large egg yolk or 2 small yolks
1 teaspoon instant coffee
4 oz unsalted butter

Swiss roll tin 8 inches by 12 inches, or paper case

Method
Set oven at 375°F, or Mark 5. Whisk the eggs and sugar at high speed until thick and mousse-like. Sift the fécule or arrowroot with the baking powder and cocoa, and cut and fold the egg mixture. Pour at once into the prepared tin, or paper case, smooth top level with a palette knife and bake for about 10 minutes in the pre-set oven.

Meanwhile prepare the filling. Heat the milk with the sugar, pour on to the egg yolk, beat well and return to the pan. Stir over the heat, without boiling, until thick, then add the coffee, allow to cool. Cream the butter until soft, then add the cooled custard a little at a time.

Turn roll out on to a sugared paper and roll up with a sheet of greaseproof paper inside. When cold, unroll carefully, spread with the filling and re-roll. Dredge with icing sugar.

How to make a paper case for the chocolate roll

Use thick greaseproof paper or non-stick (silicone) cooking paper. First, fold down a 1½-inch border on each side and crease into place. Then, cut a slit at each corner as shown (top) and fold one cut piece over the other to mitre the corners, securing each with a paper clip (bottom). Slide the case on to a baking sheet and lightly brush the greaseproof paper with a little oil or melted butter and sprinkle with flour before using

Apple and ginger pudding

1 lb cooking apples
1 oz butter
grated rind and juice of ½ lemon
1–2 tablespoons caster or soft brown sugar
1 (7 oz) packet ginger biscuits
¼ pint commercially soured cream

6-inch diameter soufflé dish or cake tin

Method
Set the oven at 350°F, or Mark 4. Peel, core and cut the apples in thick slices. Fry quickly in the butter, add the grated lemon rind and sugar, and cook until the sugar takes colour. Moisten with the lemon juice.

Arrange a layer of biscuits in the buttered soufflé dish or cake tin. Cover with a layer of the apple mixture, then a layer of soured cream. Continue with alternate layers until the dish is full, finishing with soured cream. Cover with foil and bake in the pre-set oven for 30–40 minutes. Serve hot.

COLD BUFFET FOOD

When planning a buffet party, whether for lunch or supper, it is important to have dishes which not only look attractive, but offer a choice of flavours. Eggs and tomatoes, stuffed with a variety of different fillings, make an ideal solution and the smoked trout mousse would go well with either. Chicken, too, is popular and still relatively inexpensive, so there are recipes for this also.

We have indicated the approximate number of helpings on each of these recipes. So much depends on the number of guests invited and whether they come back for seconds . . .

The tomates farcies assorties are stuffed with three different fillings: (top) bacon and curd cheese; (centre) shrimps in mayonnaise; (right) egg and chutney. The oeufs farcis maison are filled with either a pea purée or mushroom mixture, and are served on a bed of rice salad

Smoked trout mousse

To serve 8

2 smoked trout
8 oz Philadelphia cream cheese
¼ pint mayonnaise
1 teaspoon horseradish cream
salt and pepper
1 level dessertspoon gelatine
   soaked in 4 tablespoons
   white wine
2½ fl oz double cream

For béchamel sauce
1 oz butter
1 oz flour
½ pint flavoured milk

For garnish
1 pint peeled shrimps or prawns

6-inch diameter soufflé dish or 8–9-inch diameter shallow cake tin

Method
Remove the skin and all bones from the trout and pound the flesh well. Make the béchamel sauce in the usual way, and allow to cool. When cold, work it into the cream cheese, then into the fish and add the mayonnaise and horseradish cream. Adjust the seasoning, add the melted gelatine and, as the mixture thickens, fold in the lightly whipped cream.

Turn into a lightly oiled soufflé dish or cake tin. Cover. Leave to set and then freeze.
Thawing and serving Thaw for 12 hours in the refrigerator, then unmould on to a flat dish, pile the shrimps on the top and surround with Swedish cucumber salad.

Swedish cucumber salad

1 cucumber
salt
1 dessertspoon caster sugar
½ teaspoon black pepper ground
   from the mill
2 tablespoons water
1 tablespoon white wine vinegar
a little chopped dill

Method
Slice cucumber finely, sprinkle with salt and leave pressed between two plates for 30 minutes. Drain well. Mix the caster sugar with the pepper, measured water, vinegar and dill. Add to cucumber. Chill well before serving.

Tomates farcies assorties

This recipe serves 6–8 as a main course buffet dish, or more if made for a starter.

18–24 even-size tomatoes
small rounds of brown bread and butter
French dressing
watercress to garnish

For fillings
½ pint mayonnaise
2 rounded teaspoons gelatine
2 tablespoons water
salt and pepper
lemon juice to taste
½ lb shrimps or prawns (peeled)
4 eggs (hard boiled)
chutney to taste
3–4 rashers streaky bacon
3 oz curd or demi-sel cheese
1 tablespoon cream or milk
1 teaspoon chopped chives or parsley

Method
Scald and skin the tomatoes, slice off the tops at the flower end and scoop out all the seeds. Turn upside down to drain, reserving the tops.

Now prepare the fillings. Dissolve the gelatine in the water and add to the mayonnaise to use for the first two fillings. Season well. Sharpen half the mayonnaise with lemon juice and add the shrimps or prawns.

Chop the eggs, add a little chutney to taste and bind with the remaining mayonnaise. Fill 6–8 tomatoes with the prawn mixture and a similar number with the egg mixture. Replace the tops.

For the third filling, grill or fry the bacon until crisp and when cold, crush into small pieces. Sieve the cheese, soften with the cream or milk, season and add the chives or parsley and bacon; fill into the remaining tomatoes.

Set each tomato on a croûte of brown bread and butter, spoon over a little French dressing, and serve garnished with watercress.

Oeufs farcis maison

To serve 6

6 eggs (hard boiled)
4 oz green peas (cooked)
4 oz flat mushrooms
2½ oz butter
1 shallot or small onion (finely chopped)
2 oz curd cheese
salt and pepper

For béchamel sauce
½ oz butter
½ oz flour
¼ pint flavoured milk

For rice salad
6 oz long grain rice (cooked)
1 lb assorted salt or smoked fish (anchovy fillets, cooked kipper fillets or smoked haddock – cooked and flaked)
1 head celery
2 caps pimiento
French dressing (see method)

For garnish
3 black olives (halved and stoned)
6 strips pimiento
3 tomatoes (scalded, skinned and quartered)
1 bunch watercress

Forcing bag and 6-cut rose vegetable pipe

Method
Make béchamel sauce and leave to cool. Purée the peas in a liquidiser. Trim and wash the mushrooms, chop finely and cook briskly with ½ oz of the butter until all the moisture has evaporated. Add the shallot, cook a further minute; tip on to a plate to cool.

Halve the eggs lengthwise, remove the yolks and rub them through a wire strainer. Cream the remaining 2 oz butter well, pound with the yolks and curd cheese and divide into two portions. Mix one portion with the pea purée, the other with the mushroom mixture, season, and add enough cold béchamel sauce to each to bind.

Prepare the French dressing for the rice salad using 3 parts of salad oil to 1 part of vinegar, seasoning with salt, pepper, Dijon mustard and garlic.

Shred or flake the fish. Slice the celery and pimiento, mix with the rice, moisten with dressing, then fork in the fish.

Arrange the rice salad on a large round platter, place the eggs firmly on top and, using the forcing bag and pipe, fill half the eggs with the pea mixture; half with the mushroom filling. Decorate the eggs with halved olives and pimiento strips, fill the middle with watercress and place a 'tongue' of tomato between each egg.

To peel hard boiled eggs, plunge into cold water immediately after boiling. Crack shells all over with the back of a spoon, then peel off a band in the middle. The shell at each end can then be easily pulled off.

Egg salads

To serve 12

18 eggs (hard boiled)
1½ pints thick mayonnaise (see method)
1½ lb long grain rice
½ pint French dressing
1 clove garlic (crushed with a little salt)
1 dessertspoon paprika pepper
a little extra salt (if necessary)
watercress (to garnish)

salad 1
8 oz fresh or frozen prawns (shelled)
1 head celery
1 cap pimiento (shredded)
1 tablespoon chopped parsley
black pepper from the mill

salad 2
½ lb fresh or canned salmon (flaked)
1 cucumber
a little salt
1 teaspoon chopped mint or parsley
1 tablespoon tomato juice
a dash of Tabasco

salad 3
¾ lb pickled pork
1 onion (peeled)
1 carrot (peeled)
bouquet garni
8 oz firm mushroom caps
1–2 tablespoons salad oil
salt
black pepper ground from the mill
a little red wine vinegar
1 teaspoon snipped chives
1 teaspoon Dijon mustard

Method
Prepare the mayonnaise, using 3 egg yolks to every ½ pint salad oil, adding salt, pepper and white wine vinegar to taste (see page 125 for basic method, if necessary.)

Boil rice until cooked and drain thoroughly. Tip on to a large platter and turn from time to time with a fork until dry. Tip the rice into a bowl and mix with French dressing flavoured with the garlic and paprika. Cover and leave until wanted.

For salad 1, cut the celery into thick bâtons and mix with the prawns, shredded pimiento and parsley. Season with black pepper. Take ½ pint of the mayonnaise and thin with a little juice from the pimiento can. Halve 6 eggs, arrange on a large platter cut side downwards, coat with the mayonnaise and spoon the prawn mixture on top.

For salad 2, peel and dice cucumber, salt lightly and leave in the refrigerator for 30 minutes. Rinse with ice-cold water and drain thoroughly. Flake salmon (if using canned salmon, drain well before flaking). Mix with the cucumber and chopped mint or parsley. Thin ½ pint of mayonnaise with tomato juice and season with Tabasco. Halve six more eggs and arrange on the platter. Spoon the salmon mixture on top.

For salad 3, simmer the pickled pork in water with the onion, carrot and bouquet garni for 1 hour. When cold, remove skin and any bones and cut into lardons (strips). Trim mushrooms, wash and dry quickly and cut in thick slices. Sprinkle 1–2 tablespoons oil over the mushrooms and mix carefully until all the slices are coated with a film of oil, then season with salt, black pepper and wine vinegar. Mix the mushrooms with the pork. Add the chives. Flavour the remaining mayonnaise with a little mustard and thin with boiling water.

Arrange the last six eggs on the platter, coat with mayonnaise, and spoon the pork and mushroom mixture on top. Garnish with watercress.

Add extra salt as necessary to the paprika rice and serve in a large salad bowl to accompany.

CHICKEN DISHES

Chicken is a versatile bird and marries well with many different flavours. The chicken salad chinois uses rather unusual ingredients, with subtly delicious results. Mousse de volaille à l'indienne is for the more advanced cook, and would grace the most formal buffet table. Chicken raita returns to a simpler theme, using spices with yoghourt.

Chicken salad chinois

To serve 10

3½–4 lb roasting chicken
2 oz butter
salt and pepper
½ pint jellied chicken stock
1 (20 oz) can water chestnuts
1 bunch spring onions
1 head celery
6 oz firm white mushrooms
1 tablespoon oil
1 (11 oz) can lychees (stoned)
¼ pint French dressing
1 tablespoon chopped parsley

Method

Set the oven at 400°F or Mark 6. Rub the chicken with butter and put a nut of butter inside. Season well. Place chicken in a roasting tin and pour in the stock. Roast chicken until brown and sticky, about 50–60 minutes, and when cold, cut flesh from bone in chunks.

Slice the water chestnuts, wash and trim the spring onions and cut in even-size lengths. Shred the celery and keep in cold water until required. Slice the mushrooms and sauté in 1 tablespoon of hot oil for one minute only. Allow to cool.

Drain the celery and the lychees. Mix all the ingredients together, moisten with the French dressing and add 1 tablespoon parsley. Serve in a deep bowl.

Mousse de volaille à l'indienne

To serve 8

3½–4 lb roasting chicken
3 pints water
1 onion (chopped)
1 carrot (chopped)
1 stick celery (chopped)
salt
peppercorns
bouquet garni
6 oz butter (well creamed)
¼ pint double cream (partially whipped)

For curry sauce
2 oz butter
1 clove garlic (crushed with ½ teaspoon salt)
1 dessertspoon curry powder
¼ pint jellied chicken stock
1½ oz flour
½ pint milk

To finish
2 pints commercially prepared aspic or
1 wine glass sherry
1 oz gelatine
2 egg whites (lightly beaten)
4–6 oz lean cooked ham

Method

Simmer the chicken for 1–1¼ hours in the water with the vegetables, seasoning and herbs to flavour, then leave it in the liquid to cool.

To prepare the sauce: melt ½ oz of the butter and, when foaming, blend in the garlic and curry powder and cook gently for 2–3 minutes; tip on the chicken stock and simmer, covered, for 5 minutes. Strain and keep on one side. Melt the remaining 1½ oz butter in a saucepan, blend in the flour and cook very carefully for one minute. Blend in the stock and milk and stir until boiling. Allow to cool.

Remove all skin and bone from the chicken and pass the meat twice through the mincer; place in a bowl and pound well and add the sauce by degrees. Season to taste. Fold in the butter and cream.

Fill the mousse into a foil-lined cake tin, wrap and freeze.

Strain the stock from the cooked chicken, reduce by rapid boiling to 2 pints, allow to cool, then pot and freeze.

Thawing and serving Thaw mousse and stock for 24 hours in the refrigerator.

Taste the stock, season well and place in a large scalded saucepan with the sherry, gelatine and lightly beaten egg whites. Clarify and strain.

When this aspic jelly is quite cold, pour about a ½ pint on a large silver dish and leave to set in the refrigerator. Cut the lean ham into shreds and mix with ½ pint of aspic. Turn the mousse on to the aspic-lined dish and, as the ham mixture begins to set, spoon it quickly on top of the mousse. Garnish the dish with the remaining aspic, chopped, and serve with the following accompaniments.

> **To clarify stock for aspic:**
> Soak gelatine in sherry to allow it to 'swell'. Set pan containing cold stock and whisked egg whites on moderate heat and start whisking egg whites with a balloon whisk with a backwards, or anti-clockwise, movement. Once liquid is hot, add soaked gelatine and continue whisking until the liquid reaches boiling point. Stop whisking and allow liquid to rise well in pan. Turn off heat and leave contents of pan for 5 minutes to settle. Replace pan on heat and bring once more to the boil, without whisking. Remove pan from heat and strain liquid through a scalded cloth. It should be crystal clear. Discard the egg white 'filter' and allow jelly to cool.

To clarify stock, first bring cold stock up to the boil, whisking in the egg whites. When mixture reaches boiling point, stop whisking and allow to rise up before reboiling it

Prawn and almond rice

2 oz cold boiled rice
1 oz almonds (blanched, shredded and soaked overnight)
3 oz prawns
1 teaspoon paprika
2–3 tablespoons French dressing

Method

Drain almonds, fork into the rice with the prawns. Mix the paprika with 2–3 tablespoons of dressing and add to the rice mixture.

Spiced limes

4–5 limes
¾ pint water
1 whole allspice
½-inch cinnamon stick
1 capsicum
6 peppercorns
8 oz granulated sugar
1 tablespoon vinegar

Method

Slice limes thinly. Put ¾ pint water into a shallow pan, bring to boil and add limes. Cover and simmer for about 15–20 minutes. Lift out carefully with a fish slice, then add to pan the spices, tied in a muslin bag, half the sugar and the vinegar. Simmer for 2–3 minutes then replace limes and continue to simmer, with pan covered, for 10 minutes. Remove spices. Then add remaining sugar and boil gently with pan uncovered until syrup is thick. Allow to cool.
Note: A few drops of Tabasco sauce can be added in place of the capsicum.

Cucumber raita

1 large cucumber
salt
¼ pint carton plain low-fat yoghourt
black pepper
sugar (to taste)

Method

Peel the cucumber and grate coarsely on to a plate. Sprinkle with salt, cover and stand the plate in the refrigerator, or in a cold place, for 30 minutes. Then drain the cucumber thoroughly and mix it with the yoghourt and season with black pepper and a little sugar to taste.

Chicken raita

To serve 6

3–3½ lb chicken
2 oz butter
1 teaspoon garam masala
1 clove garlic
½ lemon
¼–½ pint stock made from the
   giblets

For dressing
1 large cucumber
salt and pepper
¼ pint natural yoghourt
1 tablespoon freshly chopped
   mint

Method
Set the oven at 400°F or Mark 6. Cream the butter with the garam masala. Rub the skin of the chicken first with the split clove of garlic and then with the lemon. Put a nut of spiced butter inside the bird and spread the rest over the outside. Place the bird in a roasting tin, pour round ¼ pint of stock and cook in the pre-set oven for 1–1¼ hours. Baste and turn the chicken from time to time and add extra stock as necessary. Take up and allow to cool.

Peel the cucumber, take half, chop finely, sprinkle with salt and after 10–15 minutes, reduce to a purée in the liquidiser. Cut the remaining half of cucumber into small olive shapes, blanch, drain and refresh.

Mix the cucumber purée with the yoghourt, season to taste and add the mint.

Carve the chicken, arrange in a serving dish and spoon over the dressing. Garnish with the 'olives' of cucumber and serve a hot potato salad separately.

Fresh chutney

1 large onion (thinly sliced and
   blanched)
4 sticks celery
1 large Cox's apple
1 green, or red, pepper
3 large ripe tomatoes
1 large clove garlic (crushed
   with ½ teaspoon salt)
salt and pepper
1 tablespoon wine, or cider,
   vinegar
1 dessertspoon caster sugar

Method
Chop the celery, peel, core and chop apple. Chop and blanch pepper; scald, skin and chop the tomatoes, removing the seeds. Put the onion, celery, apple, pepper and tomatoes into a pan with the garlic, cover and bring slowly to the boil. Season with salt and pepper, add vinegar and caster sugar. Stir carefully to mix, then turn out and leave until cold before serving.

The curried mousse is covered with shredded ham and garnished with chopped aspic. It is accompanied by (from left) prawn and almond rice, spiced limes, cucumber raita and fresh chutney

Garam masala means mixed spice. It consists of cinnamon, cloves, cardamoms, black cumin seeds, mace and nutmeg. It can be bought, ready-made, at Indian grocers' shops.

Hot potato salad

1 lb small new potatoes
2 fl oz white wine
salt and pepper
2 tablespoons salad oil
1 tablespoon chopped parsley
   and chives

Method
Cook the potatoes in their skins and peel quickly while hot. Sprinkle the hot potatoes with the wine, season well and then add the oil and herbs. Mix carefully and serve hot.

DESSERTS FOR THE BUFFET

Choosing a cold sweet will simplify your plan of action when preparing a buffet party. These recipes can be made in advance, kept in a cool place and need no last-minute attention. We suggest you make a choice of two sweets for your guests, so Rosemary Hume and Muriel Downes recommend the maple and walnut chiffon pie and the chestnut cream for luncheon; the coffee crème brûlée and the chartreuse de pruneaux for a formal buffet or a dinner party menu. Servings are stated on each recipe.

Top: prune and almond cream (chartreuse de pruneaux) would be ideal for a dinner party. Below: maple and walnut chiffon pie, with its crisp crumb crust, makes a delicious sweet for lunch

Maple and walnut chiffon pie

To serve 8

For crumb crust
½ lb plain digestive biscuits
2¾ oz ground walnuts
3 oz caster sugar
1 teaspoon instant coffee
5 oz butter

For filling
4 egg yolks
a pinch of salt
½ pint maple syrup
1 dessertspoon gelatine soaked
    in 2 tablespoons water
2 egg whites
a pinch of cream of tartar
2 oz caster sugar
7½ fl oz double cream

To finish
2½ fl oz double cream
6–8 walnut halves

10-inch diameter flan dish

Method
Set the oven at 375°F or Mark 5. Prepare the crust. Crush the biscuits and pass them through a wire strainer, or work in the blender to fine crumbs, and place in a basin with the ground walnuts, sugar and coffee. Melt the butter and mix into the crumbs with a fork. Press the mixture firmly over the bottom and sides of the flan dish. Bake in the preset oven for 8 minutes. Allow to cool.

Prepare the filling. Beat the egg yolks with the salt and maple syrup, pour into a double saucepan, cook and stir over hot water until thick. Remove the pan from the heat, add the soaked gelatine, stir in well and allow to cool.

Whisk the egg whites with the cream of tartar until foamy, then add the sugar a dessertspoon at a time and continue whisking until stiff and glossy. Whisk the cream until thick.

When the maple syrup mixture begins to set, beat with a hand electric or rotary beater until smooth and then fold it into the egg white mixture (meringue) with the cream.

Pile the mixture into the cooled crumb case and chill until set. Finish with a thin layer of whipped cream and decorate with walnut halves.

Chestnut cream

To serve 6

1 lb chestnuts
milk and water (to cover)

For custard
½ a split vanilla pod or the pared
    rind of ½ lemon
¾ pint milk
4 egg yolks
2 oz caster sugar
½ oz gelatine soaked in 2½ fl oz
    water
a little rum or kirsch
7½ fl oz double cream (lightly
    whipped)
2 egg whites (whipped)
whipped cream (to decorate)

*1¼–1½ pint capacity fluted moule
à manqué*

Method
Cover the chestnuts with water, bring to the boil, draw aside from the heat, take out one chestnut at a time and strip off both outer and inner skin. Put the nuts into a pan, cover with equal quantities of milk and water, and simmer until tender. Drain and press through a wire sieve. Weigh and set aside. There should be about ½ lb of purée.

Meanwhile prepare the custard. Infuse vanilla pod or lemon rind slowly in the milk. Cream the yolks and sugar thoroughly together, then strain on the milk. Blend and return to the pan. Thicken over the heat, stirring continually without boiling. Allow to cool.

Dissolve soaked gelatine over a gentle heat and add to the custard. Turn chestnut purée into a thin pan or bowl. Stir in the custard by degrees and flavour delicately with rum or kirsch.

Set the bowl on ice (or in cold water), fold in the cream and lastly the whipped egg whites. When at setting point, turn into a lightly oiled mould and leave to set.

Turn out on to a serving dish and pipe round a ruff of cream. Serve with a caramel or Melba sauce.

Caramel sauce

12 oz granulated sugar
5 fl oz cold water
½ pint warm water

Method
Dissolve the sugar slowly in the cold water, then boil rapidly until a good caramel colour is achieved. Then draw aside, add the warm water carefully and stir over heat until dissolved. Boil rapidly until it is syrupy, ie. the consistency of thin cream. Pour off and cool. If it thickens too much on cooling, add 1–2 tablespoons of warm water. Serve when cold.

Melba sauce

1 lb fresh raspberries, or frozen
    ones without sugar
8 tablespoons icing sugar
    (sifted)

Method
If using frozen raspberries buy them 2–3 days before wanted and leave them to thaw in refrigerator. Pick over fresh raspberries. Rub the raspberries through a nylon strainer and then beat in the sifted icing sugar, 1 tablespoon at a time.

The **moule à manqué** is said to have been named by a certain Paris pâtissier, who criticised a cake mixture made by his chief baker. The baker, not liking his cake being called a failure (un manqué), added butter to the mixture, covered the cake with praline, and sold the confection to a customer who liked it so much she came back for more. It was hence christened 'un manqué', and a special mould was designed for it.

Coffee crème brûlée

This very rich sweet is good served with a little fresh fruit. The nicest would be plump ripe white grapes, preferably with a muscat flavour. These should be peeled and pipped, sprinkled with soft, light brown sugar and moistened with 1 tablespoon of brandy. Use just enough to fill a large sauceboat – about ½–¾ lb grapes.

To serve 6–8

1 pint double cream
2 oz coffee beans
4 egg yolks
1 tablespoon caster sugar

To finish
2–3 oz soft light brown sugar

Method
Scald the cream with the coffee beans and infuse until a delicate coffee flavour is obtained. Cream the egg yolks well with the sugar. Strain the cream and pour on to the yolks. Return the mixture to the pan and thicken very carefully over the heat, stirring constantly. Do not allow to boil.

Strain into a shallow ovenproof dish and allow to stand for several hours, preferably overnight. The cream should be well chilled and firm.

Heat the grill. Dust the top of the cream with a thin, even coating of the brown sugar, place the dish at once under the grill. Allow the sugar to melt slowly and take colour.
Watchpoint To get an even, caramelised surface the dish should not be put too near the glowing surface of the grill.

Stand the crème brûlée in a cold place for 2–3 hours before serving.

The invention of crème brûlée is claimed by Trinity College, Cambridge, where it is still a favourite dessert. Coffee crème brûlée is a Cordon Bleu variation on the classic dish.

Chartreuse de pruneaux

(Prune and almond cream)

To serve 6–8

¾ lb prunes
½ pint red wine
a strip of orange rind
2 large tablespoons
    redcurrant jelly
1 teaspoon gelatine soaked
    in 2 tablespoons orange juice

For almond cream
2 oz almonds
½ pint milk
3 egg yolks
2 oz caster sugar
½ oz gelatine soaked in
    2½ fl oz water
½ pint double cream
2 drops almond essence

8–8½-inch diameter shallow mould

Method
Cook the prunes with the red wine and orange rind until just tender, lift from the pan with a draining spoon, allow to cool a little, split and carefully remove the stones.

Remove the orange rind from the wine, add the redcurrant jelly and stir over very gentle heat until melted, then add the prunes and simmer again very gently for 10 minutes. Tip the liquid from the prunes (there should be about ¼ pint) on to the soaked gelatine and stir until dissolved.

Arrange the prunes at the bottom of a wet mould and pour over the liquid. Leave to set in a cool place.

Blanch the almonds, dry on kitchen paper and crush in a nut mill, or use your grinder. Warm the milk to blood heat, beat the egg yolks and sugar with a fork, then pour on the milk. Strain the mixture on to the soaked gelatine and stir until dissolved. Add the prepared almonds, cover and allow to cool.

Lightly whip the cream, add the almond essence and fold into the cold custard. As the mixture begins to thicken, pour quickly on to the prunes. Cover and leave in the refrigerator to set. Unmould before serving.

CAKES FOR THE BUFFET

Easter curd cake

1 lb cream cheese
4 oz unsalted butter
4 oz caster sugar
4 egg yolks (hard-boiled)
1½ oz ground almonds
1 dessertspoon (scant ½ oz) gelatine
3 tablespoons water
1½ oz currants
1½ oz angelica (diced)
2 tablespoons brandy
½ pint double cream

8-inch plain, or spring-form, cake tin

Method
Cream butter thoroughly, add caster sugar by degrees, work in the cream cheese, beating well, then the crushed hard-boiled egg yolks and the ground almonds. (If you have bought whole almonds, blanch them and pass through a Mouli grater.) Beat until fluffy in consistency. Put gelatine in the water to soak. Wash currants well, and dry. Soak the angelica in the brandy with the currants. Partially whip the cream and fold into the butter and sugar mixture. Dissolve the gelatine over gentle heat and then add the macerated fruit, and lastly add the brandy.

Fill mixture into the cake tin. Leave in a cool place for 2–3 hours or until it is set firm. Turn out, wrap and freeze.
Thawing and serving Thaw cake for 5 hours at room temperature. Turn on to a serving dish and, if wished, pipe a ruff of whipped cream round the base.

Bombe mexicaine

3 egg whites
6 oz light brown sugar
1 rounded teaspoon instant coffee

For filling
3 oz caster sugar
1½ teaspoons instant coffee
4 oz plain dessert chocolate
½ pint double cream

Forcing bag and ½-inch plain pipe; 3 baking sheets lined with non-stick (silicone) cooking paper

Method
Set oven at 290°F or Mark 1. Whip egg whites until stiff, but not dry, add 1 tablespoon of the brown sugar and continue whisking for about 30 seconds. Stir the teaspoon of coffee into the rest of the brown sugar and, using a metal spoon, cut and fold it into meringue mixture.

Put mixture into the forcing bag and pipe three six-inch rounds on to the lined baking sheets. Bake in pre-set oven for 1–1½ hours or until the meringue is crisp.

Place the caster sugar in a small, heavy pan and cook slowly to a rich brown caramel. Remove pan from heat and add 2 tablespoons of boiling water. Rotate the pan until the caramel is dissolved. (Replace the pan on the heat, if necessary, to do this.) Tip the hot caramel on to the remaining instant coffee and set aside.

Melt the chocolate in 3–4 tablespoons of water, stirring continually to a thick cream. The chocolate should be hot, but not so hot that you cannot touch the sides of the pan. Allow to cool. Whip the cream and divide into two portions; flavour one with the coffee and caramel mixture and the other with the melted chocolate.

Sandwich the meringue rounds together with the flavoured creams. Cover with foil and polythene and freeze.
Thawing and serving Thaw for 6 hours at room temperature. Or take out of freezer the night before and leave in refrigerator, and it will be perfect for lunch.

Serve decorated with a little extra whipped cream.

Apricot cream gâteau

4 eggs
8 oz caster sugar
6 oz plain flour
pinch of salt

For filling
½ lb apricots
¼ pint water
4 tablespoons granulated sugar
¾–1 pint double cream

Two 8-inch diameter sandwich tins

Method
Set the oven at 350°F or Mark 4. Prepare the tins by brushing the base and sides with melted fat and line the base of each with a circle of greased greaseproof paper. Dust with flour. Now prepare the sponge. In your mixer, whisk the eggs and sugar together at high speed until the mixture is thick and mousse-like. If beating by hand, set the bowl over a pan of hot water to get the same result. Then remove the bowl from the heat and continue whisking until cool. Sift the flour with the salt and cut and fold into the mixture. Turn into the prepared tins and bake in the middle of the pre-set oven for about 20 minutes. Turn out and cool on a wire rack.

Meanwhile, place the apricots, water and sugar in a pan and cook gently until apricots are soft, then rub through a nylon strainer and allow purée to cool.

Whip the cream until fairly firm, then gradually add about one third of the apricot purée, whisking it in with great care.

Split each sponge in two. First sandwich the halves together with apricot cream, then reshape the two cakes into one with the flavoured cream. Cover the top and sides with any remaining cream.

Wrap the finished cake in polythene, or foil (it must be well protected) and freeze; pack the remaining apricot purée in a carton ready to serve as an accompanying sauce.
Thawing and serving Thaw overnight in refrigerator before serving.

Soured cream curd cake

For crumb crust
6 oz Break Fast biscuits
3 tablespoons sugar
grated nutmeg
a pinch of ground allspice
3 oz butter

For topping
2 eggs
4 oz caster sugar
2 tablespoons lemon juice
two 5 fl oz cartons soured cream
1 lb curd, or cream, cheese
2 tablespoons melted butter

To finish
whipped cream

9-inch diameter shallow cake tin

Method
To prepare crust: crumble biscuits and add sugar, nutmeg and allspice and bind together by beating in the butter.

Set the oven at 325°F or Mark 3. Line tin with the crumb mixture. Place eggs, caster sugar, lemon juice and soured cream in the blender. Cover and blend for 15 seconds (or beat in a bowl with a wooden spoon until smooth and well-blended).

Add the cheese gradually with the blender running at a slower speed; add the melted butter. (Or beat in cheese by degrees, then add melted butter.) Pour cheese mixture into the prepared tin over the crumb base and bake in the pre-heated oven for 35 minutes.

When cold, wrap and freeze.
Thawing and serving Thaw cake at room temperature for 4 hours, then cover the top with whipped cream or serve sugared strawberries, a cherry compote or a plum sauce separately (see the recipe for caneton rouennaise on page 22 for cherry compote).
Note: We have given the trade name of the biscuits used. They are hard and close in texture, and produce a good base crust when crumbled.

The creamy Easter curd cake has a ruff of whipped cream round the base. The bombe mexicaine is made of brown sugar meringue, flavoured with coffee and filled with coffee and chocolate creams. While thawing, the cream softens the meringue so the cake cuts 'like a dream'. This one is decorated with coffee dragées

Plum sauce
(sauce aux quetsches)

½ lb red plums (Santa Rosa or
   Early River variety)
7½ fl oz water
5 oz sugar
small glass of red wine,
   preferably claret
1 dessertspoon arrowroot

Method
Split plums and remove stones. Place water and sugar in a shallow pan, boil rapidly for 4–5 minutes, then add wine. Lay plum halves in the syrup, cut-side uppermost, cover pan and poach for a further 7–8 minutes. Purée in a liquidiser, or rub through a nylon sieve. Slake (mix) arrowroot with 2 tablespoons cold water, draw pan off heat and add to fruit. Shake pan gently to mix, then reboil. Draw aside and allow to cool.

When sauce is cold, fill into a carton and freeze. Thaw out at room temperature.
Watchpoint If the sauce is too thick, add a little more wine, or water.

PARTY MENUS:
A SPECIAL PICNIC

Individual mushroom quiches

For rich shortcrust pastry
12 oz flour
6 oz butter
2 oz shortening
2 egg yolks
4 tablespoons water

For filling
3 eggs
2 egg yolks
½ pint single cream
salt and pepper
1 medium-size onion (finely chopped)
1 oz butter
8 oz mushrooms (sliced)
3 oz grated cheese

8 small individual flan tins, 3½–4 inches diameter

Method
Prepare the pastry (see page 125) and chill while preparing the filling. Set the oven at 375°F or Mark 5. Beat the whole eggs and the yolks together with a fork, add the cream and seasoning. Cook the onion in the butter until soft but not coloured, add the mushrooms and sauté briskly for 2–3 minutes. Turn the contents of the pan into the egg mixture and stir in the cheese.

Line the flan tins with the pastry and bake blind (see page 89) in the pre-set oven for 8 minutes only. Remove beans and paper and quickly spoon in the mushroom mixture. Return to the oven and bake for about 15–20 minutes or until firm to the touch and golden brown. Allow to stand for about 10 minutes before removing from the tins.

These individual quiches can be re-warmed and packed carefully in foil in an insulated picnic box.

Fruit and chicken curry

4–5 lb roasting chicken
2–3 sprigs of tarragon
salt and pepper
¼ oz butter
4 tablespoons olive or sunflower oil
¼–½ pint stock made from the giblets
2 ripe peaches
2 ripe dessert pears
2 bananas
1 fresh mango (when available)
8 oz red or black cherries (stoned)
2 tablespoons fine caster sugar
juice of 1 lemon

For curry sauce
1 heaped tablespoon grated coconut
2 oz butter
1 onion (chopped)
1 tablespoon green ginger (grated)
1 teaspoon coriander seeds (crushed)
1 teaspoon black pepper ground from the mill
1 dessertspoon curry powder
1 teaspoon curry paste
1 dessertspoon flour
¾ pint chicken stock
8 fl oz cream

Method
Set the oven at 375°F or Mark 5. Place the tarragon, salt and pepper and butter inside the chicken and rub the outside with the oil. Set in a roasting tin and pour round ¼ pint of the chicken stock. Roast for 1–1½ hours, baste and turn from time to time adding extra stock as it evaporates. At the end of cooking the bird should be brown and sticky. Allow to cool.

Meanwhile prepare the sauce. Soak coconut in a coffee cup of boiling water for 15 minutes, then drain, reserving the water. Melt the butter, add the onion and cook slowly, uncovered, until soft – about 4–5 minutes. Blend in the spices and continue cooking slowly for a further 3–4 minutes. Draw off the heat and add the flour and stock. Stir over a gentle heat until boiling, simmer for 30 minutes, then add the coconut and water, adjust the seasoning and strain. Chill well.

Peel and slice the peaches, pears, bananas and mango, place on a shallow dish with the cherries, dust with sugar and sprinkle with the lemon juice. Cover tightly with transparent film wrap to exclude the air and keep in the refrigerator until needed.

Cut the chicken in 'bite-size' pieces and place in a deep entrée dish or china salad bowl. Partially whip the cream and mix into the cold curry sauce with the prepared fruit; spoon this over the chicken. (This can be done at the picnic site to save spills.) Serve with the following rice salad.

Cucumber, nut and rice salad

8 oz long grain rice
1 large cucumber
1 small bunch spring onions
¼ pint carton natural yoghourt
salt and black pepper ground from the mill
a little caster sugar
lemon juice (to taste)
3 oz cashew nuts or almonds (blanched and shredded)

Method
Boil the rice in plenty of salted water. Strain, rinse thoroughly with hot water, drain and dry well.

Peel and dice the cucumber, salt lightly and after 10–15 minutes drain away any liquid and dry on kitchen paper. Slice the onions very finely.

Stir and season the yoghourt with salt, pepper, sugar and lemon juice, pour over the rice and, using two forks, mix in the cucumber, onions and nuts. Wrap filled salad bowl in foil or transparent cling wrap for transporting.

Hazelnut and chocolate roulade

3 large eggs
2 teaspoons water
6 oz caster sugar
4 oz flour
¾ teaspoon baking powder
a pinch of salt
4 oz ground hazelnuts
2 tablespoons icing sugar (to finish)

For filling
8 oz raspberries
3 tablespoons icing sugar
6 oz plain dessert chocolate
1 tablespoon water
2 egg yolks
3 oz unsalted butter (well creamed and at room temperature)

Paper case 9½×11 inches×1-inch deep (see page 77)

Method
Set the oven at 400°F or Mark 6. Separate the eggs, whisk the whites with the water to a firm snow, then add the sugar a spoonful at a time and continue beating until stiff. Add the egg yolks.

Sift the flour with the baking powder and salt. Mix with the hazelnuts and cut and fold into the egg and sugar mixture. Turn into the prepared paper case, level the top with a palette knife and bake at once for 12–15 minutes, or until firm to the touch.

Turn quickly on to a sugared sheet of paper, trim the sides and roll up with a sheet of greasproof paper on the inside. Leave to cool.

Meanwhile prepare the filling. Place the raspberries and sifted icing sugar in the blender, crush them a little with a wooden spoon, then liquidize them and rub through a nylon strainer to remove the pips. Melt the chocolate very slowly in the water, remove from the heat and add the egg yolks one at a time. Beat in the butter gradually, tip into a bowl and blend in the raspberry purée.

Uncurl the sponge very carefully, spread with chocolate and raspberry cream and re-roll. Wrap and freeze.
Thawing and serving. Thaw at room temperature for 4–6 hours. Dust with icing sugar.

For a sunlit picnic meal: mushroom quiches can be served hot if you pack them in foil in an insulated box. A cold chicken and fruit curry follows with a special rice salad. We suggest lager to drink with this; for dessert, a chocolate-filled hazelnut roll

Individual asparagus mousses, with duck flan (front), sweetbread and mushroom flan (centre) and spinach flan (rear)

For you, Rosemary Hume and Muriel Downes have devised a luncheon party menu for twelve people using the freezer, but leaving some courses to be made on the morning of your party, or the day before. You can work out your own timetable from the guidelines given in the recipes.

We start with individual asparagus mousses, which are made on the day, followed by a choice of three savoury flans, each of which cuts into six generous portions. Two of these — sweetbread and mushroom and the spinach flans — can be made well ahead and frozen; the third, a rich duck flan, is put together from freezer-stored ingredients.

The dessert is a light-textured almond-flavoured cake from the freezer, served with a tangy fruit salad that's easy to prepare before the guests arrive.

Asparagus Mousse en Cocottes

Duck Flan

★ *Sweetbread and Mushroom Flan*

★ *Spinach Flan*

★ *Gâteau de Savoie Amande with Fruits Rafraîchis*

Asparagus mousse en cocottes

2 (15 oz) cans asparagus
2 pints chicken stock
½ pint béchamel sauce
½ pint mayonnaise
salt and pepper
1½ oz gelatine
½ pint whipping, or double, cream
3 egg whites
a little commercially-prepared aspic

To serve
rolls of brown bread and butter filled with chopped prawns, or small shrimps

14–16 small ramekins

Method
Make béchamel sauce and allow to cool. Prepare mayonnaise. Drain the liquid from the asparagus. Tip the stalks out carefully and cut off about 8 of the tips. Split these carefully in half and set aside on a paper napkin. Put all the tender part of the asparagus into the liquidiser (or put through a Mouli sieve) and reduce to a purée. Measure purée, adding enough chicken stock to make it up to 2 pints. Add this to the prepared béchamel sauce and when quite cold, fold into the mayonnaise. Adjust seasoning. Dissolve the gelatine in 6 fl oz chicken stock, partially whip the cream and whisk the egg whites until stiff. Add the dissolved gelatine to the mixture, stand on ice and stir until it begins to thicken creamily, then quickly fold in the cream and egg whites.

Fill into ramekin dishes to within ¼ inch from the top. Cover and leave in the refrigerator until set. Then place an asparagus tip in the centre of each and run a little cool aspic over the top to keep the tip in place and to completely fill the ramekin.

Note: Make these on the day of serving or the night before. To save time, the purée can be frozen and thawed out overnight for use in the morning. Fresh asparagus, in season, can be used and you would need two bundles.

Lining a flan ring

Lift pastry over rolling pin. Roll off any excess pastry. Push up sides from flan base

Duck flan

8 oz rich shortcrust pastry
4–5 lb duck
pared rind and juice of 1 orange
1 tablespoon oil
salt
approx. ¾ pint commercially-prepared aspic
approx. 1½–2 fl oz sherry

For filling
1½ lb cooking apples
3 tablespoons granulated sugar
1 large onion (blanched and finely chopped)
1 small carton double cream
1 dessertspoon finely chopped sage
salt and pepper

8–9-inch diameter flan ring

Method
Roll out pastry, line into flan ring and bake blind at 400°F or Mark 6, for about 25 minutes. Put half the orange rind into the duck. Rub the breast with oil and sprinkle with salt. Set on a grid in a roasting tin. Pour over the orange juice and roast in a hot oven, 425°F or Mark 7, for 50–55 minutes or until cooked. Turn frequently and baste well once the fat begins to run. When well browned, take out and leave until cold. Make up the aspic, as directed on the packet, substituting the sherry for the water needed.

To prepare filling: wipe the apples, quarter, core and slice. Put into a shallow pan rubbed with butter, cover with foil and the lid. Cook gently to a pulp, then rub through a strainer. Return to the pan with the sugar and simmer for 10–15 minutes. Meanwhile, simmer onion with the cream until soft and add to the apple purée with the chopped sage. Season and continue to cook until thick. Turn on to a plate and leave until cold. Spread the bottom of cooked flan with cold apple mixture.

Cut the breast and wing (suprêmes) from each side of the duck, and slice the meat from the legs. Shred this and cut the suprêmes into fillets. Place the leg meat over the apple and arrange the fillets on top. Shred the rest of the orange rind, blanch by placing in a small pan, covering with cold water, bringing to the boil, then draining. Refresh by pouring cold water over. Add to the aspic and, when cool and at setting point, brush the flan well with this, giving two coats if necessary. Serve cold.

Note: The duck and also the apple mixture can come from the freezer. Allow duck to thaw in fridge for 24 hours and the apple for 12 hours. The shortcrust pastry can also be taken from the freezer, but the flan case is best baked on the day of the party.

Line with greaseproof and fill with beans for baking 'blind'

Sweetbread and mushroom flan

10 oz rich shortcrust pastry
    made with:
10 oz plain flour
5 oz butter
2½ oz shortening
2 egg yolks
2½ tablespoons cold water
a little beaten egg (to glaze)

For filling
1 lb calves or lambs sweetbreads
1 medium-size onion (finely
    chopped)
bouquet garni
chicken stock or water
    (see method)
salt and pepper
½ lb button mushrooms
1½ oz butter
1¼ oz flour
2–2½ fl oz cream
1 egg
3 oz cooked ham (shredded)

8–9-inch diameter flan ring

Method

Make up pastry and chill, or remove from freezer and leave to thaw. Now prepare filling. Blanch sweetbreads in water brought to the boil, rinse, drain and press between 2 plates. When cold, trim away any skin, and put into a pan with the onion, and the bouquet garni. Barely cover with chicken stock or water, salt lightly and cover pan. Simmer until tender, about 25–30 minutes. Remove bouquet garni, pour off ½ pint of the stock and set aside. Turn out sweetbreads to cool and slice if necessary.

Halve or slice mushrooms thickly and sauté briskly in the butter for 3–4 minutes. Draw aside, stir in the flour and pour on reserved stock. Blend, adjust seasoning and bring to the boil. Add cream and simmer for 1 minute. Draw aside, stir in egg, add sweetbreads and ham. Leave till cold.

Meanwhile, roll out pastry and line into the flan ring. Gather up trimmings, roll out and cut into strips. Turn cooled sweetbread mixture into flan and place the strips across to form a lattice. Brush with a little beaten egg and bake in a hot oven, 400°F or Mark 6, for about 20 minutes. Lower heat to 375°F or Mark 5, and cook for a further 15 minutes.

Allow to get cold before wrapping and freezing.

Thawing and serving Thaw out for 5–6 hours at room temperature. Reheat at 350°F or Mark 4, for 18–20 minutes. Serve hot.

For dessert – a light, almond-flavoured sponge and a cool, fresh fruit salad (fruits rafraîchis)

Spinach flan

8 oz rich shortcrust pastry
    made with:
8 oz plain flour
4 oz butter
2 oz shortening
1 egg yolk
about 1½ tablespoons water

For filling
1 lb spinach, or a 12 oz packet of
    frozen leaf spinach
1 large onion (thinly sliced)
¾ oz butter
¾ lb curd cheese
2 eggs (beaten)
2½ fl oz cream
salt and pepper
grated cheese

8–9-inch diameter ovenproof china quiche dish

Method

Make up pastry and line into the dish. Bake blind at 400°F or Mark 6, until just set, about 15 minutes.

Meanwhile boil the spinach for 5–6 minutes, drain and press between two plates to extract all water. Soften the onion in the butter without allowing it to colour. Work the cheese with the eggs until smooth, add onion and butter and the cream. Season well.

Take the beans (used in baking blind) from the flan dish. Lift up the spinach with two forks, place in the bottom of the flan and season.

Pour the cheese mixture on top, sprinkle with grated cheese and return to the oven for a further 15–20 minutes, or until mixture is set and well browned. Leave till cold then wrap and freeze.

Thawing and serving Thaw and reheat as mushroom flan.

Gâteau de Savoie amande

5 oz fécule (potato flour), or
    2½ oz each arrowroot and
    plain flour
10 oz caster sugar
6 eggs (separated)
grated rind and juice of 1 lemon
4 oz ground almonds
icing sugar

11-inch diameter moule à manqué or 10-inch diameter cake tin

Method

If using arrowroot and plain flour, sift them together in a bowl to mix thoroughly. Prepare cake tin. Cut a round of greaseproof paper to fit the bottom. Grease the tin, put in the paper and grease it, then dust out tin with a little caster sugar and flour.

Work the egg yolks well with the sugar until light and fluffy, add lemon rind and juice. Whisk egg whites stiffly, add a large spoonful to the yolks with the almonds. Then fold in the rest of the whites alternately with the flour. Turn at once into the prepared tin and bake in a moderate oven, 360°F or Mark 4, for about an hour. Cool for a few minutes before turning out.

When quite cold, set on a cake board, slip both into a polythene bag, tie and freeze.

Thawing and serving Thaw at room temperature for 4–5 hours, then sift over icing sugar.

Note: Potato flour (fécule) is sold in 8 oz packets at many big stores and supermarkets.

Fruits rafraîchis

1 large pineapple
2 Texan grapefruit
3 ordinary grapefruit
5 seedless oranges

For syrup
½ pint water
6 oz lump or granulated sugar

Method

First prepare syrup. Put sugar and water into a pan together and set on slow heat to dissolve. Then boil rapidly for for 3–4 minutes, remove from heat and allow to cool.

Cut peel from pineapple, taking care to remove the 'eyes'. Quarter the pineapple lengthways and slice away the core. Cut across into ¼–½-inch pieces, and put them into a glass bowl. Slice rind and pith from the grapefruit and oranges. Cut out the sections between the membranes, and add to the pineapple. Spoon enough syrup over the fruit to moisten well. Cover at once with a plate just touching the fruit and refrigerate for 1–2 hours. Turn the fruit over gently just before serving.

SUMMER BUFFET FOR 8

A light supper which can be made in advance, with a choice of two starters based on the same theme. Suitable for after the theatre.

Oeufs en cocotte américaine

8 eggs
3 sticks celery
1 green pepper
4 oz shrimps (peeled)
1 shallot or 1 small onion (finely chopped)
1 dessertspoon oil
½ teaspoon paprika pepper
1 level teaspoon tomato purée
2½ fl oz tomato juice
1 level teaspoon gelatine
¼ pint mayonnaise
1 pint commercially-prepared aspic

8 cocottes or ramekins

Method
Poach the eggs and slip into a bowl of cold water until required. Finely dice the celery. Chop the green pepper, removing the core and seeds. Blanch, refresh and drain well. Mix the celery and pepper with the shrimps and divide mixture between 8 ramekins.

Soften the shallot or onion in the oil, add the paprika, tomato purée and tomato juice; simmer for 2–3 minutes. Strain, add the gelatine to strained liquid and dissolve over heat. Add the gelatine mixture to the mayonnaise.

Drain the eggs and place one in each ramekin. When the mayonnaise is thickening creamily, baste over the eggs and leave to set.

Make up aspic as directed on the packet and set in a bowl over ice. Stir gently and when on the point of setting, pour carefully over the eggs, adding enough to fill each cocotte. Chill.

Oeufs pochés bretonnaise

This alternative recipe uses the same mayonnaise sauce.

8 eggs
1 (7 oz) can tuna fish
4 tomatoes
black pepper
lemon juice
1 shallot or 1 small onion (finely chopped)
1 dessertspoon oil
½ teaspoon paprika pepper
1 level teaspoon tomato purée
2½ fl oz tomato juice
1 level teaspoon gelatine
¼ pint mayonnaise
1 pint commercially-prepared aspic

8 cocottes or ramekins

Method
Poach the eggs and slip them into a bowl of cold water. Drain and flake the tuna fish. Skin and quarter the tomatoes, scoop out the seeds and rub well in a nylon sieve, reserving the juice.

Mix the tuna fish with the tomatoes, season with black pepper and a squeeze of lemon juice and spoon into the 8 ramekins.

Prepare the mayonnaise sauce in the same way as for oeufs en cocotte américaine, but using the reserved juice from the tomato seeds.

Drain eggs, place each in a ramekin and finish as for the previous recipe.

Rich ham rolls

8 thin slices of ham
2 oz tongue (shredded)
5 oz soft liver pâté
a little Dijon mustard
1 pint commercially-prepared aspic flavoured with sherry (see method)

Method
Mix the tongue into the liver pâté and season with a mild Dijon mustard. Spread each slice of ham with the liver pâté, roll up and place side by side in a shallow oblong dish. Cover with wet greaseproof paper and keep in the refrigerator while preparing the aspic, as this will preserve the pink appearance of the ham.

Make up the commercially prepared aspic as directed on the packet, replacing about 2 tablespoons of the water with dry sherry.

When the aspic is cold and on the point of setting, remove the greaseproof paper from the ham and quickly spoon or brush the aspic over the ham rolls. Return to the refrigerator to set.

Strawberry suédoises, decorated with whipped cream and a half strawberry, make a refreshing summer dessert

Bean and pineapple salad

1 (11½ oz) can pineapple spears
½ lb French beans
¼ lb firm white mushrooms
3–4 tablespoons salad oil
a squeeze of lemon juice
salt and pepper
1 tablespoon chopped parsley
1 tablespoon chopped mint and chives

Method
Trim the beans, cut in large diamond shaped pieces, cook, refresh and drain well. Wipe and trim the mushrooms, slice and mix carefully with salad oil until every surface is coated, then season with the lemon juice, salt and pepper.
Note: Coating the mushrooms with oil before adding seasoning, particularly the salt, prevents them getting slimy.

Drain the pineapple, mix with the beans and mushrooms. Add the herbs and extra seasoning to taste.

Strawberry suédoises

1 lb strawberries
6 oz lump sugar
1 pint water
½ lb gooseberries
2 sprays elderflower (tied in a muslin bag)
2 tablespoons potato flour (fécule)

8 coupe glasses

Method
Hull the strawberries and reserve 4 for decoration. Rub half the strawberries through a nylon strainer and set aside. Slice the remaining half. Dissolve the sugar in the water over a gentle heat, add the gooseberries and cook gently until tender but not broken. Add the elderflowers and infuse for 5–6 minutes.

Strain the syrup (keep the gooseberries for a fool for another day), return to the saucepan, add the strawberry purée and bring to the boil. Draw the pan aside, add the potato flour mixed to a paste with a little water, then stir over heat to boiling point. Add the sliced strawberries, pour into the 8 glasses and cool.

Decorate each as shown.

CANDLELIT SUPPER FOR 12

Potage Crème Hawaii

Savoury Mille Feuilles

★ *Sugared Ham*

Spiced Peaches

Fennel and Cabbage Salad

or Mexican Salad

★ *Orange and Almond Gâteau*

Red wine–St Estèphe (Bordeaux)

Potage crème Hawaii

1 small pineapple
2 pints well flavoured chicken
   stock
1½ oz butter
1½ oz flour
2 egg yolks
¼ pint single cream
1 tablespoon snipped chives
salt and pepper

Method
Peel the pineapple, cut out the core and slice finely. Shred the flesh and set aside. Heat the stock to boiling point, draw aside, add the pineapple core, cover and infuse for 20–30 minutes, then strain.

Melt the butter, blend in the flour, cook gently until straw coloured, add the stock and stir until boiling. Simmer for 5 minutes. Work the egg yolks and cream together, blend in 2–3 tablespoons of the hot soup, then pour this liaison back into the pan. Stir over a gentle heat until creamy, but do not allow to boil.

Chill, add the shredded pineapple and the chives, adjust the seasoning and pour into a well chilled soup tureen.

Savoury mille feuilles

8 oz puff pastry
1 egg yolk mixed with 1
   tablespoon water and
   ½ teaspoon salt
1–2 tablespoons grated Parmesan
   cheese

For filling
2½ lb roasting chicken
1 onion (peeled)
1 carrot (peeled)
stick of celery
6 peppercorns
large bouquet garni
1 medium-size onion
1 clove garlic
1 oz butter
8 oz chicken livers
salt and black pepper
For béchamel sauce
   1 oz butter
   1 oz flour
   8 fl oz flavoured milk
4 oz butter (well creamed)
¼ pint double cream (whipped)

Method
Set the oven at 425°F or Mark 7. First prepare the pastry, if not from the freezer; roll out very thinly and cut in three strips about 12 inches by 4 inches. Place on a dampened baking sheet, prick well and brush one strip with the egg yolk mixture and dust with the cheese. Chill for 10 minutes before baking all three in the pre-set oven for 7–10 minutes, or until brown.

Simmer the chicken for 45–50 minutes in 2½ pints water with the onion, carrot, celery, peppercorns and herbs to flavour, then leave in the liquid to cool. Drain, remove skin and bone from the chicken and pass the meat twice through the mincer.

Meanwhile chop the onion and garlic finely and soften in the melted butter. Add the chicken livers and seasoning and fry together for about 3 minutes. When cool, chop finely or mince.

Place the minced chicken in a bowl with the minced liver mixture and pound well. Make a béchamel sauce and add to the meat mixture, by degrees, with plenty of seasoning. Fold in the creamed butter and whipped cream.

When pastry is cold, spread 2 layers with the chicken and liver pâté and finish with the cheese-topped piece. Place the mille feuilles on a large oval dish, surround with sliced sugared ham and spiced peaches.
Note: The pastry and the filling can be made in advance and frozen separately. Allow to thaw for 12 hours.

Sugared ham

2½ lb corner piece of gammon
1 onion (peeled)
1 carrot (peeled)
bouquet garni
cloves (see method)
4–5 tablespoons soft brown
   sugar
½ pint cider

Method
Soak the gammon for 1 hour then cover with fresh cold water, add the vegetables and herbs and simmer gently for 1¼ hours. Set oven at 350°F or Mark 4. Strip off the skin, score the fat, stud with cloves and cover with sugar. Set in an ovenproof dish, pour round the cider and bake in the pre-set oven for 35–45 minutes, or until the sugar is brown and crisp, basting occasionally. Wrap and freeze when cold.
Thawing and serving Thaw for 24 hours in the refrigerator. Cut into slices.

Spiced peaches

6 ripe peaches or 1 (16 oz) can
   peach halves
¼ pint water
small wine glass white wine
2 tablespoons white wine vinegar
2-inch stick of cinnamon
6 peppercorns
1 clove
4 tablespoons granulated sugar

Method
Skin and halve the peaches, and remove the stones, (or if using canned peaches, drain and use the syrup instead of the ¼ pint water and omit the sugar). Place the water, wine, vinegar, spices and sugar in a pan and dissolve over a gentle heat. Put in the peaches, and poach slowly for about 15 minutes until tender.

Remove the peaches carefully with a draining spoon and lay in a shallow bowl. Reduce the syrup by boiling hard until thick. Strain it over the peaches and chill well.

Fennel and cabbage salad

Fennel is a snow-white bulbous root weighing 12–16 oz; it is excellent in salads, or on its own as a cooked vegetable. Raw, it must be very thinly sliced, and only a small amount used, as the taste of aniseed is fairly pungent.

1 medium-size root of
   Florentine fennel
½–1 hard white Dutch cabbage
   (according to size)
oil (see method)
cider or white wine vinegar
salt and pepper ground from
   the mill
1 rounded tablespoon freshly
   chopped parsley

Method
Split the root in half and slice as thinly as possible. Do the same with the cabbage using a mandoline grater if available. In this way you can get really fine shreds and it saves time.

Put the vegetables into a bowl and mix carefully with salad oil until every shred of fennel and cabbage is coated. Sprinkle with the vinegar, using just less than a quarter of the amount of oil. Continue to mix, adding salt, pepper and the parsley. Taste for seasoning and turn into a salad bowl for serving.

Mexican salad

3–4 waxy potatoes (weighing
   1 lb)
2 (7 oz) cans sweetcorn
   kernels or 1 lb frozen kernels
1–2 green or red peppers
1 head celery
salt and pepper
approx. ¼ pint French dressing

Method
Boil the potatoes in their skins, then peel and cut into dice. Drain the sweetcorn, or simmer frozen kernels as directed on the packet. Drain and refresh, and add to the potatoes.

Dice and blanch peppers, drain and refresh, and add to potatoes and corn. Wash the celery and slice across thinly. Add to the bowl. Season, and mix in enough of the dressing to moisten well. Cover and leave in a cool place for about an hour before serving.

Orange and almond gâteau

3 oz whole almonds
1 tablespoon instant coffee
1 tablespoon hot water
4 large eggs
6 oz caster sugar
4 oz flour (sifted with a pinch of salt)

For filling
3 oz butter
4 oz caster sugar
3 oz almonds (finely chopped)
2 oz flaked almonds
¼ pint double cream
½ oz candied orange peel

For apricot glaze
8 tablespoons smooth apricot jam
juice of ½ orange

For glacé icing
6 oz icing sugar (sifted)
1 teaspoon instant coffee dissolved in 1 tablespoon hot water
1 tablespoon apricot glaze

8½-inch diameter spring-form mould

Method
Set the oven at 350°F or Mark 4. Grease, sugar or flour the cake tin. Blanch the whole almonds and pat dry on kitchen paper. While the almonds are still plump and juicy, put through a small cheese grater or nut mill and toast lightly in the oven — they should be a biscuit colour. Mix the coffee with the water.

Whisk the eggs and sugar until thick and mousse-like, using either an electric mixer at high speed or a wheel whisk with the bowl standing over a pan of steaming water. Cut and fold in two-thirds of the flour, add the prepared coffee and almonds and then the remaining flour. Turn into the prepared tin and bake for 40–45 minutes in the pre-set oven and cool.

Meanwhile prepare the filling. Melt the butter, add sugar, dissolve and bring to the boil. Add nuts, allow mixture to cook to a biscuit colour, pour on cream and reduce until thick. Add the blanched and shredded orange peel. Tip into a bowl to cool.

Cut the cake in three and sandwich with the cooled filling. Wrap carefully in foil to pack and freeze.
Thawing and serving Thaw for 4–6 hours at room temperature.

Prepare the apricot glaze by heating the ingredients together and then strain. Brush cake with the warm glaze which should be fairly thin and allow it to soak into the cake.

Prepare the icing. Mix icing sugar with the coffee. Add the 1 tablespoon of glaze and warm gently, beating well all the time to maintain a good gloss or shine. When cool, pour or brush lightly over the cake.

Potage crème Hawaii (top left) is served chilled. The mille feuilles is filled with chicken liver pâté, surrounded by slices of sugared ham with spiced peaches, and accompanied by Mexican salad. There's an orange and almond gâteau to finish off the meal

Whisking the sponge mixture over a pan of boiling water until thick and mousse-like. It should fall from the whisk in a thick ribbon and hold its shape

Start with lobster bouchées (centre), followed by a galantine of chicken and tongue (left), or ham roulades (behind), with a choice of salads. There's a summer salad too (right, front). For sweet, try brown sugar meringues with a special fruit salad flavoured with rum, or a freezer cake – pavé au chocolat, decorated with whipped cream and flavoured with brandy

BUFFET PARTY FOR 24

Buffet supper parties are popular, so here is one planned for twenty-four guests. Many of the dishes can be frozen beforehand. Make double the quantity of bouchées. A three-quarter pound batch of pastry is the easiest to handle and will give the best results. The galantine should yield a good 24 slices, but double the quantity of roulades. Make two gratins de légumes – these are served hot, so you will need a heat tray or trolley; alternatively, make two of the summer salads.

Double quantity of both sweets should be sufficient, provided there is a generous amount of the macédoine to be served with the meringues – or separately, if wished.

Lobster, Salmon or Prawn Bouchées

★ *Chicken Galantine with Choice of Salads*

★ *Ham Roulades*

★ *Gratin de Légumes or Summer Salad*

Meringues Créole with Macédoine de Fruits

★ *Pavé au Chocolat*

Bouchées of lobster, salmon or prawn

12 oz quantity of puff pastry (see page 125)
beaten egg (to glaze)

For filling
2 (7 oz) cans lobster meat or
8 oz salmon (cooked) or 8 oz frozen prawns

For sauce
1 oz butter
1 rounded teaspoon paprika
1 oz flour
½ pint milk, flavoured as for béchamel
salt and pepper
1–2 tablespoons cream
2–3 tablespoons hollandaise sauce

2½-inch fluted pastry cutter; 1-inch plain cutter

Method

Roll out pastry ¼-inch thick in a rectangle 10 inches long and 11 inches wide. Brush thinly with beaten egg, then, using a fluted cutter 2½ inches in diameter, stamp out 16 rounds. Take a plain cutter about 1 inch in diameter and make an incision in the centre of each round. Chill for about 15 minutes before baking in a hot oven, 425°F or Mark 7, for about 15 minutes — until well risen and firm to touch. Take bouchées off the baking sheet with a palette knife and transfer to a rack. With a small, pointed knife cut round the incision, remove top, scoop out any soft paste and replace caps. If they are not to be filled immediately, pack in boxes or cartons, no more than a double layer with a sheet of greaseproof paper in between. Cover and freeze.

To prepare filling Melt butter, stir in paprika and after 2–3 seconds, the flour. Blend in the flavoured milk, add seasoning and stir until boiling. Add cream, simmer for 2–3 minutes then draw aside and beat in hollandaise sauce. Adjust seasoning.

If using lobster meat, drain off the liquid, cut meat into large dice and fold into the sauce. This should be rich, creamy and just thick enough to coat the fish. For salmon, break into large flakes free from bone and skin, and again fold into the sauce. For frozen prawns, thaw out overnight in the fridge, draining well on a paper towel before adding to the sauce. Reheat carefully — this is best done in a bain-marie — and allow ½ hour on gentle heat for sauce to get thoroughly hot.

Thawing and serving Allow bouchées to thaw out for 3–4 hours at room temperature (if frozen) before heating in a hot oven (425°F or Mark 7) for 5–7 minutes. If using raw pastry from the freezer, thaw out for the same length of time (3–4 hours) before cutting and baking as directed above.

To fill bouchées Each bouchée should have a good quantity of filling, so split each baked pastry case, place a dessertspoon of mixture on each base and push gently up into the top half. Reshape and replace the little cap on top. Slide into a warm oven to keep hot, leaving the door open.

Note: With the exception of the prawns, the other fillings may be frozen, if wished.

'Au bain-marie'
Half-fill a large tin — a roasting tin for example, with hot water and place the dish to be re-heated in the centre. Lift into oven and leave to cook for appropriate time. This method protects the sauce from direct oven heat.

Chicken and tongue galantine

6 lb chicken, or capon
1 lb can of tongue
1 lb cooked ham (cut into slices each ¼–½ inch thick)
½ oz (about 18) pistachio nuts (blanched)
meat glaze (see below)
watercress (to garnish)

For farce (stuffing)
1 onion (finely chopped)
1 oz butter
1½ lb minced veal
3 oz fine white breadcrumbs
1 egg
5–6 fl oz double cream
salt and pepper

Method

To prepare farce: soften onion in the butter without colouring. Cool. Put the minced veal into a bowl with the crumbs, egg and cream. Mix well and season. Add onion mixture.

Bone out the chicken completely, splitting the skin down the back and cutting away the meat from the carcase, thighs and drumsticks. Spread chicken out on a board and distribute the meat evenly over the skin. Lay the farce on the meat. Cut the tongue and ham into long, finger-shaped pieces. Lay these alternately down the farce with the pistachios in between. Shape farce and chicken into a roll. Sew up the edges securely with thread. Wrap in greaseproof paper and then tightly in muslin. Tie firmly at each end and pin the edge down the middle to keep it taut.

Have ready a large pan or fish kettle half-full of boiling salted water with a slice or two of lemon added. Put in the galantine, cover and simmer from when the water reboils, for 1½ hours. Take up, cool slightly, then untie and tighten the muslin as much as possible and re-tie. Leave until quite cold, then unwrap and carefully remove the stitches.

To freeze, wrap the galantine in foil and slip into a polythene bag.

Thaw in the refrigerator for 24 hours. After about 12 hours, strip off the foil and cover with transparent 'cling wrap.

Prepare a good meat glaze or make up a mock one. Set galantine on a wire rack with a tray underneath. Warm glaze and brush galantine well. Allow to set then give a second and third coat.

To serve, cut the first 3 or 4 slices so that the checkerboard effect can be seen. Set on the serving dish and garnish with a little watercress.

Serve with either, or both, of the salads given on page 96.

True meat glaze is made from strained brown stock, boiled down until thick, syrupy and brown (a drop of gravy browning may be added to help). Cool a little before use.

Roulades de jambon

12 thin slices of cooked gammon
½ lb curd, or cream, cheese
salt and pepper
2–3 tablespoons cream
2 oz Brazil nuts (shelled)
4 oz cooked ham (chopped)

For salad
½ cucumber
salt
1 small Charentais, or ½ honeydew melon
½ lb tomatoes
French dressing
chopped parsley, mint and chives

Method

Beat the curd cheese until smooth. Season well and add cream. Slice the Brazil nuts and work into the cheese with the ham. Spread each slice of gammon with the cheese mixture. Roll up and set in a foil container or tray. Cover with transparent 'cling' wrap, or foil, and freeze.

Thawing and serving To thaw, leave for 24 hours in refrigerator.

To serve, prepare salad. Peel cucumber and cut in cubes, sprinkle lightly with salt, cover with a plate and leave to stand for 30 minutes; drain away any liquid and rinse with cold water.

Cut the melon in half, (or half again if using honeydew), remove the seeds and cut the flesh into cubes, removing from skin. Skin and quarter tomatoes, squeeze out seeds and remove core. If the tomatoes are large, cut the quarters in half again. Prepare the dressing. Mix the fruit and vegetables together, pour over dressing, cover and leave to chill. Place the roulades in an entrée dish and spoon over the salad. Garnish with chopped herbs and chives.

Mock meat glaze can be made from commercially-prepared aspic by using it double strength. Or use a can of consommé plus 1 dessertspoon gelatine dissolved in it. Use on the point of setting.

Chicory, apple and celery salad

4 large heads of chicory
3 large Cox's apples
1 large head celery
1 tablespoon freshly chopped
   parsley

For dressing
grated rind of ½ lemon
juice of 1 lemon
2 tablespoons caster sugar
3 tablespoons salad oil
4 fl oz cream
salt and pepper

Method
Wipe chicory, and cut into medium-thick diagonal slices. Quarter and core apples, and slice each quarter into 3 or 4. (Peel first if wished.) Cut celery into short bâtons, put into a bowl with the apples and chicory. Combine ingredients for dressing in the order given and adjust seasoning. Add parsley and mix dressing and salad together. Cover bowl and leave in cool place before dishing up and serving.

Sweetcorn, cucumber and new potato salad

1 or 2 cans sweetcorn kernels
½–1 cucumber
¾–1 lb new potatoes
about ¼ pint French dressing

Method
Empty sweetcorn, rinse and drain well. Peel and dice cucumber, but do not salt. Wash potatoes, boil in their skins in salted water, drain and peel while hot. Have ready the French dressing, pour a little over the potatoes and leave until cold. Add the sweetcorn and cucumber, season, and moisten again with the dressing. Cover and leave in fridge or cool place until just before serving.

Gratin de légumes

4 large Spanish onions
4 oz butter
1 lb carrots
salt and pepper
1 teaspoon sugar
1 teaspoon chopped mint, or
   parsley
¾ lb button mushrooms
1 large cauliflower
2 lb potatoes
1 egg yolk
1 tablespoon cream

For mornay sauce
1½ oz butter
1½ oz flour
¾ pint milk
4–5 tablespoons grated cheese

Forcing bag; 1-in vegetable rose pipe

Method
Peel and slice the onions, cook slowly in 1½ oz of the butter until soft and golden and place at the bottom of a 12-inch entrée, or quiche, dish. Peel and cut the carrots in thin rounds, cover with cold water, add a little salt, a teaspoon of sugar and a further ½ oz of the butter and cook steadily until all the water has evaporated; add 1 teaspoon chopped mint or parsley and spoon on top of the onions.

Wash and trim the mushrooms and sauté briskly in 1–2 oz butter, season and arrange over carrots. Sprig the cauliflower and cook until just tender. Drain, refresh and arrange among the mushrooms.

Boil potatoes, then sieve and beat to a purée with a nut of butter, 1 egg yolk and a tablespoon of cream.

To prepare the mornay sauce: melt butter gently, remove from heat and stir in flour. Pour on a third of the milk and blend well before adding the rest. Season lightly before returning to heat and stir until boiling. Continue boiling for 1–2 minutes, then gradually beat in cheese.

Spoon the sauce over the vegetables and pipe a thick lattice of puréed potato on top.

Slip dish into a polythene bag, wrap, tie and freeze.

Thawing and serving Thaw at room temperature for 3 hours, brush lightly with beaten egg. Brown in a moderately hot oven, 375°F or Mark 5, for 25–30 minutes. Serve hot.

Keep the gratin de légumes (top) warm on a heat tray. Alternatively, serve a summer salad, shown with ham roulades

Summer salad

1½ lb ripe tomatoes
¾ lb cauliflower sprigs, or one
  cauliflower
French dressing
¾ lb button mushrooms
1–2 tablespoons oil
1 large cucumber
salt
1 lb whole green beans
1 bunch spring onions (cleaned
  and sliced)

Method

Scald and peel tomatoes, cut out stalk and squeeze to remove seeds; slice. Cook cauliflower in boiling salted water until just tender. Drain, put into a bowl and moisten with French dressing. Heat oil in a pan, rinse mushrooms, wipe dry and sauté quickly in hot oil. Take out with a draining spoon and put into a bowl. Peel the cucumber and slice — salt lightly and leave for half an hour. Rinse under cold water, drain and pat dry.

Cut the green beans into 1-inch pieces and cook in boiling salted water until just tender. Drain and refresh.

Spread the beans on the bottom of a 12-inch china or quiche dish. Scatter over the spring onions and sprinkle with French dressing. Set the cauliflower sprigs on the beans with the mushrooms in between. Arrange the tomatoes and cucumber in circles over the top and sprinkle well with the dressing.

Using a forcing bag and plain nozzle, hold bag upright and pipe meringue shells on to a lined baking sheet. These are plain meringues

Pavé au chocolat

For chocolate biscuits
8 oz butter
4 oz caster sugar
2 oz sweetened chocolate
  powder
8 oz self-raising flour

For chocolate cream
6 oz block chocolate
2–2½ fl oz strong coffee, or
  water
½ pint double cream
brandy or rum (to flavour)
extra cream (for decoration)
icing sugar (for dusting)

Method

First prepare biscuits. Cream butter and sugar, work in chocolate powder and flour. Beat until smooth. Chill slightly, then divide into large 'walnuts'. Pat out on ungreased baking sheets to 3½-inch rounds, bake in a moderate oven at 350°F or Mark 4, for 7 minutes. Take out, cool a little, then lift biscuits off the baking sheets.

When cold, prepare the chocolate cream. Melt chocolate in a pan with about 2–2½ fl oz water or strong coffee; cool when thick. Whip cream, flavour with brandy or rum and fold in chocolate.

Sandwich biscuit rounds thickly together, standing them on edge. Wrap in foil and freeze.

Thawing and serving Thaw in refrigerator for about 4 hours, decorate with plain whipped cream and dust with icing sugar before serving. Cut in diagonal slices.

Meringues créole

6 egg whites
¾ lb soft light brown sugar
  (sifted)

For filling
1 orange
6–8 cubes sugar
½ pint double cream

Method

Whisk the egg whites until stiff, whisk in a tablespoon of the sugar, then quickly fold in the rest of the sifted sugar. Pipe or shape the meringue

Front: rich, dark pavé au chocolat. Behind: meringues créole with orange cream

with two dessertspoons on to baking sheets lined with non-stick (silicone) cooking paper and bake in a slow oven, 250–275°F or Mark ½–1, for about 1 hour.

After 45–50 minutes baking, lift each meringue and gently press in the underside to make a hollow and return to the oven to finish cooking. Allow to cool.

Rub the sugar cubes over the orange rind to remove the zest; crush when flavoured and dissolve in a little orange juice. Whip the cream and flavour with the orange 'syrup'. Fill the meringues with the orange-flavoured cream and serve with a macédoine of orange, pineapple and bananas flavoured with rum.

Macédoine de fruits

3 large oranges
1 fresh pineapple
4 bananas
¼ pint stock syrup (see fruits
  rafraîchis on page 90)
rum (to taste) – optional

Method

Peel oranges, using a sharp, serrated-edge knife to expose flesh. Remove segments by cutting between each membrane. Place in a glass bowl. Peel and slice pineapple into chunks, and peel and slice bananas, cutting into chunks diagonally.

Macerate fruit in the stock syrup, flavoured with a little rum, if liked, and chill in refrigerator for 1–2 hours before serving.

RECEPTION FOR 50

And for the really ambitious cook with a celebration to cater for, we have devised an afternoon or evening reception suitable for a wedding buffet, a christening party, or other family occasion. Some of the canapés can be frozen, most of the hot savouries, but we suggest making batches of cheese pastry (for the tartlets) and freezing this raw. Choux pastry is better baked, and then frozen. This will halve your preparation time on the day itself. Quantity guides are given in the recipes.

Assorted Canapes
★ *Ham and Cream Cheese Pinwheels*
Smoked Salmon Pinwheels
Asparagus Canapes
★ *Salami Cornucopias*

Savoury Tartlets
Cheese Cream Tartlets
Smoked Trout Tartlets
Smoked Cods Roe Tartlets
'Mock Caviar' Tartlets

Hot Savouries
★ *Scampi and Bacon Fritters*
★ *Mushroom Beignets*
★ *Scallops Devilled Chicken Livers*
★ *Cheese and Prawn Aigrettes with Savoury Dips*

Sweet Course
Carolines (eclairs)
Gâteaux Punch
Jacquelines (meringues)
Brandy Curls
★ *Brownies Tiny Mincepies*

ASSORTED CANAPES

Ham and cream cheese pinwheels

4 oz cooked ham (thinly sliced)
two 3 oz packets Philadelphia
**   cream cheese**
celery salt
brown and white bread
**   (buttered)**

Method
Work the cream cheese until soft and smooth and season with the celery salt. Spread each slice of ham with a layer of cream cheese and roll up. Wrap each roll in damp greaseproof paper and chill for a minimum of 2 hours, or overnight, in the refrigerator. (The damp greaseproof paper makes sure that the ham retains its attractive pink colour.)

Cut each ham roll in eight even slices with a very sharp knife, wiping the blade after each cut. Set each pinwheel on a small round of bread and butter, cut with a plain pastry cutter. Cover, wrap and freeze.

Thaw for 3 hours before serving.
Note: Ready-cooked ham in packets will be suitable for these pinwheels. Choose the kind without a rim of fat — shoulder cut should do.

Smoked salmon pinwheels

1 small loaf of brown bread
unsalted butter
½ lb smoked salmon
freshly ground black pepper
juice of ½ lemon

Method
Chill the fresh loaf in the freezer for 2 hours. This makes it easier to cut. Then cut away the rounded crust from the top and trim the side and end crusts as well. Cut 8 thin slices from length of the loaf and butter them. Cover each slice with a slice of smoked salmon, grind over a little pepper and sprinkle with lemon juice. Roll up lengthways and wrap in foil or 'cling' wrap and chill for 2 hours. Cut each roll in half-inch slices for serving. Each roll should give 5 pinwheels.
Note: If you want more than 40 pinwheels, the small brown loaf will cut into 12–16 slices and the quantity of smoked salmon can be increased in proportion. A little more lemon will be required.

The wine we chose to serve with this buffet party menu was a dry white burgundy, a Pouilly Fuissé.

Above left: ham and cream cheese pinwheels with salami cornucopias. On silver dish: smoked salmon pinwheels with 'mock caviar' tartlets. On square dish: asparagus canapés with salami cornucopias. Right and behind: cheese and prawn aigrettes, savoury dips, scampi and bacon fritters with tiny fried scallops. Left, on glass pedestal: Carolines; behind them, gâteaux Punch arranged round Jacquelines (little meringues). Right: brandy curls filled with whipped cream

Asparagus canapés

1 small brown loaf
salted butter
a little made English mustard
freshly cooked, or canned, asparagus spears
2 pints commercially-prepared aspic

Method
Prepare the loaf by cutting off crusts. Soften the salted butter and work in enough of the mustard to give it a good tang. Butter and slice the bread in generous $\frac{1}{4}$-inch slices, and place, butter side uppermost, in a swiss roll tin. Drain the asparagus, trim by the stalk ends to the same size as the width of the bread slices, and arrange side by side on the bread. Cover with 'cling' wrap and chill.

Make the aspic jelly as directed on the packet, but dissolved in the liquid from the asparagus. When cold and on the point of setting, remove the 'cling' wrap and brush aspic over asparagus. Re-cover and return to the refrigerator to set. Cut into fingers.

Salami cornucopias

8 oz packet of sliced Danish salami (10 slices)
Dutch cocktail wafer biscuits
8 oz Philadelphia cream cheese
cap of pimiento (shredded), or cocktail gherkins (sliced)

Forcing bag and $\frac{1}{2}$-inch plain pipe

Method
Remove the rind from the salami and cut each slice in two. Break the biscuits in half. Beat the cheese with a wooden spoon until soft and creamy. Fill it into the forcing bag and squeeze about a teaspoonful on to each piece of salami, curling it round into a cone shape. Place each cone on a biscuit holding it in position with a little cheese. Decorate each with small piece of pimiento or sliced gherkin and pack in a swiss roll tin. Cover with 'cling' wrap and foil, and freeze. Remove 2–3 hours before party and thaw.
Note: The Dutch cocktail biscuits should be obtainable at most good grocers'. The brand name is Roka.

TARTLETS

The following cheese pastry is excellent for making croûtes and canapés; having a high proportion of cheese it scorches easily and so when baking a large number of canapés it is wise to place them, for example, on lightly greased paper on the baking tin. In this way the whole batch can be removed at once to the cooling rack. Cheese pastry can be made in a batch, quantity as below, and frozen raw.

Cheese pastry

1 lb plain flour
10 oz butter
8 oz finely grated cheese
   (preferably half Cheddar and
   half Parmesan)
salt and pepper
a few grains of cayenne pepper
2 egg yolks mixed with 3
   tablespoons water

1¾-inch diameter shallow tartlet tins

Method
Cut the butter into the flour, add the cheese and seasoning and continue cutting with a round-bladed knife until thoroughly blended and the whole mixture looks like breadcrumbs. Beat the egg yolks and water with a fork, add to the dry ingredients and mix to a stiff dough with your fingertips. Chill well.

Take one third of the pastry, line into lightly greased tartlet tins, 1¾-inch in diameter, and chill well — for at least 1 hour in the refrigerator. Bake for about 8 minutes at 400°F or Mark 6. Remove from tins and fill when cold.

Cheese cream tartlets

1 oz butter
1 oz flour
½ pint milk
salt and pepper
4 oz grated cheese (half
   Cheddar, half Gruyère)
2 eggs
paprika pepper (for dusting)

Method
Make a sauce with the butter, flour and milk. Season well

and stir in the cheese a little at a time; add the well-beaten eggs.

When 24 bouche cups lined with the cheese pastry have had 5 minutes baking time at 400°F or Mark 6, remove from the oven, press in the middle of the pastry cases which rise a little, and pour in the cheese cream. Return to the oven for 5–6 minutes until set and brown. Dust with paprika.

Smoked trout tartlets

For filling
6 oz smoked trout
1 Demi-sel cheese
2 oz butter
1 teaspoon horseradish cream
salt and pepper
dill cucumber (sliced)

Method
Remove skin and bone from the trout and pound the flesh with the cheese. Cream the butter until soft and work into the trout mixture with the horseradish cream. Add seasoning to taste. Fill the pastry cases as described above and top each with a round of sliced dill cucumber.

Smoked cods roe tartlets

For filling
8 oz smoked cods roe
3 tablespoons fresh white
   breadcrumbs
3 tablespoons salad oil
lemon juice
1–2 drops of Tabasco sauce
10 black olives (stoned and
   halved)

Method
Soak the crumbs in the oil, add to the cods roe and blend in the liquidiser, or work in a pestle and mortar, to a smooth paste. (This can also be done by hand with a wooden spoon or a beater.) Add lemon juice and Tabasco sauce to taste. Put a teaspoonful of the mixture into each pastry case or, using a forcing bag and ½-inch plain pipe, pipe filling into cases and top with half a black olive brushed with a little extra salad oil.

'Mock caviar' tartlets

¼ pint carton soured cream
small jar lumpfish roe

Method
Take 24 of the baked pastry cases and, when cold, fill each with ½ teaspoon of soured cream and ½ teaspoon of the 'mock caviar'

HOT SAVOURIES

Fritter batter

5 oz flour
a pinch of salt
small piece of fresh yeast about
   size of a nut, or 1 teaspoon
   dried yeast
1 teacup warm water
1 tablespoon oil
1 egg white (optional)

Method
Sift flour and salt into a warm basin. Mix yeast in about half the warm water, and stir into the flour with the oil. Add the rest of the water to make the consistency of thick cream. Beat well and cover, leave in a warm place for 15–20 minutes, by which time the mixture should be well risen. If using egg white, whisk stiffly and fold into batter just before frying.

Scampi and bacon fritters

1 jumbo-size packet of frozen
   scampi
9–10 rashers streaky bacon

Method
Tip the frozen scampi from the packet on to absorbent kitchen paper and leave for 2–3 hours to thaw out at room temperature. Remove rind from bacon, stretch and flatten each rasher under the blade of a chopping knife and cut in three. Wrap each scampi in a piece of bacon, dip in fritter batter and fry in deep hot fat (375°F) until golden-brown. Cool on a wire rack, wrap and freeze.
Thawing and serving Thaw for 2 hours at room tempera-

ture. For reheating, place on a baking sheet, uncovered, and bake in a quick oven (400°F or Mark 6) for about 7 minutes.

Mushroom beignets

Choose firm, unopened button mushrooms, trim the stalks and wipe the caps with a clean damp cloth. Dip in fritter batter and deep-fat fry. Cool on a rack, wrap and freeze.
To serve Place on baking sheets while still frozen and heat in a quick oven (400°F or Mark 6) for 8–10 minutes.

Scallops

Small bay scallops can be bought in many freezer centres egged-and-crumbed and ready for frying. Scampi coated in the same way are sold in 2 lb packs. Follow the instructions on the packet.

Serve with the following two savoury dips to accompany:

Savoury dip 1

½ pint basic cream dressing
1 tablespoon finely chopped
   pickles
1 tablespoon finely chopped
   parsley
1 clove of garlic (crushed)
1 teaspoon grated onion
1 tablespoon chopped capers
1 tablespoon chopped green
   olives

Method
Mix all the ingredients together and season well.

Savoury dip 2

½ green pepper (de-seeded and
   chopped)
4 sticks of celery (chopped)
1 clove of garlic (crushed)
¼ pint basic cream dressing
¼ pint tomato chilli sauce
1 tablespoon grated horseradish
   cream sauce
3 tablespoons cream, or
   evaporated milk

Method
Mix all ingredients and chill well.

Cheese and prawn aigrettes

3 egg quantity of choux pastry
3 oz Parmesan cheese (grated)
salt and black pepper ground from mill
½ teaspoon Dijon mustard
1 lb fresh prawns (shelled)

Method
Make the choux pastry, beat in the cheese a little at a time and season well with salt, black pepper from the mill and ½ teaspoon Dijon mustard. Put the mixture out in teaspoonfuls on a wet baking tray — the mixture will make about 30. Push a prawn into each small choux and make sure that it is completely covered.

Heat the deep fat bath to 375°F and drop in the aigrettes a few at a time. As they begin to swell, raise the temperature of the fat to 400°F. (It is recommended that cooking oil should never be heated beyond 375°F for safety.) Cook until pale golden brown then drain well on a wire rack. When cold, wrap and freeze.

Thawing and serving Thaw for 1 hour at room temperature, place on a baking sheet, dust with Parmesan cheese and heat in a hot oven, 400°F or Mark 6, for 7–8 minutes.

Basic cream dressing

½ teaspoon salt
¼ teaspoon white pepper, ground from mill
1 teaspoon dry mustard
2 teaspoons sugar
1 tablespoon flour
2 fl oz white wine vinegar
4 fl oz water
1 oz butter, or margarine
¼ pint single cream

Method
Mix first six ingredients to a paste in a pan with the vinegar, add the water and stir over a gentle heat until the mixture boils. Cook for 2–3 minutes, beat in the butter and turn into a basin to cool. Cover the mixture while cooling with a buttered paper to prevent a skin forming. When cold, dilute with the cream. Makes approx. ½ pint.

Devilled chicken livers

4 chicken livers
1 oz butter
1 teaspoon chopped parsley

For marinade
1 teaspoon English mustard
1 teaspoon Dijon mustard
1 tablespoon Worcestershire sauce
2 tablespoons mushroom ketchup
1 tablespoon salad oil
1 teaspoon anchovy essence

Method
Mix together the ingredients for the marinade and leave the livers to soak for 1 hour. Sauté the livers briskly in the butter for 2–3 minutes, until browned. Pour over the marinade and continue cooking until liquid is well-reduced and sticky. Slice the livers, sprinkle with parsley and spear on cocktail sticks. Serve in bowls with tiny grilled cocktail sausages, also on cocktail sticks, with the savoury dips to accompany.

Basic choux pastry

7½ fl oz water
3 oz butter, or margarine
3¾ oz plain flour
3 eggs

Method
Put water and butter into a pan. Sift flour onto a piece of paper. Bring water and butter to the boil, and when bubbling draw aside and shoot in the flour. Beat until smooth, about ½ minute. Return to heat for 2–3 seconds to dry a little. Turn out and allow to get almost cold. Then return to pan. Whisk the eggs and add about a third at a time to the pan, beating well. Add the last third carefully to avoid getting the paste too soft. Set aside and, if wished, turn into a carton and freeze. Thaw out overnight before baking.

Cheese and prawn aigrettes, with scallops and scampi and bacon fritters, ready to serve with two savoury dips

Making choux pastry
Add flour to pan after the water and fat have been boiled, then beat flour mixture until paste is just smooth. Next, add the eggs one by one, beating them in well. Last, pipe out tiny choux on to baking sheet with a special éclair nozzle

SWEET COURSE

Carolines

**(tiny chocolate and coffee
éclairs – makes about 36)**

3 egg quantity of choux pastry
    (see page 101)
½ pint double cream (whipped)
a little sugar syrup (to thin)
1 dessertspoon instant coffee
    dissolved in 1 dessertspoon
    water
4 oz block chocolate
1 lb fondant icing

*Forcing bag and ⅜-inch diameter plain
pipe*

Method

Set the oven at 375°F or Mark
5. Make the choux pastry and
fill into a forcing bag with a
⅜-inch plain pipe. Pipe out on
dampened baking sheets in
small éclairs, about 2–2¼
inches long. Bake in pre-
heated oven for 10–15
minutes, or until really firm to
the touch. Lift off on to a rack
to cool.

Flavour half the whipped
cream with half the dissolved
coffee. Pipe this coffee-
flavoured cream into half the
Carolines. Melt the chocolate
in a pan with 1–2 tablespoons
water. Allow to cool. Then add
about a tablespoon of the
melted chocolate to the rest
of the cream. Pipe this into
the remaining Carolines.

Dilute half the fondant over
gentle heat with 1–2 tablespoons of the sugar syrup,
flavour with a little more dissolved coffee, or coffee essence, and ice the coffee
Carolines with a good coating
consistency. Then add rest of
fondant to the pan and the
melted chocolate. Mix over
gentle heat before adding a
little sugar syrup if necessary.

Coat the remaining Caro-
lines with chocolate icing.

Fondant icing

1 lb lump sugar
8 tablespoons water
pinch of cream of tartar,
    dissolved in 1 teaspoon water

sugar thermometer

Method

Place the sugar and water in a
saucepan and dissolve without stirring over a low heat.
Using a brush dipped in cold
water, wipe round pan at
level of the syrup to prevent a
crust forming. Add the cream
of tartar, place the lid on the
pan, increase the heat and
bring to the boil.

Remove the lid after 2
minutes, put a sugar thermometer in and boil the syrup
steadily to 240°F. When it has
reached this temperature take

the pan off the heat at once,
wait for the bubbles to subside, then pour the mixture
very slowly on to a damp
marble or laminated plastic
slab. Work with a wooden
spatula until it becomes a firm
and white fondant. Take a
small piece of fondant at a
time and knead with the
fingertips until smooth.

For storing, pack fondant
icing in an airtight jar or tin.
When you want to use it,
gently warm the fondant with
a little sugar syrup to make a

*The sweet course consists of
a choice of delicacies. Try
brandy curls, fruity gâteaux
Punch triangles, brown sugar
meringues with ginger cream
or (right) tiny Caroline éclairs*

smooth cream. The icing
should flow easily. Flavour
and colour it just before using.

Note: You can buy blocks or
packets of powder of fondant
icing. Simply follow the manu-
facturer's instructions.

Gâteaux Punch

Make these with trimmings of a wedding, or rich plum, cake. Weigh, and to every pound allow:

4 oz butter
2 oz golden syrup
4 oz block chocolate (melted)
2 tablespoons brandy or 1 tablespoon rum (optional)

Swiss roll tin 7½ × 11½ inches makes 30 'fingers'

Method

Crumble the cake finely in a bowl. Warm the butter, syrup and chocolate gently together. Add the brandy, or rum, and mix. Turn at once into a shallow tray ½–¾-inches deep. Press out evenly with a palette knife and leave until next day.

Run a thin coating of fondant or glacé icing over the top, flavoured with brandy or rum to taste. Leave until quite set. Then cut into fingers or triangles in the tin before taking out for serving.

Note: These are so easy and quick to make that there is no need to store them in the freezer. If, however, you have no immediate use for the cake trimmings, make up a batch of cake mixture and freeze in the tin. Thaw out, as for cakes, before icing.

Glacé icing

4–5 tablespoons granulated sugar
¼ pint water
8–12 oz icing sugar (finely sifted)
flavouring essence and colouring (as required)

Method

Make sugar syrup by dissolving sugar in ¼ pint of water in a small saucepan. Bring to the boil, and boil steadily for 10 minutes. Remove pan from the heat and when quite cold, add the icing sugar, 1 tablespoon at a time, and beat thoroughly with a wooden spatula. Add flavouring. The icing should coat back of spoon and look very glossy. Warm the pan gently on a very low heat.

Jacquelines

2 egg whites
5 oz soft light brown sugar
¼ pint double, or whipping, cream
a little caster sugar
2 stems glacé ginger (finely diced)

Forcing bag and ¼-inch éclair pipe

Method

Set oven at 275°F or Mark 1. Whip egg whites stiffly, whisk in 2 teaspoons of the brown sugar, then quickly fold in the rest.

Pipe out in 'plump buttons' on to non-stick (silicone) cooking paper or a greased and floured baking tin. Cook in the cool oven for about 35–40 minutes or until they can be lifted easily from the tin. Then, on the flat side of each one, make a dent with your finger. Put back on the tray in the oven for a further 10–15 minutes to dry. Whip cream, sweeten with a little caster sugar and fold in the ginger. Sandwich the little meringues together when cold.

Brandy curls

This quantity makes about 50 small brandy curls.

4 oz butter
4 oz demerara sugar
4 oz golden syrup
4 oz plain flour
pinch of salt
1 teaspoon ground ginger
1 teaspoon lemon juice
2–3 drops vanilla essence
1 pint double cream (to finish)

Cream horn moulds

Method

Set the oven at 325°F or Mark 3. Put the butter, sugar and syrup into a saucepan and heat gently until the butter has melted and sugar dissolved. Leave to cool slightly. Sift flour with salt and ginger into mixture, stir well, adding lemon juice and vanilla essence.

Put scant ½ teaspoons of mixture on a well-greased baking sheet 2–3 inches apart. Cook in pre-set oven for 8 minutes. Leave biscuits for 2–3 minutes, then remove from the tin with a sharp

Brownies are often praised as being the best of American cookies

knife, turn over and roll round the pointed end of a cream horn mould. Store in an airtight tin as soon as they are cold. Serve, filled with whipped cream.

Brownies

Makes about 48

4 oz unsweetened chocolate (see note below)
5 oz shortening
4 eggs
1 lb sugar
6 oz flour
1 teaspoon baking powder
pinch of salt
8 oz shelled walnuts (roughly chopped)

Two 8-inch square cake tins

Method

Set the oven at 350°F or Mark 4. Cut up or grate the chocolate, put in a saucepan with the shortening and melt over gentle heat. Whisk eggs and sugar together until light, add the chocolate mixture. Sift the flour with the baking powder and salt and stir into mixture with a wooden spoon. Stir in the nuts.

Spread into the prepared tins and bake for 30–35 minutes in the pre-set oven, or until a 'dull' crust has formed. Allow to cool and cut into small squares.

Note: If you can't obtain unsweetened chocolate, mix 4 oz cocoa with 10 tablespoons water and cook to a cream. Increase the shortening to 6 oz.

Tiny mince pies

Make these of puff pastry or shortcrust, according to your preference. Use tiny patty tins and you will find that 8 oz pastry, which normally makes approximately 18 pies, will stretch to make between 2–3 dozen, depending on the size of the tins.

Serve warm, if preferred.

WEEKEND ENTERTAINING: TICKETS FOR THE THEATRE

When having people to stay for the weekend it is essential to have your meals well-planned in advance so that you are free to spend as much time as possible with your guests. In this issue Rosemary Hume and Muriel Downes have devised menus for three separate weekends, together with plans of work to help you with the preparation.

The first is a short weekend. Your guests arrive in time for Saturday lunch, a formal three-course meal. There is no dinner menu as you have planned a visit to the theatre in the evening, but a light snack is served before you leave. You return to a piping hot gratin which has been left to heat in a pre-set automatic oven. This will serve 8, so you can invite two more friends home to supper. Sunday lunch is specifically planned to be flexible, and it can be served as late as you like. The plan of work is on page 109. All the recipes, except Saturday's gratin, serve six.

The plan of work is on page 109.

Saturday Lunch

Avocado Salad à la Grecque

★ *Poussins Boulangère*
★ *Garden Peas, French or Runner Beans*

★ *Walnut Meringue Gâteau*
with Compote of Loganberries

White wine – Pouilly-Fuissé (Burgundy)

Avocado salad à la grecque

3 ripe avocado pears
4 ripe tomatoes
1 dozen black olives
  (halved and stoned)
4 anchovy fillets (soaked in a
  little milk)
1 large tablespoon chopped
  parsley

For dressing
1 tablespoon lemon juice
1 tablespoon water
5 tablespoons olive oil
1 teaspoon sugar
black pepper ground from the
  mill

Method
First prepare the dressing: put the lemon juice, water and oil into a bowl. Add sugar and pepper, mix well and adjust the seasoning.

Scald, skin and quarter the tomatoes, remove the seeds and add to the dressing with the olives, the anchovies cut in strips and the parsley.

Peel and halve avocados, remove the stones and cut again. Place in an entrée dish or on individual plates and spoon the dressing over them.

Poussins boulangère

3 double poussins
3 oz butter
½ lb small pickling onions
6 oz firm button mushrooms
½ lb small new potatoes

For stock
1 onion (peeled)
1 carrot (peeled)
1 stick of celery
bouquet garni
salt and pepper

For marinade
juice of 1 small lemon
½ teaspoon sugar
salt and ground white pepper
1 teaspoon ground coriander
2–3 tablespoons brandy

Method
Split the poussins and cut out the backbone. Mix together the ingredients for the marinade in the order given. Spoon over the poussins and marinate for at least ½ an hour.

Place backbones of birds in pan with the onion, carrot, celery, herbs, seasoning and water to cover. Bring to the boil, skim, cover and simmer for about 1 hour, adding more

water if necessary. Set the oven at 350°F or Mark 4.

Peel and blanch the pickling onions, drain and return to a small saucepan with ½ oz of the butter and 1–2 tablespoons of the chicken stock. Cover and cook until tender. At the same time, cook the mushrooms in ½ oz butter for 1 minute and set on one side.

Scrub and dry the potatoes well and put in a small covered pan with 1 oz butter and cook for about 15 minutes over a gentle heat, shaking the pan from time to time.

Melt the remaining ounce of butter and brush over the poussins on the skin side only. Brown the birds slowly on the skin side under the grill.

Place the poussins, onions, mushrooms and potatoes in an ovenproof casserole, pour over any remaining marinade, cover and cook in the pre-set oven for 15 minutes.

Add 1–2 tablespoons of chicken stock if necessary, and continue cooking for a further 20–25 minutes Serve; or allow to cool and freeze.
Thawing and serving Thaw for 12 hours. Reheat in a moderate oven, 350°F or Mark 4, for 25–30 minutes.

Split each poussin down the front using a sharp knife

Trim away the backbone from each half with scissors

Two courses from our Saturday lunch menu – poussins boulangère, marinated in brandy and spices – served here with haricots verts, and with a walnut meringue gâteau to follow. This can be accompanied by a compote of loganberries

Walnut meringue gâteau

4 oz shelled walnuts
5 egg whites
a pinch of cream of tartar
10 oz caster sugar
icing sugar (for dusting)

For filling
2 teaspoons instant coffee
2 tablespoons soft dark brown sugar
1 tablespoon freshly boiled water
½ pint double cream
1–2 tablespoons rum

4 baking sheets lined with non-stick (silicone) cooking paper; forcing bag and plain ½-inch pipe; 8½–9 inch diameter loose-bottomed cake tin

Method
Set oven at 290°F or Mark 1.

Blanch and skin the walnuts. Grind and toast them lightly in the oven. Whisk the egg whites until foamy, add the cream of tartar and continue whisking until stiff. Take five teaspoons of the measured sugar and beat into the egg whites for about three minutes, then fold in the remaining sugar and prepared walnuts – using a basting spoon.

Pipe or spread the mixture in four 8-inch rounds on the prepared tins.

Bake in the pre-set oven for 1–1½ hours, or until dry and lightly coloured. Cool on a wire rack and, when almost cold, peel off the paper.

Dissolve the coffee and sugar in the water and allow to cool. Whip the cream until thick, add the coffee syrup and rum, and continue beating until the cream holds its shape.

Line the bottom of an 8½–9-inch loose-bottomed cake tin with foil or waxed paper, put in one meringue round and spread with one third of the cream. Continue with layers of meringue and cream, finishing with meringue.

Cover the tin with foil, or slide the tin into a polythene bag, and store overnight in the refrigerator.

Turn the cake from the tin, dust with icing sugar and decorate, if liked, with a little extra plain cream. Serve with a compote of loganberries or raspberries and redcurrants.
Note: The freezer can be used but, in this case, remove cake from the freezer four hours before serving and leave at room temperature.

Compote of loganberries

2 lb loganberries
3 rounded tablespoons granulated sugar
good pinch cinnamon
1 tablespoon arrowroot
approx ¼ pint water

Method
Put the loganberries into a pan with the sugar and cinnamon. Cover pan and set on a low heat until the juice runs freely. Draw pan aside.

Slake (mix) arrowroot with a little of the cold water, add to the pan and shake. Add the remaining water and bring to the boil. Turn into a serving dish and allow to cool.

Smoked salmon and prawn roulades

4 oz smoked salmon
1 pint fresh prawns
4 tablespoons double cream or
    mayonnaise
1 teaspoon tomato chilli sauce
juice of $\frac{1}{4}$ lemon
black pepper ground from the
    mill
Hovis or wheatmeal bread
unsalted butter
small cress (to garnish)

Method

Peel the prawns, or if using frozen ones, take $\frac{1}{4}$ lb and, after allowing them to thaw slowly in the refrigerator, dry on a paper towel. Whip the cream lightly if using, add the chilli sauce, lemon and pepper, and mix with the prawns.

Cut thin slices of brown bread and butter them; remove the crusts and lay a thin slice of the salmon on each slice. Put a teaspoon of the prawn mixture on the salmon and roll up each slice of bread.

Place the roulades on a flat dish, garnish with small cress, cover with foil or transparent film wrap and keep in refrigerator until serving time.

Smoked mackerel roulades

2 small smoked mackerel
2$\frac{1}{2}$ fl oz soured cream (or fresh
    double cream sharpened with
    lemon juice)
2 teaspoons horseradish cream
juice of $\frac{1}{2}$ lemon
black pepper ground from the
    mill
bread and butter (as for smoked
    salmon and prawn roulades)

Method

Split the mackerel open, remove the bone, lift the fillets carefully from the skin and then divide into large flakes using two forks. Mix the horseradish cream, lemon juice and pepper into the soured cream and spoon this over the fish. Leave to marinate for about $\frac{1}{2}$ an hour.

Place a spoonful of prepared fish on to each trimmed slice of brown bread and butter and roll up firmly. Dish and chill as for smoked salmon and prawn roulades.

Serve the roulades with chilled dry sherry or Muscadet before leaving for the theatre.

Ingredients for the gratin

Spooning veal over tomato coulis, before adding spinach and béchamel sauce in layers

Gratin italienne

1 lb minced veal
1 oz beef dripping or butter
1 medium-size onion (finely
    chopped)
1 tablespoon flour
2 tablespoons sherry
$\frac{1}{2}$–$\frac{3}{4}$ pint chicken stock
salt and pepper
2 lb spinach
$\frac{1}{2}$ lb noodles
béchamel sauce (see page 124)
    made with:
    1$\frac{1}{2}$ oz butter
    1$\frac{1}{2}$ oz flour
    $\frac{3}{4}$ pint flavoured milk
1$\frac{1}{2}$ oz butter
2 oz grated cheese ($\frac{1}{2}$ mild
    Cheddar, $\frac{1}{2}$ Parmesan)

For tomato coulis
1 lb ripe tomatoes, or 1 (16 oz)
    can Italian tomatoes
1 medium-size onion (finely
    sliced)
$\frac{1}{2}$ oz butter
2$\frac{1}{2}$ fl oz stock (if using fresh
    tomatoes)
1 bayleaf
$\frac{1}{2}$ teaspoon chopped basil or
    lemon thyme
1 teaspoon arrowroot slaked
    with 1 tablespoon water

Method

Set the oven at 350°F or Mark 4.

Melt the dripping or butter, add the onion and cook until soft but not coloured. Increase the heat under the pan, add the veal and stir well with a wooden fork until the meat is well broken and beginning to brown. Blend in the flour, sherry and stock and bring to the boil. Season with salt and pepper and simmer gently for 1$\frac{1}{2}$ hours until tender (the texture should be smooth and creamy).

Blanch the spinach for 3 minutes, drain, refresh and press between two plates to remove all the excess moisture. Poach the noodles until you can just break one with your thumb nail; drain, tip into a large mixing bowl and cover with lukewarm water.

Prepare a béchamel sauce with the butter, flour and flavoured milk and cover with a buttered paper to prevent a skin forming.

Make the tomato coulis. Scald and skin the tomatoes if using fresh ones, cut in quarters, scoop out the seeds and rub these in a nylon strainer to obtain the juice. Cook the onion slowly in the butter until soft but not coloured. Add the tomatoes, the juice from the seeds, stock, herbs and season with salt and pepper. Cover and simmer until pulpy and rich looking.

Draw aside, remove the bayleaf and add the arrowroot slaked (mixed) with the water. Bring to the boil again. **Watchpoint** When using canned tomatoes use the whole contents of the tin, fruit and juice, and do not attempt to remove the seeds. No stock is needed but break the tomatoes well with a wooden spoon before covering the pan and leaving to simmer.

Heat $\frac{3}{4}$ oz of the butter to a nut brown colour, add the spinach and heat gently until any remaining moisture evaporates but do not let it fry. Place half the spinach at the bottom of a deep, buttered gratin dish and cover it with half the béchamel sauce.

Drain the noodles thoroughly, place in a large pan with the remaining $\frac{3}{4}$ oz butter and toss over the heat until well coated with the butter and any water has evaporated. Season with pepper from the mill and turn into the gratin dish. Cover the noodles with the tomato coulis and then spoon in the minced veal mixture. **Watchpoint** If taking the minced veal mixture from the freezer make sure that it has completely defrosted before using – about 12 hours.

Put the remaining spinach over the meat and cover this with a layer of béchamel sauce. Scatter cheese over top.

Allow 30–35 minutes for the gratin to heat through and brown the cheese, at 350°F or Mark 4.

Note: Check the instructions of your cooker for automatic control, as it is generally necessary to add 15 minutes to the cooking time.

For dessert, serve fresh fruit and a selection of cheeses.

Serve roulades filled with smoked salmon and prawns, or smoked mackerel, with chilled Muscadet before leaving for the theatre. The gratin italienne (above) will be ready on your return. Follow with fruit and a selection of cheeses

Sunday Lunch

★ *Potage Velouté
aux Fèves*

★ *Ham Mousse
Salade de Saison*

*Obstsahnetorte
(German Fruit Flan)*

Red wine – Margaux (Bordeaux)

Potage velouté aux fèves

1 lb shelled broad beans
1¾ oz butter
1 shallot (finely chopped) or
    1 small onion
1½ oz flour
1½–2 pints veal or chicken stock
salt and pepper
2 sprigs of savory or thyme
2 egg yolks
¼ pint single cream
1 teaspoon chopped chervil
    or parsley (to garnish)

Method
Melt the butter, add the shallot and cook slowly until soft but not brown. Blend in the flour, continue cooking for 2–3 minutes until straw coloured, then add 1½ pints of stock and stir until boiling. Season and simmer gently for about 20 minutes, adding a little of the reserved cold stock and skimming well from time to time.

Meanwhile cook the broad beans with the herbs in enough boiling salted water to cover. Drain and refresh and reserve the cooking liquor. Purée beans, reserving a few.

Add the purée of beans to the velouté mixture, cover and simmer very gently for 10–15 minutes. Pour through a conical strainer before freezing.
Thawing and serving Thaw for at least 12 hours, then return soup to the pan to reheat. Mix together the egg yolks and cream; thicken the soup with this liaison, and keep warm in a bain-marie. Heat the reserved beans in their cooking liquid and add to the soup with the chervil or parsley just before serving.

Ham mousse

¾ lb cooked ham
¾ oz gelatine soaked in ¼ pint
    stock
½ pint double cream

For Madeira sauce
¾ oz dripping or butter
2 tablespoons finely-diced onion
    and carrot
½ oz flour
bouquet garni
½–¾ pint stock
1 teaspoon tomato purée
1 small wine glass Madeira
salt and pepper

For decoration
½ pint commercially-prepared
    aspic
1 tablespoon chopped truffle, or
    2 oz button mushrooms
    (cooked and sliced)

2-pint capacity soufflé dish

Method
First prepare the Madeira sauce. Cook the vegetables in the fat until about to colour. Add flour and cook to a good brown. Add the rest of the ingredients and simmer to a syrupy consistency. Strain and allow to cool.

Mince the ham twice and pound well. Sieve or work it in a liquidiser with the cold Madeira sauce and season.

Dissolve the soaked gelatine over a gentle heat and add this to the ham and sauce mixture. Fold in the lightly whipped cream. When the mixture is on the point of setting, pour it into the soufflé dish, cover with foil and place in the refrigerator or freezer.
Thawing and serving Thaw for 12 hours or overnight.

Make up the aspic and allow to cool. When on the point of setting, cover the mousse with a thin layer and allow to set. Add the truffle or mushrooms to about ¼ pint of aspic and pour over the mousse. Leave to set.

Serve with a salad.

Mussel and sweetbread casserole

An alternative main course for Sunday lunch follows. This mussel and sweetbread casserole is served hot. It may be made in advance and frozen.

When cooking the dish, you can speed up preparation by cleaning and preparing the mussels in advance, then freezing them in their liquid. Remove them from the freezer 12 hours before using, then prepare the sweetbreads and finish the dish.

As it is rich-tasting, we suggest serving it with plain boiled rice, or noodles, tossed in butter.

1 lb lambs sweetbreads
1 dozen pickling onions
2½ oz butter
1 small glass sherry
¾ pint good veal or chicken
    stock
2 quarts mussels
1 wine glass white wine
1 wine glass water
a large bouquet garni with stick
    of celery added
1½ oz flour
salt and pepper
3–3½ fl oz cream
2 tablespoons chopped parsley

Method
Soak the sweetbreads in cold, salted water for 2 hours, then drain. Cover with cold water, bring to the boil then drain again. Press between two plates, then trim carefully. Peel and blanch the onions.

Melt 1 oz butter in a flame-proof casserole and, when foaming, add the sweetbreads and onions and cook slowly for 10–15 minutes, but do not allow to colour. Add the sherry, allow to reduce by half, then add the stock; cover and simmer for 10–15 minutes.

Meanwhile, wash and scrub the mussels. Put them into a large pan with the wine, water and herbs. Cover and bring to the boil, shaking the pan occasionally. Simmer for about 2 minutes, then draw the pan aside and pour off and reserve the liquid. Strain the stock from the sweetbreads into a measuring jug and make up to 1 pint with the mussel liquor.

Melt 1½ oz butter, blend in the flour and cook to a pale straw colour, add the stock

and stir until boiling. Simmer for 5 minutes, adjust the seasoning and strain. Pot and freeze when cooled.

Remove the mussels from their shells and put in the casserole with the sweetbreads and onions. Allow to cool. Pack and freeze. Shake gently to blend all the ingredients.
Thawing and serving Thaw casserole and sauce for 24 hours in the refrigerator. Heat casserole on top of the stove. Heat sauce in a pan, add the cream and parsley and, when thoroughly hot, pour into casserole and shake to blend.

Scrub the mussels well with a small stiff brush and pull or scrape away any small pieces of weed from the sides

Any weed clinging to the sides of the shells is then scraped off

Obstsahnetorte

For pastry
3 oz flour
2 oz caster sugar
grated rind of ½ lemon
1½ oz butter
1 egg yolk
1–2 tablespoons water

For sponge
2 eggs
3 oz caster sugar
2 oz flour

For cream layer
1 rounded teaspoon gelatine
  soaked in 1 tablespoon water
2 tablespoons liqueur (kirsch,
  curaçao or maraschino)
½ pint double cream

For topping
½ lb raw or canned sharp fruit
  such as red and blackcurrants,
  dessert gooseberries or red
  cherries
redcurrant jelly glaze
  (optional)

9-inch diameter spring-form mould

The obstsahnetorte – a Cordon Bleu version of German fruit flan – is shown here decorated with rosettes of whipped cream over the fruit layer of strawberries and sliced peaches. If decorating in this way, allow an extra ¼ pint of double cream to do so

Method

Make the pastry using the same method as for pâte sucrée (see recipe for tarte aux fraises on page 36). Work it well with the heel of your hand before chilling pastry for one hour. Then roll directly on to the base of the lightly oiled mould. Bake in a moderate oven at 400°F or Mark 6, for 10 minutes. Allow to cool.

Meanwhile, whisk the eggs and caster sugar until thick and mousse-like. Using a metal spoon, fold in the sifted flour. Pour the sponge mixture on top of the cooled pastry and bake again at 375°F or Mark 5, about 15–20 minutes. Allow to cool.

Dissolve the soaked gelatine by standing the bowl or dish in a small pan of hot water; cool and add the chosen liqueur. Start whisking the cream and, as it thickens, add the gelatine and continue whisking until the cream holds its shape. Spoon the cream on top of the sponge and smooth the top with a palette knife.

Cover the cream with fruit in season. Leave quite plain or brush with a redcurrant jelly glaze if liked. Chill until required and remove mould just before serving.

May we refer you to the table of recommended keeping times for frozen food on page 126, and emphasise that it is not wise to keep food over-long in the freezer, particularly cooked meat with a stuffing.

It is far better to plan your time so that you do not freeze your dishes too far in advance. Clear labelling and coding of freezer parcels cannot be too strongly stressed.

PLAN OF WORK

Thursday
1 Make and bake walnut meringue for Saturday's lunch.
2 Make raw pastry for Sunday's fruit torte.
3 Prepare Madeira sauce for Sunday's ham mousse.
4 Cook tomato coulis for gratin. Keep in refrigerator.
5 Make ham mousse or mussel casserole and freeze. (Take veal from freezer.)
6 Make soup for Sunday and freeze without liaison.

Friday
Shop for poussins, (veal), any fish, green vegetables, soft fruit and cheese.
1 Stone olives, moisten with a little salad oil. Cut and soak anchovies. Scald tomatoes but do not peel.
2 Cook all ingredients and assemble Saturday's gratin. Cover and keep in a cool place.
3 Make loganberry compote.
4 Roll out pastry and make sponge for torte and bake.
5 Whip cream, fill meringue. Cover and keep chilled.

Saturday morning
1 Marinate poussins for ½ hour.
2 Prepare roulades. Leave covered in refrigerator.
3 Finish poussins. Cook accompanying vegetable.
4 Meanwhile, prepare avocado salad and dish up.

Before leaving for theatre
Place gratin in pre-set automatic oven. (Remove Sunday's mousse or casserole and soup from freezer.) Set out fruit and cheese.

Sunday morning
1 Finish ham mousse with aspic and truffles (or place mussel casserole to heat).
2 Whip cream, prepare fruit and finish fruit torte.
3 Make salad. Prepare soup liaison before reheating soup. Cook noodles.

A SPECIAL CELEBRATION

An autumn weekend and your guests, possibly your daughter's fiancé and his parents, arrive in time for dinner on Friday evening. All the preparation for the main course is done in the morning, even as far as placing the trout in their serving dish ready for baking, and with a cold first course and sweet, there is plenty of time for a relaxed drink before dinner.

Saturday lunch is a straightforward two-course meal, a simply-prepared lamb casserole followed by a cold sweet. However, you may prefer to serve cheese and fresh fruit for dessert, especially as a celebration dinner party is planned for the evening. The main course of this, and the pancakes for the pudding, can be taken from the freezer.

A cold main course, preceded by a warming soup, is suggested for Sunday lunch, causing no inconvenience for either churchgoers or late risers. The sweet can be put together during the course of the morning, so there's a minimum of preparation to attend to before the meal. Follow our plan of work on page 116. Menus have been planned for six people.

Friday Dinner

★ *Pâté de Porc*

Truites Farcies aux Tomates

Fish Potatoes

Tangerine Charlotte

Red wine – Côte de Beaune (Burgundy)
White wine – Chablis (Burgundy)

From the top: pâté de porc served with freshly made toast; truites farcies aux tomates and, for dessert, a creamy tangerine charlotte

Pâté de porc

½–¾ lb salt belly pork
1 onion (peeled)
trimmings of celery
6 peppercorns
1 bayleaf
4 oz pigs liver
2 oz fresh breadcrumbs
1 clove garlic crushed with
    ½ teaspoon salt
6 oz fresh pork (minced)
2 tablespoons brandy
¼ teaspoon ground allspice
pepper freshly ground from mill

To serve
Melba toast (see page 10)

Method

Cover the salt pork with cold water, add the onion, celery, peppercorns and bayleaf and simmer gently for 1 hour. Allow to cool in the liquid.

Set oven at 350°F or Mark 4. Remove the skin and any ducts from the liver, chop coarsely and work for a few seconds in the liquidiser, or use a mincer fitted with the large-holed disc. Beat the crumbs and garlic into the liver and work this mixture into the minced fresh pork. Add the brandy, allspice and pepper.

Drain the salt pork, remove the skin and any small bones, cut the meat in ½-inch cubes and mix carefully into the liver mixture. Turn into a small casserole or terrine with lid, seal the lid with luting paste and place in a roasting tin. Pour in enough hot water to come halfway up the sides of the casserole and place in the pre-set oven. Cook for 1½ hours.

Remove the lid, cover the pâté with a double thickness of greaseproof paper or foil and press lightly until quite cold. (A small plate with a 1 lb can of fruit or vegetables from your storecupboard on top will do admirably if you have no weights.) Freeze if wished.
Thawing and serving. Thaw for 12 hours, or overnight, in the refrigerator.

This pâté can be served in the casserole, or turned out and sliced. Melba toast, freshly-made toast placed in the folds of a napkin, or crispbread should be handed separately. We also recommend a pot of Dijon mustard to accompany this pâté.

Truites farcies aux tomates

6 trout
2 tablespoons seasoned flour
2 oz butter
1 teaspoon lemon juice
2 teaspoons chopped parsley
½ teaspoon chopped tarragon

For stuffing
6 ripe tomatoes (peeled)
1 clove garlic
1 shallot, or 1 small onion
1 oz butter
1 green pepper (finely chopped)
½ lb spinach
salt and pepper
1–2 tablespoons beaten egg

Method

Bone out the trout. Wash and dry, and set aside.

To prepare the stuffing: remove the seeds from the tomatoes and chop flesh coarsely. Peel and finely chop the garlic and shallot or onion, and cook until soft with the butter in a small sauté pan. Increase the heat, add the tomatoes and cook briskly for 2–3 minutes.

Blanch the finely chopped green pepper, refresh and drain well. Blanch the spinach for 1 minute, drain and press between two plates to remove all the moisture, then chop finely. (If using frozen spinach, allow to thaw and then press between two plates.)

Mix the green pepper and spinach with the tomato mixture, season well and add the beaten egg, a little at a time, to bind.

Set oven at 350°F or Mark 4. Fill the trout with the farce (stuffing), pass each fish carefully through the seasoned flour and lift into a well-buttered ovenproof dish. Pour over a little melted butter (about ½ oz from the measured butter) and cook trout in the pre-set oven for 15–20 minutes. If necessary, slide the dish under a hot grill for 2–3 minutes to crisp and brown the skins. Keep warm.

To finish: melt the remaining butter to a nut brown colour in a small pan, add the lemon juice and herbs and pour quickly over the trout.

Boning a trout

First snip off the fins and van dyke (cut a V-shape in) the tail with scissors. Then cut off the head as shown above

Slit each fish down the back, keeping the knife on top of the backbone. Open up fish until it lies flat, then slip knife under bone at the head end and cut down to just above the tail. Lift out the backbone

---

'Fish' potatoes would be ideal to accompany the trout dish. Use large even-size potatoes, peel and cut in four lengthways and trim the cut edges only with a potato peeler. Steam until tender, then sprinkle lightly with salt and chopped parsley before serving.

Luting paste for pâté
Put 3–4 oz flour into a bowl and mix quickly with enough cold water (approximately 2½ fl oz) to make a dough similar in consistency to a scone dough. This amount is enough to seal the lid of one casserole or terrine.

Tangerine charlotte

4 tangerines
6 sugar lumps
¾ pint milk
3 egg yolks
1½ oz caster sugar
1 teaspoon arrowroot
1 dessertspoon gelatine
    soaked in the strained juice of
    1 tangerine and 2 tablespoons
    water
2½ fl oz double cream
1 egg white (whipped)

To finish
1 packet langues de chat
    biscuits
¼ pint double cream

1½-pint capacity charlotte tin

Method

Rub the sugar lumps over the rind of the tangerines to remove all the zest and then dissolve the sugar lumps in the milk over low heat. Beat the egg yolks with the caster sugar and arrowroot until thick and light, then add the milk. Return to the pan, or use a double saucepan, and thicken the custard, without boiling, stirring continually. Strain into a bowl and allow to cool.

Dissolve the gelatine over gentle heat and add to the tangerine custard. Lightly whip the cream and whisk the egg white until stiff.

Stir the custard mixture over ice until it begins to thicken, then fold in the whipped cream and egg white. Pour at once into the lightly oiled mould, cover with foil or transparent film wrap and leave in the refrigerator to set.

To serve: cut the rind, pith and first membrane from the tangerines leaving the flesh exposed. This is best done with a serrated-edge knife and, if you cut round with a sawing action, you should not lose any juice. Slice the tangerines. Whip the cream until thick.

Turn the tangerine cream on to a dessert plate, spread the sides with part of the whipped cream and use what is left to fix the langues de chat biscuits just overlapping each other round the sides. Arrange the sliced tangerines on top.

Saturday Lunch

*Lamb and Tomato
Casserole
Mexicaine
with Pilaf*

Danish Apple Sweet

Red wine – Vin Ordinaire

Lamb and tomato casserole mexicaine

1½ lb fillet of lamb
2 teaspoons paprika
4 rashers streaky bacon
1 (8 oz) can tomatoes
2 tablespoons oil
½ oz butter
2 medium-size onions (sliced)
1 clove garlic (finely chopped)
1 tablespoon flour
1 tablespoon tomato purée
1 wine glass red wine
¼ pint good stock
salt and pepper
½ teaspoon sugar
bouquet garni
4 oz flat mushrooms
1 rounded teaspoon fécule or
   arrowroot, mixed with 1
   tablespoon water (to thicken)
1 tablespoon chopped parsley

For pilaf
4 oz long grain rice
1 oz butter
1 (11½ oz) can Mexicorn

Method
Slice the lamb fillet across in 1-inch pieces and roll them in the paprika. Cut the bacon into lardons (strips) and blanch. Tip the canned tomatoes with their juice into the liquidiser and work until smooth, or rub through a nylon strainer.

Set the oven at 350°F or Mark 4.

Heat the oil in a flameproof casserole, add the butter, and brown the lamb on all sides. Lower the heat, add the onion, garlic and bacon and cook until all are golden brown. Dust in the flour, mix and add the sieved tomatoes, purée, wine and stock. Bring slowly to the boil, season with salt, pepper and sugar, add the herbs, cover and cook gently in the pre-set oven for about 1 hour or until tender. After 50 minutes' cooking time reduce the heat to 325°F or Mark 3 and put in the mushrooms.

If freezing, cook for a further 10 minutes, then cool, pack and freeze.

Thawing and serving Thaw overnight in refrigerator. Re-heat for 40–50 minutes at 350°F or Mark 4.

Meanwhile cook, drain and dry the rice for the pilaf. Butter generously a deep gratin dish and spoon in the rice; season with salt and pepper from the mill and mix in the corn with a fork. Cover with a thickly-buttered paper, or foil, and put on a shelf under the lamb for 15–20 minutes.

If the gravy in the casserole is a little thin, or if there is any fat on the top, bind with 1 rounded teaspoon of fécule (potato flour) or arrowroot mixed with water. Pour this round the sides of the casserole and gently shake the casserole to blend it in. Return to the oven for about 1 minute, then serve dusted with chopped parsley.

Remove the foil from the rice and stir it carefully with a fork. Serve with the lamb.

Clarified butter
To clarify butter, take 8 oz butter and cut it into a thick saucepan. Melt over a slow heat and, once melted, continue to cook until it is foaming. Skim well, strain through a piece of muslin into a basin and leave to settle.

Pour into another basin leaving the sediment behind. The butter will then form a solid cake which can be used at once, or melted down into pots which should be covered before storing in the larder or refrigerator.

Clarified butter gives a better flavour and colour to food cooked in it, and is less apt to burn when heated as the moisture and salt have been removed.

Danish apple sweet

2 lb cooking apples
½ oz butter
grated rind and juice of ½ lemon
4 oz granulated sugar
2 oz clarified or unsalted butter
   (see left below)
2 oz wholemeal breadcrumbs
3–4 tablespoons strawberry jam
¼ pint double cream
1 teaspoon vanilla sugar

This simple sweet is sometimes known as 'Peasant girl in a veil'.

Method
Wipe the apples, remove the stalk and 'eye'. Rub the butter over the base of a thick pan. Peel and quarter the apples and slice into the pan. Add the lemon juice and rind and press a double sheet of grease-proof paper on to the apples. Cover the pan, set on low heat and cook until the apples are soft; rub through a fine strainer.

Return the purée to the rinsed pan, add the sugar and stir until dissolved. Cook carefully until the apple purée is thick. Allow to cool a little, turn into a glass bowl and smooth the top with a palette knife.

Heat the butter in a small frying pan and, when foaming, put in the crumbs and stir until golden brown; turn on to a plate to cool. Spread the strawberry jam over the apple purée and cover with the fried crumbs.

Whip the cream, sweeten with the vanilla sugar, and when it is just holding its shape, pile it on top of the crumbs.

Vanilla sugar
Vanilla sugar is made by leaving a vanilla pod in a jar of caster sugar for several days. The subtle vanilla flavouring permeates the sugar, which is used for cakes and puddings.

Saturday Dinner

*Shrimp Cocottes
Armoricaine*

★ *Pigeons Farcis
en Casserole*

Potatoes Normande

★ *Braised Celery*

★ *Crêpes Fourrées
Lorraine*

Red wine – Gevrey-Chambertin
(Burgundy)

Shrimp cocottes armoricaine

8 oz peeled shrimps or small
   prawns
1 (16 oz) can tomatoes
a strip of lemon rind
4–6 peppercorns
a clove of garlic (well bruised)
½ bayleaf
salt and sugar to taste
1 tablespoon gelatine soaked in
   3 tablespoons water or
   white wine
2–3 drops of Tabasco sauce
¼ pint partially whipped cream
brown bread and butter (to
   serve)

6 ramekins or cocottes

Method
Put the tomatoes in a pan with the lemon rind, peppercorns, garlic and bayleaf. Add salt and sugar to taste and bring slowly to the boil. Simmer for 10–15 minutes until thick and well-reduced, then press the pulp through a nylon strainer. Add the soaked gelatine and stir until dissolved, then leave to cool. Adjust the seasoning, and add the Tabasco.

When the mixture is thickening creamily, fold in the mayonnaise, or cream, and pour into 6 ramekins. Leave to set.

Arrange the shrimps in a pyramid on top of each ramekin and serve with brown bread and butter.

For a special dinner party — individual shrimp cocottes are followed by stuffed pigeons casseroled with mushrooms and onions. *Serve this with potatoes normande (front) and braised celery. Finish with pancakes filled with coffee crème and raisins*

Pigeons farcis 'en casserole'

4 pigeons
½–¾ oz butter
1 tablespoon flour
1 wine glass white wine
¾ pint brown jellied stock
salt
bouquet garni
½ lb pickling onions (peeled)
6 oz flat mushrooms
1 teaspoon arrowroot (to finish)

For stuffing
½ lb bacon pieces
1 medium-size onion (finely chopped)
2 tablespoons chopped parsley
fresh white breadcrumbs
½ beaten egg
a little white pepper freshly ground from mill
a little grated lemon rind

Method
Set oven at 350°F or Mark 4.

Cut the pigeons down the back and remove the backbone and rib cage from each.

Now make the stuffing. Remove the rind from the bacon, cut the bacon into small pieces and cook slowly until frizzled and brown. Remove from the pan with a draining spoon, add the onion and cook slowly until soft.

Mix the onion, bacon and parsley together, add just enough crumbs to hold the bacon and bind with beaten egg. Season with pepper and flavour with lemon rind.

Fill the pigeons with the stuffing and sew up. Brown slowly in the butter in a flameproof casserole, blend in the flour, allow to colour then add the wine and stock. Season, add the bouquet garni, cover and cook in the pre-set oven for 1 hour.

Meanwhile blanch the peeled onions for 5 minutes and drain well. Trim the mushrooms, add to the casserole with the onions after an hour's cooking, and continue cooking for 15–20 minutes.

Take up the pigeons, remove the string and cut each bird in half. Reduce the liquid in the casserole a little and lift out the bouquet garni. Add arrowroot, slaked with a little cold water, to thicken lightly if necessary. Replace the pigeons to reheat. Keep warm.
Note: This dish could be prepared in advance, kept in the refrigerator for two days or even frozen and then reheated.
Thawing and serving Thaw for 24 hours, or overnight, in the refrigerator. Reheat in a pre-set moderate oven, 350°F or Mark 4, for 40–50 minutes.

Serve with potatoes normande, which means there's no saucepan to wash after dinner, and braised celery, which again can be prepared in advance and reheated with no loss of flavour.

Potatoes normande

2 lb potatoes
2 oz butter
salt and black pepper freshly ground from mill
1 pint milk

Method
Cut the potatoes in thin, even slices and arrange, overlapping, in a well buttered fireproof dish. Season between the layers, pour over the milk and cover the top with the remaining butter cut into tiny pieces. Bake in a moderately hot oven, 400°F or Mark 6, for about 50–60 minutes.

Braised celery

6 large sticks of celery
2 large onions (diced)
2 large carrots (diced)
2 oz butter
1 pint jellied stock
salt and pepper
bouquet garni

Method
Wash celery, split sticks in two, blanch in boiling, salted water and drain.

Dice the onion and carrot, sweat them in butter in a pan. Then add the celery, stock, seasoning and bouquet garni. Cover and braise for 1–1½ hours, or until tender, in an oven at 325°F or Mark 3. Baste well from time to time.

When cooked, the gravy should be well reduced and the celery glazed. Dish up and strain gravy over the celery.
If freezing, thaw for 4–6 hours at room temperature before reheating for 30 minutes in the oven below the pigeons.

Crêpes fourrées Lorraine

4 oz flour
pinch of salt
1 egg
1 egg yolk
½ pint milk
½ oz melted butter

For filling
4 oz seeded raisins
2–3 tablespoons black coffee and/or brandy
1 egg (separated)
1 egg yolk
2 oz caster sugar
¾ oz flour
½ oz cornflour
¾ pint milk
1 teaspoon instant coffee

To finish
icing sugar (for dusting)
a few walnut halves
¼–½ pint maple syrup

Method
First prepare the batter. Sift the flour and salt into a bowl. Make a well in the centre, add the egg and egg yolk, and begin to add the milk slowly, stirring all the time. When half the milk has been added, stir in the melted butter and beat well until smooth. Add the remaining milk and set aside.

Cover the raisins with the coffee and/or brandy and leave to soak while preparing the filling.

Cream the 2 egg yolks with a third of the sugar and the measured flours, then dilute with a little of the milk. Scald the remainder of the milk with the coffee, pour on to the flour mixture, blend and return to the pan. Stir until boiling, draw aside and allow to cool. Whip the egg white, add the rest of the sugar and continue to whip until stiff. Fold into the coffee mixture and add the raisins.

Fry paper-thin pancakes, spread each one with a large spoonful of the filling and roll up. Cool, pack and freeze, if wished.
Thawing and serving Thaw for 4–5 hours at room temperature. Stack crosswise in a buttered ovenproof dish, dust with icing sugar and scatter over broken walnuts.

Bake at 400°F or Mark 6 for 6–7 minutes. Serve hot with the maple syrup poured round just before serving.

Make a well in the flour and add one egg and an egg yolk

Pour milk slowly into flour and egg mixture, stirring well

Tilt pan while pouring in the batter so it spreads evenly

When underneath is a good colour, flip the pancake over

Cream of leek soup

8 large leeks
1½ oz butter
1 pint chicken stock
salt and pepper
¾ oz flour
½ pint milk
3 tablespoons single cream

Method

Trim and wash the leeks thoroughly under a running tap and reserve the pale green top of one for garnish. Slice the leeks into thin rounds and stir over gentle heat for 7–8 minutes in a large pan with half the butter. Tip on the stock, season with salt and pepper, cover and simmer for 10–15 minutes. Rub the leeks through a fine sieve or work to a purée in the liquidiser.

Melt the remaining butter in the rinsed saucepan, draw aside, add the flour, blend in the milk and stir until boiling. Add the leek purée and simmer 3–5 minutes. Pot and freeze.

Shred the leek top garnish into fine strips each about 1 inch long and blanch for 5 minutes, drain well. Freeze.

Thawing and serving Thaw for 12 hours, before reheating to boiling point.

Put the cream at the bottom of a warmed tureen, pour in hot soup, scatter warmed garnish on top and serve.

Chicken and tongue galette

4 thick slices cooked tongue
3 lb roasting chicken
2½ pints water
1 onion (peeled)
1 carrot (peeled)
salt
6 peppercorns
bouquet garni
½ pint béchamel sauce
   made with
   1½ oz butter, 1½ oz flour and
   ½ pint flavoured milk
salt and pepper
1 dessertspoon gelatine soaked
   in 2½ fl oz chicken stock
4 oz butter (well creamed)
2 tablespoons lightly whipped
   double cream
4 oz cooked ham (shredded)
slices of tomato and cucumber
   (to garnish)

6¾-inch diameter cake tin with loose base, lined with a disc of waxed or greaseproof paper

Method

Place the chicken in a pan with the water, onion, carrot, seasonings and bouquet garni and simmer for about one hour. Leave in the liquid to cool.

Meanwhile, prepare a béchamel sauce; leave to cool.

Remove all the skin and bone from the chicken and pass the meat twice through the mincer. Place in a bowl, pound well and add the béchamel sauce by degrees with plenty of seasoning. Dissolve the soaked gelatine over gentle heat and set aside. Mix the butter into the chicken, then add the cool gelatine and finally fold in the cream and ham.

Place a slice of tongue at the bottom of the prepared cake tin and cover with a third of the chicken mousse. Continue in this way until the tin is full, finishing with a slice of tongue.

Cover the tin with foil and keep in the refrigerator or freeze until ready to serve.

Thawing and serving Thaw for 24 hours. Turn the galette out on to a round serving dish and garnish with sliced tomato and cucumber.

Serve with potato and watercress salad, and hand Cumberland sauce separately.

The cold chicken and tongue galette for Sunday lunch is ready to serve with Cumberland sauce and a potato and watercress salad

Potato and watercress salad

2 lb even-size potatoes
1 large bunch watercress
French dressing:
   2 tablespoons white wine
   vinegar
   salt
   black pepper from the mill
   ½ teaspoon Dijon mustard
   8 tablespoons salad oil

Method

Cook the potatoes in their skins. Peel, slice thickly and spoon over half the dressing while the potatoes are still warm. Meanwhile, wash and drain the watercress, reserving the best of the leafy sprigs and strip away any leaves from the remaining stalks.

Dry the stalks, snip with kitchen scissors and add to the dressing. Spoon over the potatoes when they are cold. Add the reserved sprigs of watercress just before serving.

Cumberland sauce

2 oranges
8 tablespoons redcurrant jelly
juice of 1 lemon
2 wine glasses port wine

Method

Remove rind from half of one orange with a potato peeler. Cut into needle-like shreds and cook in boiling water until tender, then drain and rinse well.

Heat the redcurrant jelly until dissolved, then stir in the lemon juice, wine and strained juice of both oranges. When cold, add the orange rind and serve in a sauceboat.

Bananes au caramel à la crème

6 ripe bananas
8 sugar lumps
2 large oranges
2 tablespoons Grand Marnier liqueur (optional)
1 packet of 4 sponge cakes
½ pint double cream

For caramel
6 oz granulated sugar
6 fl oz water

6 coupe glasses

Method

First prepare the caramel. Dissolve the sugar slowly in half the water, then boil rapidly until a good brown colour. Check boiling by dipping the bottom of the pan into cold water, then pour out a quarter of the caramel on to an oiled tin. Add the remainder of the water to the pan and set over slow heat until melted and boiling. Pour into a bowl and leave until cold.

Watchpoint when making caramel it is essential to dissolve the sugar very slowly. Keep the heat under the pan very low and do not allow the water to boil until every grain of sugar has dissolved. Do not stir. The sugar can be moved from the bottom of the pan by drawing a spoon carefully through it. When all the sugar has dissolved, bring to the boil and then cook steadily to a rich brown caramel. This may take some time, but do not let the caramel get too dark or it will burn!

Rub the lumps of sugar over the skin of the oranges, and, when full of zest, crush them with a rolling pin and dissolve in the juice of both oranges. Add the liqueur.

Break up the sponge cakes and divide among 6 coupe glasses. Slice the bananas, pour the orange juice over them and divide between the coupe glasses. Whip the cream lightly, adding the caramel syrup by degrees, then spoon this over the bananas. Crush the set caramel and sprinkle over the cream on each coupe.

A Cordon Bleu concoction quickly put together from bananas, oranges, liqueur, sponge cakes and caramel-flavoured cream

PLAN OF WORK

Wednesday or Thursday
1 Make pancakes. Interleave with greaseproof or waxed paper. Wrap and keep in refrigerator or freezer.
2 Prepare breadcrumbs for pigeon stuffing and Danish apple sweet.
3 (Prepare and cook pigeons for Saturday and freeze.)
4 Make caramel topping and syrup for Sunday's sweet and store topping in polythene wrap in an airtight tin.
5 (Prepare and cook lamb casserole and freeze.)

Thursday
Shop for all meat and game, fruit and root vegetables; check storecupboard for biscuits, rice, cans etc.

1 Prepare and cook pâté for Friday's dinner.
2 Make custard for tangerine charlotte, but do not add gelatine. Leave carefully covered in a cool place.
3 Cook tomatoes, blanch and prepare peppers and spinach for trout stuffing but do not mix together.
4 Make apple purée for Danish apple sweet.
5 Cook chicken for Sunday's galette. When cold, remove skin and bones. Keep in a cool place.
6 Make Melba toast and store in an airtight tin.

Friday
Shop for fish and green vegetables.

1 Add gelatine to custard, finish tangerine charlotte and keep in the refrigerator.
2 Cook Saturday's lamb casserole, but not pilaf, (if not already in freezer).
3 Make coffee filling for pancakes.
4 Stuff pigeons, (if not in freezer) trim celery and prepare mirepoix ready for cooking. Check on brown jellied stock.
5 Make chicken mousse from cooked chicken and assemble galette. Keep in refrigerator until Sunday. Make Cumberland sauce.
6 Make leek soup for Sunday, if not in freezer.
7 Cook tomato mixture for Saturday's cocottes. Put in a cool place to set.
8 Mix together ingredients for stuffing trout, finish dish and leave ready for cooking. Prepare fish potatoes.
9 (Remove pigeons and lamb casserole from freezer.)

Saturday morning
1 Cook rice for pilaf, mix with corn and put ready for reheating at lunchtime.
2 (Take pancakes from freezer ready for filling.)
3 Fry breadcrumbs and whip cream to complete Danish apple sweet.
4 Fill pancakes with coffee mixture, leave ready for heating.
5 Reheat lamb casserole and pilaf.

Saturday evening
1 Finish cocottes and cut brown bread and butter.
2 Put pigeons and celery to cook or reheat.
3 Cut potatoes and arrange in dish ½ hour before putting into oven.
4 (Take Sunday's soup from the freezer.)

Sunday morning
1 Make banana and caramel dessert.
2 Slice cucumber and tomatoes. Turn out and garnish the chicken and tongue galette.
3 Make the potato and watercress salad to accompany.
4 Reheat soup just before serving.

SOUPS

Home-made soups are always welcome when the family arrives home, or guests drop in for an informal lunch. If you have left-over meat stew or even the remains of a cauliflower cheese, purée it and freeze it, ready for making into a soup with any suitable left-over cooked vegetables. Some ideas are given on this page — nothing need be wasted. Again, you do not need a freezer if you purée left-overs and cook them straight away.

Cauliflower cheese soup

1 medium-size onion
1 oz butter
enough cooked cauliflower to fill a ½ pint basin
cooked potatoes (preferably mashed) or the scooped out pulp of baked potatoes
salt and pepper
approx ¼ pint milk

To finish
1½ oz grated cheese

Method
Peel and slice onion thinly, soften in the butter and add the left-over cauliflower and potato. Season and blend, or put through a Mouli sieve, adding enough milk to make a thick purée. Measure and put into a carton or pot for freezing.

To make the soup, allow to thaw, or hold the carton under a running cold tap for a few minutes, then tip contents into a saucepan. Set on low heat and dilute with chicken stock (or milk) to make a soup of good consistency. Allow to boil, then draw aside and by degrees whisk in about 1½ oz grated cheese. Adjust seasoning and reheat without boiling.

If watercress has been bought for a salad and is good, keep the end stalks and snip them finely. Add a tablespoon of these to the soup after adding the cheese.

Mock mulligatawny

Small quantities of a beef ragoût or goulash make a good Mulligatawny type of soup. So measure the amount of stew left. To every ½ pint take:

1 onion (finely chopped)
1 tablespoon dripping
1 level dessertspoon curry powder
½ teaspoon cumin
1 medium-size cooking apple (peeled and sliced)
1 dessertspoon tomato purée
¼ pint stock
salt and pepper

To finish
¾ pint brown stock
1 teaspoon arrowroot slaked with 1 tablespoon water
½ oz butter
1–2 tablespoons double cream

Method
Soften onion in the dripping and allow to colour slightly. Then add both spices and, after a minute, the peeled and sliced apple. Add tomato purée and stock. Season and simmer for 5–6 minutes. Add left over stew, mix and blend (or rub through a Mouli sieve). Turn into a carton and freeze.

To heat, turn into a saucepan and heat gently. Dilute with brown beef stock and thicken lightly with 1 teaspoon arrowroot slaked in 1 tablespoon water. Finish with about ½ oz of butter and a tablespoon or two of double cream.

Top: cauliflower cheese soup. Below: mock mulligatawny

Cooked carrots also purée well for making into a soup. If a few Jerusalem artichokes are left in the vegetable rack, peel, slice and soften with the onion before adding the carrots. Use a crumb 'panade' (½ pint of breadcrumbs soaked in a little stock) as a thickening if cooked potato is not to hand. On reheating, dilute with stock and flavour with chopped mint.

Watercress stalks, which would normally be thrown away, can be kept and added to the outside leaves of a lettuce to make a green soup. The stalks give a pleasant, peppery flavour.

Cooked peas (about a cupful) can also be added to the lettuce to give body and flavour. Finish with a little chopped mint, if available.

WITH AN ACCENT ON SUMMER

This is a weekend in summer, when your guests arrive on Friday evening for dinner. Then, after a traditional English breakfast on Saturday morning, you will all be out for the day, perhaps attending some local function such as a hospital fête or garden party, or a sports meeting, where lunch and tea will be available. Alternatively, you could provide a hearty soup from one of the recipes in this book, with bread and cheese, leaving both you and your guests free to come and go as you please.

Saturday evening's menu takes the form of a fork supper party for 12 people, with a choice of two main dishes and two sweets. These, and the starter, can all be prepared in advance.

Sunday lunch has two hot dishes, but both can be produced with the minimum of effort. The kebabs make a welcome change from the usual roast joint and the cold sweet takes only a few minutes to put together. So follow the plan of work on page 123. Menus are planned for six.

Welcome your guests with a summer soup, followed by fillets of sole stuffed with cods roe and soured cream; to follow, there's a tart of pears flavoured with orange juice and brandy in crisp almond pastry. The centre is filled with whipped cream

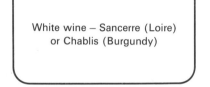

Friday Dinner

★ *Potage Vert*

Filets de Sole Farcis
New Potatoes

★ *Tarte aux Poires*
Armagnac

White wine – Sancerre (Loire)
or Chablis (Burgundy)

Potage vert

outside leaves of 2 lettuce
1 large handful spinach, sorrel or
  young nettles (well washed)
stalks of 2 bunches watercress
1 oz butter
1 medium-size onion (finely
  chopped)
¾ oz flour
1 pint chicken stock
salt and pepper
½ pint milk (scalded)
3 tablespoons garden peas
  (cooked)
2–3 tablespoons cream
1 teaspoon freshly chopped mint

Method
Shred the lettuce and spinach leaves, and coarsely chop the watercress stalks. Melt the butter, add the onion and cook until soft, without colouring. Stir in the flour and continue to cook for one minute. Draw the pan away from the heat, blend in the stock and stir until boiling. Season, put in the shredded 'greens' and simmer gently for 15–20 minutes.

Pass through a Mouli sieve or work to a purée in a liquidiser and return to the rinsed pan with the scalded milk; adjust the seasoning and add the peas.

Spoon the cream into a warmed tureen, pour in the hot soup, stir gently, add the mint and serve.

If freezing, freeze before adding the cooked peas. Thaw for 12 hours in refrigerator. Reheat to boiling point. Add peas.

Place the pears in the uncooked pastry case with the stalk ends pointed towards the centre

Filets de sole farcis

6 double fillets of sole, or
  plaice (skinned)
3 oz butter
3 tablespoons fresh white
  breadcrumbs
watercress (to garnish)

For farce
6 oz smoked cods roe
6 tablespoons fresh white
  breadcrumbs
1 teaspoon juice from a grated
  onion
a dash of Tabasco
3 tablespoons soured, or fresh
  cream
lemon juice to taste
white pepper from the mill

Method
Set oven at 350°F, or Mark 4. Wash and dry the fish. Prepare the farce. Pound the cods roe with the breadcrumbs, onion juice and Tabasco, or blend until smooth in a liquidiser; work in the soured or fresh cream and lemon juice, and season with pepper.

Spread the farce along half the skinned side of each fillet of fish, then fold in half lengthways and lift carefully into a buttered ovenproof serving dish.

Melt the butter, allow to cool and spoon a little over the fish. Sprinkle breadcrumbs on top of the fillets and pour the remaining butter over the crumbs.

Bake in the pre-set oven, basting occasionally, for 20–30 minutes. Garnish with a little crisp watercress and serve with new potatoes, plainly cooked and finished with butter and chopped parsley.

Tarte aux poires Armagnac

For almond pastry
8 oz plain flour
4 oz caster sugar
4 oz butter
3 egg yolks
1–2 drops almond essence
4 oz ground almonds

For filling
2–3 ripe dessert pears
1 tablespoon caster sugar
grated rind and juice of ½
  orange
2 tablespoons Armagnac

To finish
a little egg white
1 teaspoon caster sugar
3–4 fl oz double cream

8-inch diameter flan ring

Method
First prepare the pastry. Sift the flour on to a board or slab, make a well in the centre and in this place the sugar, butter, egg yolks and almond essence; sprinkle the almonds on the flour. With the fingers of one hand work the ingredients to a firm paste. Place in a polythene bag and chill in the

Roll the ring of pastry lightly over the tart with a rolling pin, then seal rim and bake the tart

refrigerator for about 1 hour. **Note :** This pastry can be made in advance and frozen.

Now prepare the filling. Peel, core and quarter the pears, sprinkle with the sugar, orange rind and juice and Armagnac. Cover and macerate for ½ hour. Set the oven at 375°F, or Mark 5.

Roll out a good third of the pastry to the same diameter as the flan ring. Stamp out a round from the middle with a 2½-inch cutter and put with the remaining two thirds of the pastry. Roll this out and line the flan ring.

Drain the pears and reserve the juice. Fill the tart with the pears and cover carefully with the pastry ring. Press and trim around the edge. Bake for 35–40 minutes in the pre-set oven.

About 5 minutes before the tart is cooked, remove it from the oven, brush with the lightly-broken egg white and dust quickly with the caster sugar. Return it to the oven to frost the top. (Freeze.)

Whip the cream lightly and add the reserved juice from the pears. The cream should just hold its shape but not be stiff enough to pipe. Allow the tart to cool and, just before serving, pour the cream into the centre.

Thawing and serving Thaw for 6 hours at room temperature. Warm through in a moderate oven, 350°F, or Mark 4, for 10–12 minutes. Pour in cream.

Cream cheese and tomato jelly ring

2 (16 oz) cans Italian tomatoes
1 bayleaf
1 medium-size onion (sliced)
1 pint chicken stock
1 tablespoon tomato purée
6 peppercorns
salt
a pinch of sugar
1 oz gelatine dissolved in ¼ pint stock or water
1 bunch watercress (to garnish)

For cheese mixture
¾ lb Philadelphia cream cheese
2 green peppers (blanched and chopped)
1 tablespoon snipped chives
salt and pepper
8 fl oz single cream
1 tablespoon gelatine soaked in 4 tablespoons white wine or water

2½-pint capacity ring mould

Method

Turn the tomatoes into a pan with the bayleaf, onion, stock, tomato purée and peppercorns. Season with salt and a pinch of sugar and simmer for 5–10 minutes. Pass through a strainer and cool.

Dissolve the gelatine in the water or stock and add to the tomato mixture.

Meanwhile prepare the cheese mixture. Beat the cream cheese with the chopped peppers, chives and seasoning and work in the cream. Melt the gelatine in the wine or water over a gentle heat, and stir gently into the cheese.

As the tomato mixture begins to thicken, pour about half of it into the wet ring mould and, when just set, spread the cream cheese mixture on top. Smooth with a knife and then carefully pour on the remaining tomato mixture. Cover with transparent film wrap and leave in the refrigerator to set.

To serve dip the mould into hot water and turn out. Fill the centre with watercress and serve with anchovy bread.

Hot anchovy bread

2 medium-size French loaves
8 oz unsalted butter
2–3 tablespoons anchovy essence
a little black pepper from the mill
1 teaspoon lemon juice

Method

Work the butter until soft with a wooden spoon and beat in the anchovy essence, pepper and lemon juice. Cut the bread in ½-inch slices and spread generously with the anchovy butter. Reshape the loaves, spreading any remaining butter over the top crust. Wrap each loaf in foil and freeze or keep in the refrigerator.

Bake for 10 minutes in a hot oven, 400°F or Mark 6, then open up the foil and leave in the oven for a further 3 minutes until crisp. If frozen, bake without thawing for 20–25 minutes. Turn the slices on to a hot platter.

Chicken japonais

4–5 lb roasting chicken
2 oz butter
salt and pepper
½ pint jellied stock made from the giblets (for roasting)
½ small fresh pineapple or 1 (11½ oz) can pineapple chunks (drained)
caster sugar (see method)
½ head celery
2 oz walnut kernels
2 large ripe pears
½ lb red cherries (stoned)
French dressing

Method

Set the oven at 400°F, or Mark 6. French roast the chicken with the butter and stock until brown and sticky, about 1¼–1½ hours.

When cold, cut flesh from the bone in 'chunky' pieces.

If using fresh pineapple, cut away the skin and core, slice flesh and dust lightly with a little fine sugar. Wash and slice the celery. Soak in ice-cold water until crisp, and then drain and dry. Blanch and skin the walnuts. Peel and slice the pears.

Mix all the ingredients together and moisten with French dressing. Serve in a deep bowl with tarragon cream dressing served separately.

Tarragon cream dressing

3 eggs
6 tablespoons caster sugar
9 tablespoons tarragon vinegar
a pinch of salt
¾ pint double cream (whipped)

Method

Beat the eggs and sugar together until light, add the vinegar and cook in a basin over a pan of boiling water until thick. Add a pinch of salt. Fold in the lightly-whipped cream when cold.

Salade aux saucissons

1 lb 'pork and beef' sausages
4 frankfurters
1 small white Dutch cabbage (approx 2 lb)
7–8 tablespoons oil
salt and pepper
2 tablespoons white wine vinegar
1 bunch spring onions (sliced)
4 oz salami
4 oz Polish krakowska or ham sausage
4 oz mortadella
4 oz liver sausage
½–¾ lb new potatoes
1 teaspoon made English mustard
a pinch of sugar
1 lb ripe tomatoes (to garnish)

Method

Fry the 'pork and beef' sausages slowly until brown on all sides, allowing 20–25 minutes cooking time, and poach the frankfurters for 5–8 minutes, then remove the skin. When cold, cut in diagonal slices.

Meanwhile, shred the cabbage very finely, mix with 4 tablespoons of the salad oil, turning thoroughly until all the cabbage is coated. Season with salt, pepper and I tablespoon of the vinegar and add the sliced spring onions; cover and chill.

Slice, skin and shred or dice the continental sausages. Scrape and cook the potatoes, slice and mix while hot with a dressing made with the mustard, the remaining 3 tablespoons oil, salt, pepper and sugar and the remaining tablespoon of vinegar.

Mix all the sausages with the cabbage salad and the dressed potatoes. Check the seasoning, adding extra French dressing if necessary.

Scald, skin and thickly slice the tomatoes.

Serve the salad 'en pyramide' in a deep dish and surround with the tomatoes.

An attractive party spread with (left) cream cheese and tomato jelly ring, (behind) chicken japonais, (front) salade aux saucissons, and Jamaican torte

Jamaican torte

8 oz unsalted butter
8 oz soft brown sugar
4 egg yolks
¼ pint hot strong black coffee
4 bananas
2–3 tablespoons rum
½ pint double cream
2 packets Boudoir biscuits

9-inch diameter angel cake tin

Method
Cream the butter until soft, add the sugar a little at a time and continue beating until soft and fluffy. Beat in the egg yolks and the hot coffee, and allow to cool. Work the bananas in the liquidiser with the rum, fold into the partially whipped cream and then add to the coffee mixture.

Line the bottom and sides of the tin with the biscuits and pour in the filling. Cover well with foil and leave in the refrigerator overnight.

Turn on to a serving dish and tie a narrow ribbon round the side.

Raspberry rod grod

1½ lb raspberries
pared rind and juice of 1 orange
1½ wine glasses red wine
2 pints water
10–12 oz granulated sugar
1 rounded tablespoon potato flour (fécule), or arrowroot
caster sugar (for dusting)
whipped cream (for serving)

Method
Put the rind and juice of the orange into a pan with the wine. Cover and boil gently until reduced by half, then strain. Return to the pan, add the water, sugar and approximately half the raspberries. Bring to the boil, cover and simmer for 15–20 minutes.

Rub through a nylon strainer. Adjust sweetness. Add remaining raspberries, return to the pan and simmer for 5–6 minutes. Draw aside. Slake (mix) 1 rounded tablespoon fécule or arrowroot with 3–4 tablespoons water. Blend into the pan and reboil. Pour into a glass bowl and dust the surface with caster sugar. Do not refrigerate before serving with lightly-whipped cream, if wished.

Oeufs en cocotte Arnold Bennett

1 lb Finnan haddock on the bone, or 12 oz smoked haddock fillet
7 new-laid eggs
¼ pint double cream
white pepper ground from the mill
a little butter
1 tablespoon each finely grated dry Cheddar and Parmesan cheese
a little salt

6 cocottes or ramekins

Method
Set the oven 400°F or Mark 6.

Place the smoked haddock in a pan. Cover with cold water, bring slowly to the boil, draw the pan aside and leave for 10 minutes. Flake the fish, removing skin and bones.

Separate one egg, reserving the white, and mix the yolk with 4 tablespoons of the cream. Add this to the fish, season with a little white pepper and spoon an equal amount into each of six buttered cocottes. Lightly whip the remaining cream, add the cheese and adjust seasoning. Stiffly whisk the egg white and fold it into the cheese mixture.

Break an egg into each cocotte, cover with the cheese mixture, and bake for 5–6 minutes in the pre-set oven.

Kebabs à la grecque

1½ lb lamb fillet or lean shoulder (weight without bone)
½ teaspoon paprika
½ teaspoon dried oregano
black pepper ground from the mill
6 tablespoons olive oil
4 medium-size onions
a few mint leaves

6 long kebab skewers

Method
Cut the lamb fillet into ¾-inch slices (if using shoulder meat, cut this into cubes). Lay these in a flat dish, dust with the paprika, oregano and black pepper, pour over the oil and leave to marinate for at least 1–2 hours, although they can be left longer.

Slice the onions in the thinnest possible rounds and keep in a covered basin.

Thread meat, onion rings and mint leaves on to each skewer allowing 2–3 mint leaves for each kebab. Brush well with the oil from the dish.

Cook under a hot grill for 8–10 minutes, turning the skewers once or twice to ensure even browning.

Serve with the following piquant brown sauce, pilaf and a green salad.

Piquant sauce

¾ oz butter
1 dessertspoon flour
½ pint stock (this can be made with a bouillon cube)
2 tablespoons soy sauce
2 tablespoons piquant fruity sauce
1 dessertspoon tomato purée
1 clove garlic (crushed with a little salt)
salt and pepper
1 teaspoon made English mustard
1 large tablespoon fruit chutney (peach or mango)
2 sweet cocktail gherkins (finely chopped)

Method
Brown the flour lightly in the butter, add the stock, sauces, tomato purée and garlic. Stir until boiling, season well with salt, pepper and mustard and simmer for 4–5 minutes. Add the chutney and chopped gherkins and serve.

Lamb kebabs, served with pilaf and a simply-made piquant sauce, will be greatly enjoyed for Sunday lunch

Pepper and mushroom pilaf

½ lb long grain rice
2 oz butter
1 medium-size onion (finely sliced)
1¼–1½ pints chicken stock
salt and pepper
1 bayleaf
4 oz small flat mushrooms (finely sliced)
2 caps pimiento (cut in small strips)

Method
Set the oven at 350°F or Mark 4.

Melt two-thirds of the butter in a flameproof casserole, add the onion and cook, uncovered, very slowly until soft but not brown. Stir in the rice and cook a little more briskly for about 2 minutes, or until the grains of rice look transparent. Pour on 1¼ pints stock, add salt, pepper and the bayleaf and bring to the boil.

Cover the casserole and put in the pre-set oven for 20–30 minutes or until the rice grains are tender and the stock absorbed. Add the extra stock only if necessary.

Remove the bayleaf and stir in mushrooms and pimiento with a fork. Dot the remaining butter over the top. Replace the lid and leave the casserole on top of the stove to keep warm while grilling the kebabs.

To serve: place the kebabs, still on their skewers, on a hot dish and garnish with watercress. Keep the rice in its casserole; pour the sauce into a gravy boat. Toss the green salad.

Green salads usually have a basis of lettuce — cos, cabbage, Webb's or iceberg — or can be a mixture of greens, such as watercress, sliced cucumber, endive, chicory, green pepper and spring onions.

Flavour with garlic in the traditional way by rubbing the salad bowl with a peeled clove. Sprinkle with chopped fresh herbs and toss in dressing at the last moment.

Granadilla mousse

1 (16 oz) can granadilla pulp
2 egg yolks
3 eggs
3 oz caster sugar
¼ pint double cream
1 dessertspoon gelatine soaked in 4 tablespoons granadilla juice or water

Method
Rub the granadilla pulp through a nylon strainer to remove the seeds, and measure ¼ pint of the purée. Freeze what is left for another time.

Put the egg yolks and whole eggs in a basin, add the sugar gradually and whisk at high speed with an electric beater until very thick and mousse-like. (If using a hand whisk, stand the basin over a pan of hot water and when mixture is thick, remove from the heat and continue whisking until the mixture is cold).

Lightly whip the cream and dissolve the gelatine over gentle heat.

Fold the fruit purée with half the cream into the mousse mixture, stand the basin in ice-cold water and quickly stir in the gelatine. As the mixture begins to thicken, pour into a glass bowl, cover with foil or transparent film wrap and leave in a cool place to set.

Spread the remaining cream over the mousse with a palette knife.

Note: If granadilla pulp is difficult to obtain, ½ lb strawberries, puréed, may be substituted.

Granadilla
Granadilla is the name of various species of passion fruit and flower. Succulent and highly perfumed, it is eaten as a dessert fruit and used for making sweets, drinks and ices.

PLAN OF WORK
Do the main bulk of your shopping on Thursday, but leave vegetables, salading and soft fruit until Friday.

Thursday
1 Make pastry for pear flan, if none in freezer, and store in the refrigerator.
2 Make Jamaican torte; complete French loaves for anchovy bread; either freeze bread, or store in the refrigerator.
3 Make tomato mixture for Saturday's jelly ring, but do not add the gelatine; store in the refrigerator.
4 Cook and flake haddock for Sunday lunch starter, keep in a covered basin in the refrigerator.
5 Make breadcrumbs for stuffed sole for Friday evening.
6 Make tarragon cream dressing to accompany Saturday's chicken dish and keep in a cool place.
7 Make all the French dressing you will need and store in an empty wine bottle.

Friday
Shop for salad vegetables and soft fruit and, on return, wash and pick over watercress and leave head down in a basin of cold water. Wash lettuce and trim off all outside leaves and reserve these with watercress stalks for soup.

1 Roast chicken for Saturday evening.
2 Shred and dress cabbage for Saturday evening; cover and store in a cold larder or the refrigerator.
Cook and dress potatoes.
Prepare all the sausages, but do not mix with vegetables.
Scald tomatoes but do not peel.
3 Prepare sole for evening meal and leave in dish covered with butter and breadcrumbs ready for baking.
4 Take tomato mixture for jelly ring from the refrigerator; prepare cream cheese then add gelatine and complete the dish. Cover mould with transparent film wrap and store in the refrigerator.
5 Make and bake pear flan for dinner.
6 Prepare pineapple, celery and walnuts for Saturday's chicken japonais.

Friday evening
1 Set oven at 350°F or Mark 4.
2 Scrape and cook new potatoes and chop parsley.
3 Bake sole in pre-set oven.
4 Whip cream for flan.
5 Make soup (if not from freezer).
6 Place torte in oven to gently reheat before serving first course.

Saturday
Before breakfast
1 Remove Jamaican torte from refrigerator.
2 Make raspberry rod grod.

After breakfast
1 Cut chicken and complete chicken japonais.
2 Mix prepared ingredients for sausage salad.

On return from outing
1 Put anchovy bread in oven to heat.
2 Turn out and garnish tomato ring and whip cream for raspberry rod grod.

Sunday
1 Take haddock from refrigerator.
2 Cut meat for kebabs and marinate for 1–2 hours before cooking.
3 Make up granadilla mousse and leave to set.
4 Prepare salad, make piquant sauce and pilaf.
5 Complete cocottes Arnold Bennett just before serving.

BASIC RECIPES

Brown stock

3 lb beef bones (or mixed
    beef/veal)
2 onions (quartered)
2 carrots (quartered)
1 stick of celery
large bouquet garni
6 peppercorns
3–4 quarts water
salt

*6-quart capacity saucepan, or small
fish kettle*

Method

Wipe bones but do not wash
unless unavoidable. Put into a
very large pan. Set on gentle
heat and leave bones to fry
gently for 15–20 minutes.
Enough fat will come out from
the marrow so do not add any
to pan unless bones are very
dry.

After 10 minutes add the
vegetables, having sliced the
celery into 3–4 pieces.

When bones and vegetables
are just coloured, add herbs,
peppercorns and the water,
which should come up two-
thirds above level of ingredients. Bring slowly to the boil,
skimming occasionally, then
half cover pan to allow reduc-
tion to take place and simmer
4–5 hours, or until stock tastes
strong and good.

Strain off and use bones
again for a second boiling.

Although this second stock
will not be so strong as the
first, it is good for soups and
gravies. Use the first stock for
brown sauces, sautés, casseroles, or where a jellied
stock is required.
Note: Stock can be kept in
the refrigerator for up to one
week, but chicken stock must
be reboiled every day.

White stock

This stock is made in the same
way except that bones and
vegetables are not browned
before the water is added, and
veal bones are used. Do not
add the vegetables until the
bones have come to the boil
and the fat has been skimmed
off the liquid.

Chicken stock

This should be made from the
giblets, but not the liver, which
imparts a bitter taste. Dry fry
giblets (neck, gizzard, heart
and feet, if available) with an
onion, washed but not peeled,
and cut in half. Add 2 pints of
cold water, a large pinch of
salt, a few peppercorns and a
bouquet garni and simmer
gently for 1–2 hours.

Béchamel sauce

Makes $\frac{1}{2}$ pint

$\frac{1}{2}$ pint milk
1 slice of onion
1 small bayleaf
6 peppercorns
1 blade of mace

For roux
1 oz butter
1 rounded tablespoon flour
salt and pepper

Method

Pour milk into a saucepan, add
flavourings, cover pan and
infuse on gentle heat for 5–7
minutes. Strain milk and set
aside. Rinse and wipe out pan
and melt butter. Stir in flour
off the heat. Pour in half the
flavoured milk and blend until
smooth, using a wooden
spoon. Add the rest of the milk,
season lightly and stir until
boiling. Boil for about 2
minutes.
Note: Use basic method, but
where different ingredients or
quantities are specified in the
recipes, follow these.

Demi-glace sauce

Makes 3 pints

2 carrots (peeled and diced)
2 medium-size onions (peeled
    and chopped)
2 sticks celery (diced)
6 tablespoons oil
3 tablespoons flour
a handful of mushroom peelings
    and stalks
1 tablespoon tomato purée
$3\frac{3}{4}$ pints jellied stock
bouquet garni

Method

Fry vegetables slowly in oil
until they begin to shrink. Stir
in flour and continue to cook
until a good brown. Chop
mushrooms and add with
tomato purée and 3 pints of
the stock. Add bouquet garni,
stir until boiling and partially
cover pan with the lid. Simmer
for $1\frac{1}{2}$–2 hours.

Draw pan aside take out
bouquet garni, add the remaining stock in three parts,
bringing the sauce to the boil
between each addition and
skimming well.

Continue to simmer for a
further 10 minutes, and strain
before using. Pot and freeze in
$\frac{1}{2}$ pint quantities.

Basic puff pastry

8 oz plain flour
pinch of salt
8 oz butter
1 teaspoon lemon juice
scant ¼ pint water (ice cold)

Method

Sift flour and salt into a bowl. Rub in a piece of butter the size of a walnut. Add lemon juice to water, make a well in centre of flour and pour in about two-thirds of the liquid. Mix with a palette or round-bladed, knife. When the dough is beginning to form, add remaining water.

Turn out the dough on to a marble slab, or a board, dusted with flour. Knead dough for 2–3 minutes, then roll out to a square about ½–¾ inch thick.

Beat butter, if necessary, to make it pliable and place in centre of dough. Fold this up over butter to enclose it completely (sides and ends over centre like a parcel). Wrap in a cloth or piece of greaseproof paper and put in the refrigerator for 10–15 minutes.

Flour slab or work top, put on dough, the join facing upwards, and bring rolling pin down on to dough 3–4 times to flatten it slightly.

Now roll out to a rectangle about ½–¾ inch thick. Fold into three, ends to middle, if necessary pulling the ends to keep them rectangular. Seal the edges with your hand or rolling pin and turn pastry half round to bring the edge towards you. Roll out again and fold in three (keep a note of the 'turns' given). Chill pastry for 15 minutes.

Repeat this process, giving a total of 6 turns with three 15-minute rests after each two turns. Then leave in the refrigerator, or wrap and freeze until wanted. Thaw overnight before using.

Pastry quantities

When terms such as 8 oz pastry or an 8 oz quantity of pastry are used, this means the amount obtained by using 8 oz flour not 8 oz of prepared dough.

Roll out puff pastry, lay butter on centre and turn in sides

Fold pastry into three, ends to middle, like a parcel

Flatten lightly with rolling pin before rolling out puff pastry

After each rolling, the pastry is folded into three again

Rich shortcrust pastry

8 oz plain flour
pinch of salt
6 oz butter
1 egg yolk
2–3 tablespoons cold water

Method

Sift the flour with a pinch of salt into a mixing bowl. Drop in the butter and cut it into the flour until the small pieces are well coated. Then rub them in with the fingertips until the mixture looks like fine breadcrumbs. Mix egg yolk with water, tip into the fat and flour and mix quickly with a palette knife to a firm dough.

Turn on to a floured board and knead lightly until smooth. Chill in refrigerator (wrapped in greaseproof paper, a polythene bag or foil) for 30 minutes before using.

The recipe for **French flan pastry** (pâte sucrée) can be found under tarte aux Fraises Cordon Bleu on page 36.

The recipe for **basic choux pastry** can be found on page 101. In either case, increase the ingredients in proportion for larger amounts.

Kneaded butter (beurre manié) is a liaison of butter and flour worked together as a paste and added to liquids to thicken them. Work twice as much butter as flour into a paste with a fork, and add in small pieces to the cooled mixture off the heat. Stir, shake the pan and reboil. If still not thick enough, add more kneaded butter in the same manner.

French dressing

1 tablespoon wine or tarragon vinegar
½ teaspoon salt
½ teaspoon black pepper ground from the mill
½ teaspoon freshly chopped herbs
3–4 tablespoons salad oil
good pinch of sugar (optional)

Method

Mix the vinegar with the salt, pepper and herbs. Add the oil. When the dressing thickens, taste for correct seasoning; if it is sharp yet oily, add more salt. Add a pinch of sugar if liked. **Note**: A true French dressing does not contain sugar, but a pinch may be added for English tastes.

Double the quantity given above to make about ¼ pint, using 6–8 tablespoons oil to 2 tablespoons vinegar.

Mayonnaise

Makes ½ pint

3 large egg yolks
salt and pepper
½ pint oil
approx. 1 tablespoon lemon juice or white wine vinegar

Method

Work the egg yolks and seasoning with a small whisk or wooden spoon until thick, then start to add the oil drop by drop. When 2 tablespoons of oil have been added the mixture will be very thick. Now carefully stir in 1 teaspoon of lemon juice.

The remaining oil can then be added a little more quickly, either 1 tablespoon at a time and beaten thoroughly between each addition until it is absorbed, or in a thin, steady stream if you are using an electric beater.

When all the oil has been absorbed, add the remaining lemon juice to taste, and add extra salt and pepper as necessary.
Note: If ¼ pint mayonnaise is required, use ¼ pint oil and 2 small egg yolks; for ¾ pint use ¾ pint oil and 4 large egg yolks.

Two basic sauces, demi-glace and tomato, with some of their raw ingredients, and light and dark jellied stocks from the freezer

If you have a freezer, it is a good idea to cook a large batch of mince and divide it into different-size packs. Thaw out thoroughly before using in recipes such as those on page 52.

Basic mince

3 lb best quality mince
3-4 tablespoons dripping
1 large onion (finely chopped)
2 large tablespoons flour
2 pints good stock or water
salt and pepper
a little arrowroot, slaked with
1 tablespoon cold water

Method
Choose a large thick-based saucepan, put in the dripping and, when hot, add the onion. Fry until it is just turning colour, then crumble in the mince. Using a metal spoon, stir mince frequently, frying briskly all the while. When mince is well separated, draw pan aside and stir in the flour. Moisten with a good pint of stock or water, season, cover and simmer on the top of the stove or in the oven for 2 hours or longer, if necessary. The mince must be very tender and is difficult to overcook.

During the cooking time, stir occasionally and add the rest of the stock as the mince thickens. When the meat is tender, bind with a little slaked arrowroot, if necessary. Allow to cool, then pack and freeze in portions in aluminium foil dishes.

Useful left-overs A stock of these are real time-savers.
Fine white breadcrumbs Make them in a liquidiser, using stale bread taken from an unsliced loaf and cut in 1 in. squares after removing crusts. Spread out squares and leave for an hour or so before blending into crumbs.
Cheese Save small end pieces of Cheddar cheese and grate when hard and dry. Like breadcrumbs, it can be frozen in bulk. Use for sauces and toppings.
Chicken carcases, raw or cooked, can be packed with vegetable trimmings and a bayleaf and frozen. These can be taken straight from the freezer and placed in a saucepan or pressure cooker and covered with cold water to make stock. The carcase bones of 1 chicken will give you ½ pint of really good strong stock.
Egg The smallest quantity of beaten egg is worth keeping. Add a good pinch of salt to it and mix well until the egg darkens a little in colour. This will prevent the egg drying and getting hard; tip into a tiny preserve container and freeze.

Invaluable for brushing the tops of pies and potato crusts. Add a few drops warm water before brushing it over pies.
Egg whites freeze beautifully. Collect them in a covered container in the refrigerator, then freeze them 4 at a time.
Fish Save small quantities of cooked white fish and sauce for making soups.

How long can frozen foods be kept?

Baked cakes, flan and tartlet cases	6 months
Pastry (uncooked)	3 months
Dairy Produce	
Butter (salted)	3 months
(unsalted)	6 months
Cheese (hard)	3 months
(soft)	8 months
Cream (not less than 40% butterfat)	3–4 months
Eggs (separated)	10 months
Fish	
Fish (oily – salmon, trout etc)	4 months
(white – fresh water)	6–12 months
Fruit (packed in syrup or dry sugar)	up to 12 months
Meat	
Meat (cooked)	2 months
(cooked and stuffed)	1 month
(uncooked)	1 month
Bacon rashers & steaks	4 weeks
(joints, smoked)	8 weeks
(joints, unsmoked)	5 weeks
Beef	12 months
Lamb	12 months
Mince	2 months
Offal	2 months
Pork	9 months
Sausages	6 weeks
Poultry and Game	
Chicken	12 months
Duck	6 months
Giblets	3 months
Game (must be hung for usual time before freezing)	6 months
Sauces	4 months
Soups	4 months
Vegetables	up to 12 months

Note: food will keep in good condition for long periods at −18°C (0°F), but it is usual to limit storage time for best eating qualities. The above times are the recommended ones. There is no risk to health if food is stored for longer, but the flavour and quality will gradually deteriorate.

Headspace
When freezing any liquid, or food in a liquid or syrup eg. purées or casseroles, leave room in the container for expansion during freezing, otherwise the contents may burst the container. Leave about 1 inch for a pint container; 2 inches for a quart.

INDEX